In This Fo

Suzie Hull lives in Northern Ireland with her family and numerous rescue cats. She originally had notions of being a ballet dancer, but after that didn't work out, she trained as a Montessori Nursery teacher and has spent the last thirty years working with children. She has always had an enduring passion for history and books, and as she came from a family of creative women it was only a matter of time before she turned to writing her own. A member of the RNA, *In This Foreign Land* is her debut novel.

In This Foreign Land

Suzie Hull

First published in Great Britain in 2021 by Orion Dash,
an imprint of The Orion Publishing Group Ltd.,
Carmelite House, 50 Victoria Embankment,
London EC4Y 0DZ

An Hachette UK Company

1 3 5 7 9 10 8 6 4 2

A CIP catalogue record for this book is
available from the British Library.

ISBN (Paperback) 978 1 3987 1057 3
ISBN (eBook) 978 1 3987 0781 8

Typeset at The Spartan Press Ltd,
Lymington, Hants

www.orionbooks.co.uk

To my family cheer squad.
I hope I did you proud.

Prologue

No 5 British Red Cross Hospital, Abbeville, France, March 1916

The motor ambulance ground to a halt on the road; ice clinging to the rims and windshield, grains of snow driven into every possible crevice. An officer was waiting in front of the low wooden hut. Grey bushy eyebrows almost hidden under his peaked cap, dusted white with the snowfall. His face was heavily lined from years spent soldiering under the blistering sun, and he chewed silently on an empty pipe. He strode round to the rear of the vehicle when the doors were opened, gloved hands clasped behind his back.

A nurse and an orderly sat in the vehicle, both well covered up, warding off the intense cold which had slunk in from the east and threatened to overwhelm everyone. The patient on the stretcher could have been a ghost there was so little of him. The skin over his skull was paper thin, and every vein was outlined like the map of the Nile delta. His body was hard to discern under the mound of blankets covering him.

'Is this my boy?' the colonel asked, all clipped tones, brusque and business-like.

'This is Lieutenant Edward Dunwoody, sir, Royal Irish,' the nurse answered, clambering down.

The older officer dipped his head so she wouldn't see the glimmer of an unshed tear in his eye. 'That's him.' He cleared his throat. 'You're safe now, my boy.' He stood back and waited whilst the orderlies carried his son into the hut.

'You may come in now. Two minutes only,' the nurse said, holding the door ajar against the bitter wind.

He stamped his feet to get the blood flowing through his toes again and removed his empty pipe, thrusting it deep into his pocket. Following the back of the nurse who had accompanied the patient from Belgium, he came to a halt next to his son, almost invisible within the small iron bed frame.

The colonel sat, uncomfortable, on the wooden chair. The mound in the bed didn't resemble his son. His last memories of Edward, eighteen months ago, were of a tall, strapping, muscular man, with a healthy tan to his skin from his months living in Cairo. Now, the spindly arms reminded him of twigs they used for kindling back home in Ireland.

At least his boy was clean now.

Not everything was clean though. He saw small scraps of grubby paper within his son's finger and thumb and bent forward to examine it. A face perhaps, it was hard to tell, faded and discoloured. He prised it from his hands.

'Don't touch that,' the nurse shouted. 'Please don't.'

Too late; the inert body sprang to life, defying the disease which had ravaged it.

'Isobel.' The words got louder, until he was roaring, disturbing the whole ward. His body convulsing with the disturbance. 'Isobel!'

The nurse deftly intervened and retrieved the small filthy photos, giving them back to the son. She closed his fingers around them, whispering soothing words. When he was calm, she stood again and spoke to the older officer.

'Please don't do that. He can't be without them. It's his

wife and son, you must understand that. He needs to hold onto his photographs.'

The colonel stood, straightened his shoulders and slowly, but with great authority, spoke to her. 'She's not his wife, and she's dead.' He snatched the small photos from his son's hand and stuffed them into his pocket. 'The sooner he accepts that the better it is for everyone.' Back ramrod straight, he exited the hut, ears deaf to the commotion that erupted behind him.

Chapter One

RMS Oceana, *March 1914*

The doors to the first-class salon burst open onto the deck and a fug of smoke and perfume spilled out, dispersing in the night air.

'Come and dance, Isobel,' Cecily called, as she raced across the wooden deck, her chiffon dress billowing in the breeze. She slithered to a stop and reached across to take a quick draw on her sister's cigarette.

Isobel admired the stamina of her younger sister. 'My feet hurt. Don't yours?'

'Never! Whilst Mother isn't here to spoil our fun, I could dance all night.'

Isobel laughed, but refused to move. 'I'm keeping Alice company. Go back inside, darling, I'll see you later.'

Cecily handed back the cigarette to Isobel and then dashed off again towards the dance floor inside the salon.

'Find me later,' Isobel called.

Cecily fluttered her fingers in response before being swallowed up by the gay laughter and dance music.

Isobel stayed by the ship's railing with Alice, as the *Oceana* sliced through the dark Mediterranean waters. They had already been dancing for hours, but it was only just past midnight. The resident band would be playing a few more hours yet as dance partners waltzed and quick-stepped their way around the dance floor, ladies in their silk dresses and the men in military dress jackets, regardless of how stuffy the room was.

'You can dance if you want to. I shan't mind,' Alice said, holding her champagne cocktail and standing next to her friend.

'No, really. All those eager young lieutenants are getting a bit annoying.' It was the way they spoke about the other non-British passengers on board, and the crew, that she didn't like. The horrid things they said and in such loud voices. Isobel turned to look out at the sea, dangling her head over the rail, inhaling the salty air and delighting in the refreshing spray from errant waves which broke at the front of the ship. 'Will it be like this in Cairo?'

'Like what? Being over-run with more dance partners than you can get used to? I should think so. There are plenty of regiments in Egypt.'

'No, I meant...' she didn't finish. Her friend had grown up with a father who had served in the Colonial Service, their house had probably been over-run with visiting military men and their wives, so she wouldn't understand. 'When will you see Wilfred?'

'Hopefully he and Edward will be waiting for us when we dock in Alexandria, but he said not to count on it. You will write when we return to his regiment, won't you?'

'Of course I will, silly. Nervous?'

Alice shrugged, but stared out at the velvet blue sky, suspended with dewdrops of sparkling stars. 'Wouldn't you be if you hadn't seen your husband for months?'

Isobel hung over the railing even further. A gust of warm night air tugged against her peacock-feathered headdress, dislodging it, and it disappeared overboard. 'Golly! How unfortunate!' Her laughter echoed around the empty deck.

'Anyway, I'm not getting married. I've told you countless times. I'm going to be stunningly successful and exhibit at the Royal Institute in London and everyone will talk about my paintings.'

'You don't fool me, Isobel,' Alice teased. 'Edward wouldn't have pleaded with you to come to Cairo if he wasn't interested!'

'We're old friends. Edward doesn't think of me in that way. Besides, his letters are full of a Miss Lucy Hartington now.' She barely concealed her disquiet. She and Edward had been friends since childhood, Wilfred too, although he'd always been the older, stuffy brother. No, despite what her heart ached for, she had convinced herself that Edward had just been friendly when he'd encouraged her and her sister Cecily to accompany Alice out to Egypt. 'Anyway. I'm not getting married and that's that.'

'Really.'

'Alice, can I ask you something?'

'Of course.' She chuckled. 'Is it about Edward?'

'Yes, and no. I mean, I've travelled all this way with you, and it's been lovely. More than lovely – it's been everything I've always wanted, but it's not as though anything is going to happen. I mean ...' She blushed deeper, thinking about him. She still didn't know if Edward liked her in that way and it made everything so much more complicated. 'Just suppose someone did ask me to marry them, someone I liked?'

Alice's eyebrow rose, but she was smiling. 'A man doesn't contrive to invite you half-way across the world if he *doesn't* like you, Isobel!'

Inside she was a mass of doubts. She lifted her glass and swallowed down the last of her cocktail, then nibbled on the cherry while she thought things through. 'But that's not all I meant to ask. It's about marriage, you see. I always said

7

I'd never get married. I frustrated every attempt Mother made to find a suitable young man for me. I was rude, I was unladylike, I was downright shocking sometimes.'

'You were afraid,' Alice said quietly.

Surprised, she looked closer at her friend. 'Weren't you?'

Alice didn't answer to start with, looking out at the sea that had carried them from Naples all this way to a new continent. 'Of Wilfred? No, I think you have his character wrong.'

Isobel barely managed to stop herself snorting in disagreement. There were plenty of words she could think of that described him ...

'You think he is ...'

Isobel was going to say stuffy, or stuck up, but she decided upon a less harsh-sounding word. 'Serious.'

'He's shy,' Alice said.

'He's not.' Shy was the last word she'd pick. Snooty, imperious, conceited ... plenty of words that meant he was awkward or looked down on her. There were numerous occasions when he'd been too quick to correct her, she could think of a dozen right now. The New Year's Eve party back in Belfast just before the two brothers had sailed back to Egypt sprang to mind.

Edward had asked her for the first dance as he normally did, and then she'd had to wait until supper to see him again. She'd lifted more than a few glasses of champagne during the evening; nerves as usual had caught her on the hop. Wilfred had appeared at her elbow just as she'd been about to lift yet another glass and his impeccable vowels had sliced through the air. *I'd say four glasses was enough, wouldn't you, Isobel?* His words and the insinuation behind them wounded her, her cheeks still heated thinking about it now. *Why don't you dance with me instead of waiting for Edward and getting yourself improperly drunk?* No, she wouldn't say he was shy.

'Yes, he is. And slightly jealous of you both, if you really want to know.'

Isobel clutched the ship's railings and just stared, open mouthed at her friend.

'He said that you and Edward fitted together so seamlessly as children that he always felt jealous of your friendship, and your confidence. Yes, he did.' Isobel was shaking her head. 'I believe he recognises that you are talented but believes that talent threatens Edward's happiness.'

'He does disapprove!' Isobel grasped this with glee. 'I always knew it. His mother too. She dislikes me. It's my painting, isn't it?'

'They do love Edward, you know,' Alice said, touching her gently on the arm. 'His parents just want the best for him, even if that is slightly misleading.'

'But we're getting away from my question.'

'We are. Which was...?'

'Are you afraid of losing yourself now that you are married? Having to put your own needs last?'

'I see.' Alice hesitated, taking the opportunity to fix a stray dark curl that had escaped her elaborate hairstyle. She turned, allowing Isobel to help her thread it back under the headband she wore. 'Well, the answer is, Wilfred is warm and funny and kind, even if you can't see that. I didn't fear marriage to Wilfred, but I am a little afraid of marriage to the army. Getting stuck in some far away place, with stupefying heat and being lonely. I fear my parents will miss me dreadfully and I ... them.' Her voice broke, shattering the myth that Isobel had carried that her friend was always strong. 'Look after them for me, won't you?' Unshed tears glittered in her eyes.

9

'I will. Truly I will.'

The two women stood side by side, holding on to one another, both thinking of their futures, as the silver-white moon hung low over the sea and lit up their path to Alexandria. The sounds from the raucous dance were muffled inside the ship. Here, beside the rail, the noise of breaking waves mingled with the waterfall of beads that trimmed both ladies' dresses, tinkling in the breeze.

Isobel breathed in the night air – a heady mixture of sea salt, Turkish cigarettes and Alice's new perfume she'd bought in Paris. Isobel tried to imprint it all in her mind. Their last night together before they arrived in Egypt.

'Let's not go to bed tonight, Alice! Let's stay up and watch the sun rise for the first time over Egypt.'

'You have your head in the stars, Izzy, but I like it. We'll need more champagne though, and blankets. I'm not prepared to see the sun rise with cold feet. Deal?'

Isobel's insides squirmed with delight. In a matter of hours, a new day would dawn, and her head was spinning with the opportunities it might bring her. 'Absolutely, Alice. A night like this calls for more champagne.'

Chapter Two

Standing on the promenade deck, Isobel squinted into the distance. A dark smudge appeared where minutes earlier it hadn't existed. In a matter of hours, she would be standing on a whole new continent, and who knew what sort of life might be waiting for her?

After starting out overcast and drizzly when they left Naples, the wind had picked up for the first day of their sailing but improved yesterday, and last night had been a balmy, perfect night, followed by this equally calm morning. Mrs Finch and Cecily had resigned themselves to staying in their cabins for the first day and resting, and only Mr Finch, Alice and Isobel had bravely marched around the open promenade deck. When she had felt a little better Cecily had joined them, sitting on the veranda in a lounge chair, doing her best not to move. She'd been in high enough spirits last night for the dance though, and Isobel had noted the interest with which one young lieutenant had paid her younger sister.

Isobel and Cecily were travelling with the Finches and their daughter Alice, Mother having declared that Egypt was far too hot and dusty to suit her and Rosalie, their younger sister, and she'd point blank refused to cross the Mediterranean by sea. Instead, the pair of them had taken the opportunity to travel around Europe, visiting all the main capital cities. Isobel was delighted. It meant she would be able to see Edward again without the cloying, soul-destroying presence of her mother. Now, as she leant on the rail, watching the water splash under the bow of the ship, she could feel a thrill of excitement building inside her – how would it be between the two of them?

Mrs Finch joined them on deck as the morning slipped past and they observed the African coastline looming up ahead. Little boats with large white sails bobbed about under the bow of the ship and by eleven o'clock in the morning they were guided towards the harbour.

'Your first voyage across the Mediterranean, my dears,' Mr Finch commented to the two sisters. 'How did you find it?'

'Wonderful, Mr Finch, a delight!' both sisters replied.

'Shame on you, dear, for asking. Can't you see how they feel by the way their eyes are shining?' his wife commented. 'This is a little more exciting than the volcanic stones of Ireland, wouldn't you say?'

'Absolutely!' Isobel still hadn't got over her good fortune at having been introduced to Alice and her parents. They had fallen into a friendship that was as comfortable as a well-worn pair of kid gloves. Alice hadn't waited long before suggesting that both sisters join her on her trip out to Egypt.

'Mr Finch, Mrs Finch, Mrs Dunwoody and ladies, I have come to say goodbye.' Lieutenant Fitzsimmons made a sharp bow to the small group, but it was plain to see his eyes were focused only on Cecily. 'As I am stationed in Cairo, I was hoping we might meet again for tea, or dinner perhaps?'

'Of course we will. As soon as we are settled, we'll send you a card,' Mr Finch replied.

'Mr Finch, ladies.' Lieutenant Fitzsimmons bowed again, before returning to his fellow officers who were also returning to their respective battalions of the British Army, at present stationed in Cairo.

Isobel squeezed Cecily's arm as they stood next to each

other watching the miniature figures just in sight on the quayside below them, scurrying back and forth with a numerous number of boxes, bags and bundles.

'He's very sweet, Cecily.'

Cecily, who was avoiding eye contact with her sister, merely nodded.

'Oh, look at the two men over there,' Mrs Finch remarked. 'Is that Wilfred, do you think?'

'It couldn't be. He said not to get my hopes up.'

'Are you sure, my dear? There are two men down there and the one in uniform looks remarkably like your Wilfred.'

'Honestly, Mother, you think every man in uniform is Wilfred. How many times this trip have you remarked, *doesn't that man look remarkably like your Wilfred?*'

'I have binoculars, Alice, do look.' Cecily handed over a pair that she had borrowed. Alice took them and peered down at the two men.

'Oh, Mother, it is. He came out early to surprise me.'

'There see, he's missed you already. And who else is with him, alongside the native gentleman in the tarboosh? The man in the pale suit?'

'Why, I think it's his brother,' Alice grinned at her friend. 'Well, Isobel, Edward has arrived to see you too.'

Heat flooded into Isobel's cheeks, leaving her lost for words. The moment she had been waiting for, dreaming of for weeks was finally here. Her heart hammered in her chest. What if he was different again after the few months apart? What if he no longer desired her company? Oh, what would she find to say to him?

'Isobel, I do believe your cheeks match the colour of your dress and your hair. At least you have a cream lace collar on it, otherwise it might be a little difficult finding you under it all,' teased Cecily.

13

'They're here,' she whispered to nobody but herself. The wait while the two men navigated the inside of the steamer before appearing out on deck felt like more than a thousand summer days. But the many nights spent dreaming of this moment was swept aside as Edward appeared breathless by her side.

'Isobel,' he said gently, peering under her summer hat. 'How lovely to see you.'

Regardless of the company standing around them, he lifted her hand gingerly to his lips, holding her gaze. Like a butterfly, his lips touched the back of her hand and her legs turned to jelly. 'Hello, Edward,' was all she could whisper back, gazing into his bronzed face. Those amber eyes that gazed back were so familiar. His smile seemed to begin within his heart and radiate out from his very soul. 'This is very pleasant, isn't it?' Instantly, she cringed. Why hadn't she mentioned something more interesting?

Distracted for a second by the noise to their left, they joined in the laughter as Wilfred had Alice in his arms and was spinning her around the deck. It was hard not to feel overwhelmed by good fortune and love. Isobel had a whole month at least to spend in Egypt and hoped she would see Edward most days.

He laughed at her. 'Well yes, I suppose the day is pleasant. More so for seeing you though. No daring escapades on the way over? No pirates or storms to alarm you?'

'No, none at all, but now you're teasing me.' Blushing even more, she cast her eyes to the deck rather than meet his own and fiddled with her gloves.

'Sorry, Izzy. It is nice to see you again though, all the same.'

'Now, my dears, all this emotion! It is so nice to see you two gentlemen. It is a pity you missed Lieutenant

Fitzsimmons, Edward and Wilfred.' Mrs Finch dabbed her eyes with her lace handkerchief.

'You don't mean Tom, do you, Mrs Finch?' Wilfred asked.

'Yes, I do.'

'I met him as we boarded the ship. He and I were in Sandhurst together. I told him to call on us as soon as he could. Now, ladies, if are you ready, I am to escort you to lunch, whilst Edward will assist Mr Finch here in gathering all your luggage.' Wilfred held both his arms out, one for Alice and the other for his mother-in-law. 'Isobel and Cecily, stick close behind me.'

Isobel held tight to Cecily as they descended the gangplank and landed in the melee of the quayside. People of every nationality crushing in around them, going about their day, calling in all sorts of different languages. The two sisters dodged donkeys with overloaded panniers sticking out either side as they tried to keep up with Wilfred. Isobel jumped when a camel opened its mouth and let out an enormous bellow right in front of them. The smell of human sweat and warm animals and a constant haze of dust as the animals jolted along, swinging their tails and scattering more dust and dirt as they went was nearly more than she could cope with. *Be brave, Izzy*, she muttered. You wanted an adventure, and this is it.

'Come along, Isobel,' Cecily pleaded, as she stopped for a moment, taking it all in. Men wearing flowing gowns were pulling on a camel next to them, forcing it down to the ground. Perched precariously on its back was an elaborately carved large wooden box with colourful silk curtains. The door in the side opened and Isobel could make out the lady's eyes, sharply defined with black lines around them, and a ring through her nose but the rest of her was covered from her head to her toes in black silk. The lady emerged, head and shoulders first, then hands, reaching out to hold onto the door, the sound of her jewellery tinkling against itself reaching Isobel's ears. Then came her legs, and a flash of silk hidden under the black, before Isobel gasped with admiration when she saw her feet; bare within her leather sandals except for beautiful silver rings around her toes. She climbed down, and the crowd pressed in around and she disappeared as the tide of people carried on. The camel rocked as it lumbered to its feet and then it too set off again.

Cecily pulled her along, determined they wouldn't lose sight of their own party, the backs of whom they could still see in front of them. Mesmerised by everything she saw, Isobel's eyes darted all around, trying to take it all in. Flies were a constant nuisance around their faces, and she wished she'd pulled a muslin scarf over her hat to protect herself like Mrs Finch and Alice had.

Just as quickly the crowd thinned, and they stopped, breathing in the fresh air, Wilfred raised his arm indicating the direction they were going. 'Follow me, ladies. Isobel, do keep up!' They crossed the road avoiding cabs, carts and other tourists and walked towards the calm of the hotel. They rested themselves on rattan chairs sipping cocktails and refreshing lime juice while they waited for Edward and Mr Finch to arrive.

After lunch they boarded the train for Cairo. It was only Cecily and Isobel who exclaimed over the countryside, as the train clattered along. The two young ladies were given the window seats, so they might get the best view. Mr and Mrs Finch were too busy nodding and saying hello to acquaintances they had made on the *Oceana*, everyone it seemed was travelling on to Cairo.

'Oh, look, Isobel,' Cecily said as they passed isolated villages made up of small mud huts, with families sitting outside them. 'I'm very glad we don't have to wear those veils. I imagine they are very hot covered up like that.'

'The fabric looks light, Cecily. See how it blows in the breeze, I imagine it might be cool.' She tried not to fidget with her own linen dress. The rust-coloured skirt soaking up the sun's rays was already warm to the touch, and her petticoat and stockings below made her legs burn up. Or perhaps it was because Edward was sitting so close.

Cecily continued to comment on every new thing as they rattled through the desert; a camel train, loaded up with bags and sacks and rolls of cloth, the cloudless cobalt sky, and then the splashes of green where the marshes existed, and the different vegetation that grew there.

Cairo rose majestically out of the desert; elegant minarets, elaborate mosques and fortified buildings appearing in front of them. The golden domes glinted in the afternoon sunshine. Isobel drank it all up, wishing she had the ability to record it all directly upon her drawing pad, and capture the intensity of the colours, so different to the Irish countryside back home, and different even to the shapes and atmosphere of the Riviera. Egypt was as though God had opened an entirely different paint box made up of a unique colour palette that didn't exist anywhere else except here. There was a pulse to it; a rich boldness that overtook everything she had ever known before.

'Happy?' Edward leant gently sideways in his seat, with the lightest of touches on her gloved hand. His breath tickled her cheek – her heart could not get used to his proximity. If she had to describe how she felt compared to a colour, she would have to pick a shade of scarlet. It was as though there was no longer blood in her veins, but living, breathing vermillion paint, ready to explode out of her and proclaim itself over a pristine white canvas. She had a desire to express how she felt right this minute, but words were not enough. She could only whisper 'yes'. His hand so close to hers, not even skin to skin, aroused a passion in her she hadn't even known could exist. The brakes screeched and juddered as they made their way closer into the city and the station. Edward straightened up and put a little distance between them again.

Mrs Finch piped up. 'Isobel, Cecily, I have been thinking what is best to do now that your mother isn't here.' Mrs Harris had written to them when they were still in Cannes to say she and Rosalie *would* join them after all in Cairo and had booked two adjoining suites for them at Shepheard's. Isobel had retorted to Cecily that Mother seemed perfectly capable of getting a boat once she thought they were having more fun than she and Rosalie were having. Then they had received a wire in Naples before they boarded the *Oceana* to say that she was delayed, as they had met up with delightful American friends, and not to expect them for a few more weeks.

'Indeed, Mrs Finch, I was thinking the same. It wouldn't be suitable for us to be in Shepheard's alone.'

'You have read my mind, Isobel. You always were a sensible girl. So, unless your mother has managed to arrive before us unexpectedly, I suggest Mr Finch and I should stay in Shepheard's with you, just until she does, and we will cancel our booking at the Continental.'

'I believe you are right, Mrs Finch. If Wilfred hadn't surprised Alice turning up unexpectedly like he did, I had imagined that Alice would stay with us, but,' smiling at Alice, 'she will be enjoying the company of her husband again.'

'My thoughts too, Isobel. So, for that matter, I shall instruct Mr Finch to send your luggage and ours over to Shepheard's immediately and see if we can reserve a table there for dinner. Alice and Wilfred might wish to dine alone this evening. However, we would welcome your company, Edward, very much indeed.'

'Thank you, Mrs Finch. Dinner invitation accepted. Shepheard's have dancing every evening during the week too, so I'm certain Isobel and Cecily will not lack for dance partners tonight. And tomorrow you can start with a little sight seeing. Although, I should mention that Mother is also in Cairo.'

Isobel didn't have the manners to stop her true feelings being expressed on her face. Cecily kicked her ankle and spoke before her. 'How nice, Edward. We shall look forward to meeting her again soon. Will she be dining with us?'

'Not tonight. I know she already has plans, but she intends to call on you very soon, Mr and Mrs Finch. I expect we shall see her at the dance though.'

'How pleasant. We shall look forward to it, Edward,' Mrs Finch replied with perfect manners.

Isobel tried to nod and look agreeable, but inside she was fuming. *His mother*! She'd managed to have time apart from her own mother who was always criticising her actions, and instead Edward's mother was here. Oh, life was utterly unfair. Mrs Dunwoody had not figured in any of her pleasant daydreams in the slightest. She spent the rest of the ride into the station thinking uncharitable thoughts about the woman.

Chapter Three

Shepheard's Hotel, they were soon to discover, had a European look to the building, with its raised sun terrace in front of it and glass canopy; whereas inside, the hotel was quite unlike anything Isobel or Cecily had ever seen before. As they progressed through the lobby, they tried valiantly not to stare at the grand lamp stands, designed as sculptures of half-naked young women, placed symmetrically to each other, their breasts on show for everyone to see. The décor was terribly grand in an oriental style with huge columns and carvings, gold decoration and colourful tiles, a glass dome and Persian rugs adorning the floors.

'Well, this is quite unique, isn't it?' Cecily declared.

'That is an understatement. Mother may wish she had kept our booking at the Continental after all. Imagine passing them every day on your way to breakfast.'

'Don't mention it, Isobel, really you mustn't!'

'Well, I'm quite sure, rich American friends or not, she'll wish she had gone for a European hotel, and not the exotic. Mother isn't into exotic anything, she may faint.'

The girls tried not to stare as a couple sauntered past them arm in arm. 'Isobel, isn't that ...?'

'Yes, but don't look. We read about them in last week's *Times*. I didn't expect them to be still here. His divorce hasn't even come through.'

'Why Mrs Finch and you even worried about us being

properly escorted is a mystery. The hotel doesn't seem to worry. Isobel, is that man selling things, right here in the lobby?' An Indian man sauntered past with various bags and encouraged the hotel guests to peruse his silk fabrics and even precious gems which he produced out of his pockets for anyone who had the time to engage with him. The girls' wide-eyed gaze continued as an Arab passed them with a monkey sitting on his shoulder nibbling a piece of fruit as they waited for Mr Finch to book them into their rooms.

'Isobel,' Edward said, catching her arm. 'I shall return in an hour or so for dinner, if you have nothing else to do, would you join me for a drink on the terrace?'

Flashing him her most winning smile, Isobel's shyness briefly disappeared. 'Yes,' she whispered back. This was a new city in a new country, and as such, she must make the most of every opportunity before Mother arrived. This would be her first evening in Cairo, and it was going to be a wonderful opportunity to be with Edward by herself, and opportunities like that didn't come around very often.

Their adjoining rooms were plentiful and decadent. The pale green curtain fabric had a delicate print of Chinese pagodas and perfect little bridges, finished with a heavy brocade trim. The coverlets on their beds matched, as did the armchairs and sofa in the sitting area. Each room had elegant writing desks, wardrobes and chests of drawers and it was only the addition of the mosquito nets over each bed which reminded them that they were in Egypt and not in Europe. The tall windows had white painted shutters to let in air but not the sun.

'Look at our bathroom, Isobel!' Cecily exclaimed, flinging doors open as she explored their suite. Their shared bathroom was extravagantly fitted out with hot and cold running water, gold taps and gold trimmed tiles. 'Even the walls are painted gold, Izzy!' Cecily continued to call out everything she saw, especially the pelicans and flamingos that she could hear from their open window. Their maid, Minnie, was already unpacking their smaller cases, but their trunks hadn't arrived yet.

'Did you know Shepheard's has its own post office, Isobel? Imagine that. And shops downstairs, and a library.' Cecily chatted away to her sister as Isobel rushed through her toilette, determined to get back downstairs as quickly as she could. 'What shall I wear, Cecily? I want this to be perfect.'

'Have we got any dresses, Minnie, or are they stuck in customs?'

'We do, miss. I have one each for you as I feared this might happen. Mr Finch said your trunks will arrive to-morrow. Now, Miss Isobel, here's your dress.'

'Let's have fun, Izzy, before Mother and Rosalie arrive,' Cecily called as she twirled around Isobel's room. 'I want to go dancing every night if we can.'

'My thoughts exactly. This is as far away from Belfast as the moon might be. Let's enjoy ourselves, for I have the strangest feeling that it won't last long.'

'It's Mother. She has that effect on everyone. Somehow, she manages to find fun unsuitable.'

Chapter Four

Edward was waiting for her on the terrace when she arrived downstairs. He waved her across to his table where he'd been sitting watching the world go by.

'Isobel,' he said, beaming at her. 'I'm so glad you came. There's so much I want to show you. How do you find Alice?'

'She's a dear. It was fortuitous that you introduced us, else I'd never be here.'

He grinned back. 'That was the plan, but I didn't want to say so outright. I thought you'd get on with Alice and her parents, they're very straightforward people. No airs and graces.'

'Like me?'

'And me. I'm not fond of being tied to tradition and society. I'm just so relieved I never joined Father and Wilfred in the Royal Irish Regiment. Not that I would shirk my duty, if it came to a war with Germany, but I like what I'm doing now.'

'There isn't going to be a war is there?' she asked, glancing at the waiter who had arrived at their table. He was busy pouring champagne for the two of them.

'No, Isobel. Of course there won't be a war, but if there was I would join up. Now, here's to our first night together in Cairo and to our adventures!'

Her heart sank. Toasting their adventures together wasn't

the romantic platitude that it could have been. Silly of her, of course. She tried to smile back, all the while noticing how many young people he constantly waved to as they walked in or out of Shepheard's. He must think of her as just a friend after all.

'I was thinking you might like to take afternoon tea at the pyramids tomorrow. The Mena House Hotel has an excellent veranda for you to relax on, they even have a swimming pool if you care for a swim.'

Isobel burst out laughing. 'Gracious, a swimming pool! At the pyramids.' She wondered if she would be brave enough to go in the water with him. Her nerves were getting the better of her, sitting beside him and the slight tremble in her hand meant she slopped the champagne a little. Embarrassed, she hoped he didn't notice, whereas he didn't seem nervous in the slightest, just friendly like he'd always been. 'When do you have to work, Edward? We can't be selfish and keep you away from it.'

'I arranged for a few days off since you have just arrived. But after that, I'm afraid I will only be free in the evenings. There is so much to look forward to, Isobel. Do you care for the opera? Verdi's "Aida" is being performed. I have heard it myself once before. I hope to get tickets if you would care to go.'

'That would be wonderful.'

'And then there are so many parks and gardens you will enjoy and the museums, especially the Egyptian one; artefacts from the pyramids, Isobel. And balls and dances every evening, and we can take boat trips under the stars, and watch the sun setting. There is so much to show you.'

'A month hardly seems long enough, Edward,' she replied, her words catching in the back of her throat. She had a strange sensation as though this was her only time. She didn't deserve to be this happy, with so much to look forward to. She wondered how long it would last, particularly once her mother arrived.

'You look sad, Isobel? Is something wrong?' he asked.

'No, not at all. I wish I could preserve this moment forever, right before we start our holiday, where I know I will take great delight in exploring everything. I am just so grateful to be here, that is all.'

'That is a relief, and just what I'd expect an artist to say. I can't wait for you to try painting out here.'

'It will be delightful, Edward. All of it is going to be an adventure. I can't wait.'

'Ah, here are the rest of our party. May I escort you into dinner?'

Isobel nodded. She was happy, of course she was, but she was a bundle of nerves and she knew it would be a few more days until she relaxed around him.

Dinner was practically perfect, but her nerves stopped her eating as much as she would like. Edward escorted her onto the dance floor for the very first dance of the night. She never lacked for dance partners the rest of the evening, but she excused herself to find the ladies room and powder her nose. When she returned it was hard to find her group, and when she did spot them, her confidence instantly left her. Edward was dancing with someone else.

Edward's partner was small, with glossy dark chestnut curls and perfectly arched eyebrows. The young lady lifted her chin to look up at Edward. Isobel tried not to stare as they quick-stepped across the floor. Edward continued to sweep the lady around the dance floor, but his eyes locked onto Isobel once he spotted her. Every time he moved and disappeared behind another couple, his eyes still sought her out. Isobel breathed in sharply and a pain settled into her chest.

Stop it, she chided herself, of course he's free to dance with other ladies – but the damage was done. She stood back into a corner for a few minutes in order to get a firm grip on her emotions. Mrs Dunwoody glided past deep in conversation with a lady Isobel didn't know, halting right in front of her hiding place.

'Excellent dancing as ever, Lavinia,' the other woman with a wrinkly neck and too much face powder said. 'Shepheard's always did know how to hold a dance. Who is that divine young woman with Edward?'

'She,' Mrs Dunwoody raised her chin a little to get a better view, 'is Miss Lucy Hartington. We have great hopes of a match between her and Edward. Her father is the Colonel Major of the Highlanders, and her mother is the sister of the 5th Earl of Bantry.'

Isobel froze behind the palm, her hands trembling against her body after hearing the agonising words. The older lady now laughed behind her fan, not knowing Isobel was behind them.

'Mrs Harris won't be pleased about that. She's made it well known how fond Edward is of her girls, particularly the oldest one. God help you.'

Lavinia Dunwoody sighed. 'Mrs Harris might be acceptable company in Belfast when there are few other women for me to socialise with, and they do have a sizeable fortune, but a marriage between our families? How unthinkable.'

Her tittering reached Isobel's ears and the shame of those words burnt through her skin like the sun in the desert. But the lady wasn't yet finished.

'Edward might be soft on their oldest girl, she seems to

have an unreasonable hold over him, but I've already had a word with him about his duty to the family and how unfair it is to keep encouraging her. Honestly, I was incensed when I heard she and her sister were coming out with the Finches. I hastened out here as soon as was possible. I'll keep his mind where it should be.' Lavinia Dunwoody's friend nodded in agreement. '*She* happens to be the most unsuitable of the lot, have you seen the size of her feet? And she calls herself an artist, of all things. Her mother may as well just put her on the stage and be done with it. Even as a child she was far too strong-willed and boyish.'

The two ladies stretched their necks to examine the group of young people on the far side of the ballroom. Cecily had just danced with Tom Fitzsimmons, and the couple had stopped next to Edward and Lucy Hartington. From her spot behind the palm, Isobel could see her sister leaning towards Edward and making conversation, then, as the military band struck up the next tune, Edward held out his hand and led Cecily onto the dance-floor, leaving Lucy and Tom together.

Mrs Dunwoody snorted. 'Even the younger sister seems to be intent at throwing herself at Edward. Time to intervene, I believe. We'll foist her on that awful Tutty Fanshore from Eton. Vulgar man by all accounts, but unbelievably rich.' She laughed with her companion then, both seeming to congratulate the other with the new match for Cecily. The two ladies strode away from Isobel's hiding place and crossed the room with the confidence of females who knew their place in society.

Hot tears slid down Isobel's cheeks from their harsh words. She didn't fit in – they'd just confirmed that. Even her mother with all the money that her marriage entitled her to, didn't fit in exactly as she wanted. Oh Edward!

She knew she would never be able to compete with Lucy Hartington now.

One tune finished, then the next before Cecily found her. 'What are you doing here, Isobel? Edward has been looking for you.'

Inhaling deeply to control her emotions, she answered as quickly as she could. 'Mrs Dunwoody doesn't like me.'

'How do you know?'

'I overheard!' Isobel exclaimed, her voice breaking, trying not to cry.

Cecily peered intently at her. 'You mean … she actually said those words, about you, just now?'

'Yes.' Isobel gesticulated, jabbing her hand in the direction she'd gone.

'Well, the woman is plain rude, and we are not. Neither is Edward. Smile now and don't let on. We'll talk about this later. He wanted you here, remember, no matter what his mother said about you. You've obviously rattled her, or she wouldn't have crossed a continent to be here. Are you going to let her put you down?'

Isobel gulped, hard, thinking about it. 'Well no. But–'

Cecily interrupted. 'No buts. Pretend you are confident, and everyone will believe it. Ignore her. Look, here he comes. And for goodness sake, smile!' She nudged her sister, forcing her to stand taller and carry on.

'Hello, Izzy, I thought I'd lost you for a while. Mother insisted I danced with Lucy. I couldn't get out of it, you know how it is.' His cheeks flushed as he said it. 'Might I dance with you once more before supper? You might want an early night if you don't mind me saying. You look a little tired.'

Forcing herself to smile, Isobel accepted his hand and

followed him onto the dance floor. Her stomach twisted in knots. It was all so difficult to know what he really thought.

He swept her into his arms, one hand in the small of her back, the other hand holding hers as the music started. They were virtually the same height, eye to eye, and his seemed to bore straight into hers. 'I can't tell you how much I've waited for this, Izzy. Time together, just us. Just like the old days.'

'Oh,' she said, her cheeks burning. She was so confused. His hand on her back tightened just a fraction, enough for her to feel it. He smiled that lopsided grin of his that always melted her heart – half bashful, half encouraging. The one he'd always used when they'd been younger, and they'd spent long summer holidays together down at Strangford Lough. The picnics and trips to the many small islands or building hideouts or camping in the woods eventually came to an end about the same time Isobel was forced into long skirts and corsets. Unscheduled scrapes were replaced by tennis fours and tea on the lawn and Mrs Dunwoody who had returned with her husband from being stationed in India, made it abundantly clear her boys were headed for better things.

Isobel sighed thinking back on their childhood. She'd taken up painting not long after Wilfred and Edward had departed for Eton and then Cambridge. Painting had given her the required space she'd needed away from the pressure of socialising with more young people her mother would invite over and the monotony of sitting still and being polite.

Edward gently squeezed her fingers with his. 'You're day-dreaming.'

'I was. How did you know?'

'I know you so well, or at least I hope I still do. You had that faraway look in your eye that I remember from our childhood when you were up to something.'

She laughed. He was nearly right. 'Your mother doesn't like me.'

'Of course not, but don't let it bother you. Wilfred doesn't either.'

'Doesn't that worry you?'

'Not at all. If Mother did like you, then I should fear I was friends with someone entirely boring and sensible. And you are none of that. As for Wilfred, I think you scare him. You are a woman with an abundance of talent and a brain as sharp as a pin, and he is so used to being in charge, that you frighten him.'

'Alice has a brain too.' She halted for a second.

'Of course she does, but she soothes Wilfred, didn't you notice? She carefully manipulates him, so that he agrees to whatever her plan had been in the first place.'

'Unlike me.'

'Unlike you, Izzy. Impulsive, creative, vibrant and untethered. You scare him.' Edward had stopped too, and was holding her so close in his arms, his breath tickled her cheeks, fanning the heat that burnt within her. He locked eyes with her, his lips dipping closer and closer towards her. 'You scare me too,' he said so quietly she had to move even closer to hear.

Isobel forgot to breathe. For a moment, the rest of the dance floor vanished, and it was just the two of them. Inches apart, bodies being drawn closer to each other, hearts beating in tandem. He swallowed, and she watched his eyes drop to her lips. He moved his head a fraction lower, he was going to—

'There you are, Izzy,' Cecily interrupted. 'Shall we go to supper?' Edward pulled back immediately, but Isobel saw a ruddiness to his cheeks too. He looked away, then back again, smiling, as though they had shared a secret between them.

That same bashful smile she desired. Squeezing her fingertips once more he released them, before placing her hand firmly on his arm so he could lead her to the heavily laden supper tables. As they walked across the room, she caught sight of Mrs Dunwoody standing next to her companion. Holding herself that little bit taller, Isobel nodded in her direction, and couldn't quite manage to stifle the smug smile. She was with Edward, and he did like her, no matter what plans his family had for his future.

Chapter Five

Isobel woke to the sound of the muezzin calling the faithful to prayer. It was still dark, so she lay on, listening to the sounds undulating and warbling in a way she found hauntingly beautiful. As it faded away, she untangled herself from her mosquito net and crept out of bed, padding across the Persian rug to the window and flinging back the shutters.

Their rooms overlooked the internal garden, which right now lay in inky darkness. Perching on the window seat she gazed at sky above her, one side of which was the deepest indigo blue, the opposite side flushed with the palest pink. Isobel lingered by the window until the cool early morning air chilled her skin, before returning to bed wrapped in her favourite shawl. She'd intended to write more in her diary, but the emotion of yesterday had her quite exhausted and very soon her eyes closed.

She woke again to bright sunshine and the day had already started. Isobel felt very daring walking down to breakfast by herself. Cecily was still lounging in bed, and there was no sign of Mr and Mrs Finch. Enormous urns of overflowing white flowers sat on sideboards around the edge of the garden room where breakfast was laid out, the heavy sweet fragrance filling her nostrils as she nervously waited at the door to be escorted to her window seat. As the tall waiters passed by her table, she inhaled something different, perhaps an oil they used on their skin or hair, something dense and woody, possibly with sweet overtones and then heavy clouds of smoke from cigars and pungent cigarettes as men reclined back in their basket chairs, exhaling as they read the morning papers.

Seated next to an open window, she gazed out onto the lush green garden that she'd seen this morning. It was filled with more exotic blooms, most of them she recognised from a week on the south coast of France. Billowing bright pink, frothy flowers tumbled out of pots accompanied by long, trailing foliage of every shade of green. And then there were peculiar plants, with a multitude of long spiked leaves that shot straight from the base with flowering buds so unlike anything she'd seen before, her hand itched to sketch them. Yellow Wagtails hopped and crept across the verdant green lawn, hiding in the shade or dipping in and out of the water droplets splashing out of the stone fountain, and green birds swooped and dived from their perches in the trees, catching insects in their beaks. She must ask the Finches what they were called. In a brief gust of wind, warm gritty air blew into her face and reminded her of where she was now.

Cairo! An exciting new city with so many things to see. A waiter stopped by her table bringing a silver teapot, then another offering a plate of luscious, juicy fruit slices.

'Good morning, Isobel. Are you here long?'

'Mr Finch, Mrs Finch. Good morning. I thought you were still asleep, so I came down alone.'

'Not at all, my dear. We've been up for hours, we like getting out before the day warms up, but I don't believe it's too overpowering now. Shall we join you?'

'Oh, please do. I don't like sitting by myself. Cecily refused to get up, but I couldn't stay a minute longer, not with so many things to see.'

The couple both laughed before settling themselves in the extra seats around the table. 'Edward said to say he'll call for you and Cecily in an hour to take the pair of you sightseeing. Then later this afternoon we are meeting up with Alice and Wilfred and taking a drive out into the desert. We shall dine out this evening, Edward has it all arranged.'

'That's kind of him.'

'Isn't it?' Mrs Finch replied, smiling from behind the rim of her teacup that had just been poured. 'Well, eat up, my dear. You have to keep your strength up if you're involved in matters of the heart.'

Isobel tried not to wince at the words. She fiddled with her napkin, laughing it off but inside her stomach felt like butterflies dancing. It was so hard not to get her hopes up on the trip over, waiting and wondering if Edward was interested in her. Then yesterday she'd been so tongue-tied around him she'd felt her insides shrivel up and die it was so embarrassing; even after he'd asked her down for a drink on the terrace she'd been overcome with nerves for the entire evening. Oh, why couldn't she be all natural and easy-going like Cecily?

Isobel thought of the previous evening when they'd danced together in the hotel. Edward had been warm and friendly, and she'd been convinced he'd almost kissed her, but it was as she had feared – there were plenty of other attractive ladies also vying for his attention, and it was so obvious now that his family wanted him to marry Lucy Hartington. But how did he feel about it? She could hardly ask him outright.

They sat a while longer with Mr Finch doing most of the talking, filling Isobel in on various people he recognised or who he'd heard were in town, and who they must leave cards in with before Isobel excused herself to return to their rooms and ensure she and Cecily would be ready for Edward.

★

'Now, ladies,' Edward said as they stood in the cool of the white tiled entrance hall. 'I thought it would be best if we did a short walking tour this morning, so you can get your bearings. Not too long though, you'll find this afternoon's expedition tiring enough. Follow me.' He led them through the busy lobby, and past the veranda outside the front of the hotel. The warm air immediately hit them, Isobel's nose wrinkling from the desert air and the waft of unpleasant pong of animal it brought with it. The noise of the street was louder than she'd remembered from yesterday, the constant honking of motor car horns, locals calling out for trade, even the noises of donkeys braying as they trotted past assaulted her ears. Edward pushed through street vendors outside the hotel shouting their wares; hats, parasols, bottles filled with oils and perfume, one man even had handbags with crocodile feet attached. Following behind the pale grey suited back of Edward, Isobel was grateful he was with them, but her heart still felt anxious.

Cecily squeezed her arm. 'Come on, Izzy, isn't this remarkable? Where are we now, Edward?' her sister asked as they paused on the pavement a little further down from their hotel. It was a wide boulevard, similar to many that they'd seen in Paris and on the south coast of France; indeed, it was hard to imagine, except for the dust and the unfamiliar Arab voices that they were so far away from home.

Edward gestured left and right. 'Now, your hotel is behind us, the Continental is just up there, and opposite is the Ezbekiya gardens which will be very easy for you both to walk in. If you want to go out together, there are plenty of cabs outside the hotel, you'd be quite safe to travel together. The Gezirah club is only ten minutes away, and the mosques or the Egyptian museum will be easy for you to visit. If

35

you ever need any assistance, just ask in the hotel for a dragoman who will be your guide. Make sure you ask inside the hotel though; I don't want you getting caught out with a disreputable local.'

'What about sightseeing? I want to see the bazaars, and the Old City, and the minarets and palaces.' Her words fell out in such a rush she promptly blushed.

'The porters, or Mr Finch, could arrange a sightseeing trip in one of the cabs, but please, Isobel, never go on your own. And never venture into the other areas of the city by yourself on foot. I know how impulsive you are.'

'Why not? I'm perfectly capable of looking after myself.'

Gently touching her arm, he gazed straight into her eyes. 'Isobel, you'll get lost. Yes, even you, the intrepid explorer that you are.' She dropped her eyes. 'The back streets are a maze of tiny twisted alleys, you'll get completely lost, and, being practical, the British aren't always liked by everyone. So please don't.' She tilted her head a tiny bit, annoyed at being told what to do. 'Promise me, Izzy. I don't want you to get into trouble, I'd be heartbroken if anything happened to you.'

'Oh?' Her breath caught in her throat. Had she heard him correctly? He'd be heartbroken, but she so desperately wanted to explore by herself.

'Isobel!' He stopped, folding his arms across his chest and staring straight at her. 'Promise me, Isobel. I don't mean to be annoying, but you must accept that right now in a new city I do know more than you.'

She thought of her Baedecker guide, and the hours she'd spent reading it. It didn't seem too hard according to the book – it even gave a full description of which bazaars to go to and how to conduct yourself. She was sure she could manage, but taking in the expression on Edward's face he didn't think the same. Slipping her left hand behind her back and crossing her fingers, she nodded quickly. What he didn't know wouldn't hurt him. He paused; she knew him well enough to know he was considering her attitude.

'Hand! No, not that one!' He grinned at her, as she held out her right hand. 'Don't try and trick me, Izzy!'

Reluctantly she drew her other hand forward and she thought her heart would stop as he took her hand gently between his own and carefully uncrossed her fingers, before holding her gaze for the longest time.

'Don't go by yourself, Izzy, because I would feel responsible if something happened. I know you too well.'

They set off down the street taking in a circular walk past the Grand Continental Hotel, then right around the outside of the Ezbekiya Gardens, Edward pointing out shops they might like, clubs, places they might like to have tea, and then back home through the gardens themselves. All three of them were exhausted by the time they stopped under an enormous rubber tree. Another little group waved over to them, calling Edward's name.

'Ah, I do apologise, I need to pay my respects to Miss Hartington and her family. Please excuse me,' and he walked over to greet the three gentlemen and the young lady.

Isobel didn't miss the way the lady inclined her head towards him, smiled in that certain way, even twirled her parasol. With his back to them it was hard to see how Edward responded to her, but they could hear him refer to them as 'old friends'. 'Oh, Cecily! Is that Lucy Hartington, *again*?' Isobel bit her lip to stop herself crying in despair. It was so frustrating. It was like being on a boat in a gale; one minute she was up, the next she was down. She had so little faith in her attractiveness, she couldn't believe that Edward liked her as a woman, and not just a friend.

'How has this happened, Cecily? I can never compete

with her, she's just like Rosalie; all petite and perfect and she always manages to laugh at the correct moment. I feel like a carthorse when I'm around her. It was supposed to be a pleasant excursion, our first in the new city and now I'm desolate again.'

Cecily spun round, her face etched with compassion. 'You must be sensible, Izzy. Of course Edward knows lots of people, please just try and focus on the positive things he said. Have confidence in yourself too. You can't be up and down all the time, it will drive him crazy. It drives me crazy for a start!'

'You exaggerate, Cecily, I can't be that bad.'

'Sadly, you are. Mother did you no favours because of the way she's always been sterner with you, but you must find an inner balance and confidence.'

'Now you're insulting me!'

'I'm sorry, I don't mean to. But you must be sensible. Just be yourself. Well,' she hesitated, 'your normal self when you get excited about new things and drawing and museums and the like. I think that's why Edward is friends with you. You seem to wear your heart on your sleeve and it's refreshing. The rest of us,' she exhaled painfully, 'the rest of us well-brought-up young ladies are too polite for our own good. We say yes when we must and no when we have to, and we've been trained never to have an independent thought in our heads. But please, try to be calm and not jump to incorrect conclusions.'

'What if he proposes to her, like his mother wants him to?'

'Then you will smile and continue to be his friend, just as you've always been.'

Isobel frowned at her sister before turning away and pretended to study the flower bed near them. Cecily was correct, but it still hurt. She mustn't let her despair spoil her friendship with Edward. She didn't own him, he could speak to whoever he chose, but she couldn't rest easy until she knew for certain he wasn't going to be swayed by his mother. Oh, if she didn't love him so badly this wouldn't hurt so much. They barely spoke another word until Edward returned to escort them back to the hotel, and then the words were on her lips before she could stop herself.

'Your mother was hoping for a match between you and Lucy, is that correct?' She watched the colour drain from his face and instantly regretted it.

He ran his finger around the front of his collar before answering. 'My parents and Lucy's parents are good friends, they think we will be well matched.'

'You're not a pair of horses!' she snapped.

Edward half-turned away. 'I'm sorry, Izzy, this isn't something I should be discussing with you, but it doesn't change how I feel about you. We've been friends for years. I did, do,' he corrected himself, 'want to show you all that Cairo has because I know it will improve your art and, well, I just know what interests you. Forgive me if I have been less than clear.'

She couldn't speak. Just nodded in reply.

'Of course, Edward, you've been more than clear.' Cecily stepped in to rescue her. 'And so kind to show us around. We're looking forward to the trip this afternoon. Good day.'

He didn't walk them into the hotel but waved them off after depositing them on the front steps, with a quick goodbye and promise to see them at three with Wilfred and Alice. Shunning her sister's company, Isobel marched through the lobby and straight up to her room, tears stinging her eyes as she went. No sooner did she reach her bedroom than she slammed the door shut and threw herself on the bed, tears of self-pity sliding down her cheeks.

Chapter Six

A slight breeze wafted through the open window, but there was little noise floating up from the gardens that their room overlooked. It was the click of the bedroom door being opened that wakened Isobel, who had fallen into a light slumber.

'Izzy! There you are. You've missed lunch completely. I knew you were upset, but I thought you'd recover enough to join us in the dining room.' Isobel barely moved her head and couldn't even look her sister in the eye. 'I've been such a fool, haven't I? What did you say to the Finches?'

'I said you had a headache after being out this morning.' She perched next to her sister on the bed, reaching across and stroking her forehead, pulling aside her hair. A stray curl of Isobel's strawberry blonde locks had escaped and was tangling itself across her cheek and around her neck. 'Are you feeling sorry for yourself now?'

Rolling onto her side, Isobel looked morosely at her dearest sister. 'I just don't like this feeling of not knowing how things stand between us.'

'And you react badly, I know. You always have. It's your worst fault, as we all know.'

'Oh, Cecily!' Tears welled up in her eyes as she reached across to her sister. 'All these months I've been imagining what might be between us, hoping, dreaming about him, and now I have to wait on the sidelines knowing his mother wants him to marry Lucy. What if she forbids him to see me?'

'Dearest, that's another one of your faults. You have a very vivid imagination. Now,' Cecily said, smoothing back the hair from the rest of Isobel's face. 'Whether he likes you in that way or not is out of your hands, but you have every reason to be the best friend to him that you can possibly be. Just start talking to him again like you used to. You hardly exchanged a word with him last night either.'

'I was too shy. Silly I know, but I couldn't think of an interesting thing to say, and last night and this morning I saw the way Lucy Hartington reacted to him. Why on earth would he like someone like me in that way, I'm a disaster.'

'You silly goose. All Edward wants is for you to be your normal self. Well,' she hesitated, 'not the normal grumpy sister I'm exposed to far too often. The nice one who is full of life and bubbling over with enthusiasm. Just be yourself, that's all.'

Sighing heavily, Isobel flopped onto her back. 'You make it sound so easy but it hurts. I really wanted there to be something more, and now there won't be. I just need time to get over it.'

'Yes, you do,' she said, stroking her sister's hand. 'Now, come on. Get up and tidy yourself and change your dress. I'll ring for a pot of tea and some cold meats to be brought up, and you'll feel better in no time. We're going to see the pyramids, remember. That's exciting.'

Isobel roused herself from her bed, desperately trying to follow Cecily's good advice, but, deep in her heart, she despaired of the future. Her behaviour today had reminded her of why she was so often chastised at home. Men didn't like emotional or opinionated women; her mother had drummed that into her so many times. She must get a better grip of herself while she was here. But she was jealous of Lucy and it was going to be hard being around Edward now.

The tea and cold meat refreshed her, and, with Minnie's help, she changed into a practical walking skirt and cream blouse, suitable for visiting the pyramids. She debated whether to bring her drawing book, but Cecily talked her out of it.

'It'll be nearly four o'clock by the time we are there, Izzy, just time for a short walk. You'll have no time for drawing today.' Reluctantly she obeyed, but her fingers twitched, wanting to hold a pencil again. But Cecily was right. Even though it was late March, the sun had started setting last night by just after five; she'd have precious little time for sightseeing, let alone sketching. It would have to wait for another day.

By the time she and Cecily descended the stairs, the rest of their party were assembled on the front veranda, raised up from the cacophony of the street but with an ample viewpoint of all the Arabs selling their goods. Isobel was subdued meeting Edward again and could barely meet his eye.

'Isobel, Mother said you had a headache, are you quite well?' Alice greeted her friend with a kiss on the cheek and Isobel smiled despite how she was feeling. Alice was beaming with happiness.

'I'm much better, thank you.'

'That would explain why you were so quiet last thing,' Edward said, stepping towards her.

Biting her lip to ensure she didn't make things worse, lightly she said, 'Indeed it must.' She caught Cecily glaring at her, and although it pained her to say it, she continued. 'I do apologise if I wasn't very polite. The sunlight was hurting my eyes.' He simply smiled in reply. They had brushed the engagement issue out of sight for now, but it was going to be hard to not let it mar her holiday and their friendship.

'Now, dears, come on, let's get going or this afternoon will be over. Wilfred here has brought us all invitations to a dance at the Continental this evening. Won't that be splendid?'

'Lovely,' several people replied. Mrs Finch bustled them down the steps then, obviously eager to get going. Isobel followed behind her, keeping ahead of everyone else – she felt just as frustrated as she had this morning. Ignoring all efforts of assistance, she climbed into the front of one of the motor cars that Wilfred and Edward had borrowed for the afternoon and sat down. Edward slid into the driver's seat right next to her.

'Oh,' she said, surprised.

'All set?' he asked. 'I really mean it when I say I've been looking forward to showing you the city and the pyramids for so long, Izzy. Don't let Mother, and what she wants, affect the time we do have together. Let's just enjoy ourselves right now.'

Mrs Finch, Cecily and Mr Finch all climbed into the back of the large Rolls-Royce, while Wilfred and Alice took the two-seater Renault. Unsettled by his closeness, she couldn't say another word but perched upright, trying to control her nerves. A brief jerk as the car started made her topple slightly against his arm and she sprang back, embarrassed in case he thought she was too close. Whether he noticed or not she couldn't tell, for as the cars set off in the direction of the Opera House and the Continental, Edward started up a commentary, pointing out places of interest as they drove south through the city towards the Nile, crossing the swing bridges, and out towards the desert. She was glad she had

43

remembered to bring a scarf and wrapped it tightly around her pith helmet.

'You're very quiet,' he said to her at one point as they sped across the English bridge.

'I'm drinking it all in.'

'Well said,' he replied, chuckling at her. 'Such an Isobel expression too.'

'Is the car new? It's very grand.' Isobel stroked the shiny black leather on the front seat.

'I believe so. Gerry had it shipped out with his last consignment of wines, sherry and champagne. A Silver Ghost, he said. He's quite precious about it, so I better not run into anything.'

There was so much to observe, she started to relax. The ornate buildings, some solid and square built by the British and the French; enormous Egyptian palaces with white marble columns and gold trimmed roofs; and everywhere she looked were palm trees and bright exotic flowers. She was glad the hood was down, even if it was quite warm, as she didn't want to miss a single thing. Even watching the boats with their single sails bobbing on the river was a delight. The sun that shone in her face was pleasant, and she didn't mind the dust that was kicked up as the cars drove along a long straight road out into the desert. The giant pyramids looming before them made her heart race. Words could hardly do them justice. She imagined trying to explain them to Mrs Cox back home. Awe was the best word, and even then, it seemed inadequate.

'Enjoying yourself now?' Edward said.

'Yes, of course I am. How could you doubt it?' So long as she didn't think about him and Lucy, she could be happy.

'With you, Isobel, anything is possible.' He nudged her playfully. 'Here we are. Mena House Hotel.'

They rolled through the gates, the car tyres crunching on the stony path and proceeded slowly up the drive, coming to a stop in front of a well-manicured scene. Palms grew out of planters, and two curved beds full of flowers sat either side of the broad steps. A unique building, it reminded her in some way of Summer Hill; an extensive, low building, the white walls dazzling in the sunshine, but with the addition of the mashrabiya screens. Isobel had seen similar carved wooden fretwork back in the large hall in Shepheard's. The roofs were on different levels, creating a unique feel to the place.

Mr Finch and Edward stepped down first, and Isobel accepted Edward's hand as he helped her out, her long skirt blocking her view of where she should put her foot. Again, he offered her his arm and he walked her up the steps and through the entrance hall, on towards the gardens. Rooms which had seemed dark compared to the bright sunshine from outside brightened again, as he led her onto a beautiful terrace, with rattan chairs and tables and the most stunning view. Her mouth fell open as she came to a complete halt. 'Oh, Edward!' was all she could muster. 'Oh, Edward!'

'I knew you'd like it. Come on.'

A few more feet and they were on the steps of the veranda. In front of them rose up the Great Pyramid, an enormous edifice to those that had gone before. Her eyes wide open, she squeezed his arm with excitement. 'Can we go?' Now that they were so close, she could only see one pyramid in front of her. The undulating sandy desert and the constant movement of the palm trees just emphasised the extraordinary geometric lines of this man-made monument. 'It's extraordinary. I can't believe it.'

'I can see you're excited, Isobel, but the pyramids have sat here for thousands of years, they will wait a little while longer.' He teased her gently. 'Let's take a few minutes first to get our bearings and then we will explore.'

She could barely contain herself and edged further outside, impatiently waiting for everyone to be ready. A long caravan of camels dipped and swayed along the desert road only yards in front of her. Their long necks bobbed up and down and each camel was heavily laden with what she presumed were rugs strapped to their backs. The Arabs leading them seemed impervious to the sun and the sand, stepping along beside the beasts. Isobel walked off the terrace; even in her tightly laced boots, she could feel the shifting sand under her feet and hear the whispers of it as it blew hither and thither by the breeze.

'Fancy one of those do you?' Edward said, coming up beside her elbow.

'Gosh, I'm not sure. Camels seem rather noisy and awkward.'

'It's not like you to turn down a challenge.'

'Well now, I didn't say I wouldn't.' She grinned. 'Shall we?'

'Yes. Wilfred is arranging transport for you now. We don't have long, I'm afraid, but a gentle amble up towards the base of the pyramid and to the far side just to get a feel of the area, and then back in time for tea.'

'Thank you. I mean that.' She hesitated. 'I was a trifle rude with you this morning. Sorry.'

He grinned. 'Forget it, Izzy. Let's enjoy ourselves, and I promise I'll bring you back plenty of times whilst you're here. We could even book rooms for a few days. You'd enjoy riding out in the morning. They keep an excellent stable here. We'd have a fine time.'

'Thank you.' She beamed. 'Now, can we go?'

Cecily said the smell from the camels was too much and Mrs Finch downright refused. Those ladies borrowed horses

46

instead and followed on behind with Mr Finch. But Edward and Wilfred joined them, and after an energetic haggle to fix the number of piastres they had to pay, they set off. Despite the extra height, and a saddle which was different to what she was used to, Isobel found it remarkably easy.

'Managing, Isobel?' Edward called out.

'Of course. It's quite comfortable. It's not so different to side saddle when I hook my leg around the front post.' The saddles were covered in heavy wearing fabric, nearly like a carpet, and all the reins were trimmed with colourful tassels. The camel she was on let out an enormous bellow and tiny drops of spittle showered Isobel's skirts. Throwing her head back, she laughed; it was an experience she wouldn't forget. She flapped at the flies that were insistent on following them, and they trekked through the sand closer to the stone pyramid.

Isobel longed for a camera to capture the scene since she had been unable to bring her sketchbook. When they got up close the stones were quite rough, not as she'd expected at all, and each one reaching up to the waist of a man or woman. They watched a small party of Europeans, ladies included, standing on blocks about four layers up. 'Wilfred, are they climbing up or down?'

'Down I should think at this hour of the day.'

'Oh, good gracious!' Mrs Finch exclaimed as one of the ladies was in the process of being hauled up to the next block by two men above her, and at the same time being pushed from behind. 'What a way to climb!'

'It's not very elegant, is it?'

'No, indeed. Skirts do hold you back rather.' Isobel decided she might look in the shops for a divided riding skirt. Surely they'd be far more useful for climbing the stones. 'They'll not go further, I imagine. They're probably going to watch the sunset for a little while before descending. It wouldn't be safe in the dark.'

'No, I can imagine!' Mr Finch agreed.

'Fancy it, Isobel?'

'Will you take me, Edward, if I wanted to?'

'Of course, not that you'd make it to the top though. You'd be exhausted.' She craned her neck, seeking the summit, but it was impossible this close. 'Is that a challenge?' She winked at him. Perhaps Edward didn't think she was capable, but she'd have a decent shot at it. They watched for a little longer before the other ladies decided it was time to return to the hotel for tea and a rest.

Coming home through the soft, sooty darkness, Edward was next to her again in the motor. They didn't talk much but she was all too aware that he had slowly and cautiously edged his hand over hers, hidden as they were by the high back of the seat, no one would see. The desert breeze was cool, and she pulled her wrap close around her shoulders, moving her hand for a moment. As soon as she settled again, Edward moved away, as though it had never even happened. They were rushing back to their hotel to get changed for the dance that evening, and there'd been no mention of Lucy Hartington joining them; her mind and her heart whirled with everything from today. It was all so confusing.

Chapter Seven

By the time they returned to Shepheard's, Minnie had pressed their dresses, and laid them out on their beds. She ran a bath for each of them, and today Isobel took her time with her toilette. Both girls were wearing white dresses with matching long white gloves; Cecily's was silk organza with a delicate gold stripe running through the skirt, and Isobel's was a silk satin empire line, trimmed with a sage-green sash and the same green edging to her chiffon sleeves. Minnie brushed out their hair and arranged it, finishing Cecily's with a gold butterfly comb and for Isobel she pinned a small spray of silk lily of the valley behind her ear and tucked another into her sash, stitching it in quickly so it wouldn't come loose as she was dancing. 'Now, very nice if I do say myself,' Minnie said, when she was finished, inviting Isobel to check her appearance in the long mirror.

Isobel gasped. For once she did feel beautiful, as she turned in different directions to admire herself. The dress accentuated her figure, falling softly around her long limbs.

'Come, Izzy, we mustn't be late. They said to meet them on the loggia, where the band plays. We'll have to walk to the Continental for dinner and the dance.'

Holding onto her sister for moral support, they descended the staircase, searching for their party as they walked amongst the other hotel guests. 'Where are they, Cecily? I can't see them.'

'Be calm, Izzy. Look, Edward has seen you already.'

Striding across the hall, moving aside for other people, Edward made a beeline for the two of them. It was hard not to notice the admiring looks which other women gave him as he walked straight past them and right to her, his white dinner jacket enhancing his good looks. 'Good evening, Isobel.' He lifted her hand and kissed her fingertips, his eyes were locked on hers, and they never left; not even for a second. 'May I accompany you to dinner?'

'Of course you may.' Her pulse raced as he took her hand and secured it on his arm.

'Shall we?' He led the way back to their group where they were having a cocktail before walking over to the Continental for the rest of the evening.

Exquisite decorations made from fresh flowers adorned the colonnades and sideboards in the ballroom of the hotel. 'Such fancy dresses, Cecily,' Isobel said as she stopped briefly beside her sister, gasping for breath.

'And the jewels! Have you seen the size of the emerald that young lady is wearing, the one with auburn hair and the green marabou trim on her dress?'

Isobel hardly had time for a rest before another young man arrived to take her back onto the dance floor. Neither young lady had sat down for more than one dance at a time, partners being in plentiful supply, many of the men being in mess dress from some of the local British battalions stationed in Cairo.

She was dancing the foxtrot with Edward when he spoke. 'Can I spirit you away somewhere a little quieter?' His breath around her earlobe was so delightful she wished he would do it again.

'Not too far, Edward, I don't think I am as brazen as some of the ladies we have seen.'

He chuckled, his hand in the small of her back, and the other holding her hand tightly. 'I am not about to make you the talk of the town, Isobel, but perhaps a little cool night air might be pleasant.'

'Well, just for a moment then. It is rather warm in here. Your mother isn't here this evening?'

'Thankfully, no.'

Placing her hand on his arm, he escorted her off the dance floor and out into the gardens that looked like fairyland. Electric lights hung between the trees casting a wondrous glow. The night air was warm against her bare skin, and the perfume from the exotic flowers floated across the garden, delighting her with their fragrance.

Selecting a small terrace area which was still within sight of the glass doors, Edward led her to stand next to a fountain.

'Isobel, every time I see you, I am reminded just how beautiful you are.'

'Oh, Edward.' She was astounded. She'd hoped and hoped this would happen, but after this morning she'd convinced herself he didn't feel the same way.

'It's true, Isobel. I have thought of nothing else but you since we parted in Belfast, and your mother made you wear that ridiculous lemon dress that didn't suit you in the slightest.'

'Imagine you remembering my dress.'

'Trust me, Isobel, I remember everything there is about you. From the way your eyebrows rise just above your hazel eyes to the new freckle that must have come out whilst you were in Nice. I know how you rub your left ear when you are a tiny bit nervous, and the way you bite your lip when you are trying not to speak back to your mother. Or me.'

'Edward! How did you know that? Even I didn't realise

that, but it's true. I do. Mother infuriates me so much some days, I don't know how on earth I ever keep my—'

'Shh, Isobel. I'm going to kiss you.'

Her lips parted in a gasp of 'oh', but he was quicker than she was and as their lips met each other for the first time it felt like a shower of stars passing through her. She stared, her eyes locked intimately with his, and he parted from her lips just as quick. 'I've wanted to do that for a very long time, Isobel. You can't imagine how I feel to have you so close to me right now.'

Her head felt so light she thought she might float away. They stood the designated distance for propriety's sake, but it made no difference. Her skin burnt as though his fingers were trailing up one arm and across her shoulder blades and back down the other side, but she was not stupid. She took a deep breath. 'Don't trifle with my emotions, Edward. I like you, really I do, but you're not being fair to me. If you have no intention of marrying me, then you don't get to kiss me like that again. It hurts.' His eyes flooded with guilt, but she turned and walked away. No matter how much she liked him, and how much he said he liked her, his family still expected him to marry Lucy. Her heart wasn't strong enough to survive being tampered with this way.

'Isobel, Isobel!' His voice rang in her ears, but she couldn't turn back. She wouldn't. She loved him, but she still had some self-respect left.

Edward swore under his breath. Isobel was right, she always was, and he'd deserved everything she'd said.

Wilfred was leaning against a column and stood up as Edward walked towards him. He caught his brother as he headed back to the bar. 'A word in your ear, Edward.'

'Really? What now? You sound like Mother.'

He went to walk away, but Wilfred grabbed his arm. 'Yes really.'

Edward reached into his pocket for a cigarette and lit it whilst he trailed after his older brother, his head was still spinning after the kiss and then the rebuttal from Isobel. By the look on Wilfred's face, he had seen the whole thing. Edward took a long draw on his cigarette.

'What exactly are you playing at, Edward?' Wilfred's voice was low but intense. 'Kissing a lady, in public? Have you completely lost your mind? As far as Mother led me to understand, you are only days away from announcing your engagement with Miss Hartington, and yet ...' His face puffed up like a boiled lobster. 'Here you are, dancing and being intimate with another woman.'

Edward exhaled, rolling his eyes at his brother. 'I hoped you'd be on my side. And she's not some other woman, she's Isobel.'

'All the more reason you don't get to play with her affections.' Wilfred's nostrils flared above his moustache. 'We've both known her for a very long time, can't you see how much she likes you? Honestly, Edward, I expected a whole lot more from you.' He paced in front of his brother. 'You got to choose your own career, disappointing Mother and Father in the process, you've picked your passion over duty already. Now it's time to put duty first and do the right thing. Do not trifle with Isobel's affections. I will not allow it. Back off gently and remember your family obligations.'

He bristled. 'In heaven's name, why can't I choose my own bride? You did.'

Wilfred exhaled slowly. 'Alice is a very sweet girl, whom I know I will be happy with, but whom I picked purely for the fact that she would make a suitable wife for an army fellow like myself. Our parents guided me with that choice, and I agreed with them. Duty, that's what I put first. I have always put duty first, to family, to King, to country. Something that you obviously have no understanding of.'

Edward's blood was pumping hard now. He was so tired of having his loyalties questioned, by Wilfred and his parents. Why couldn't he choose exactly what he wanted to do with his life and who to fall in love with? 'So, tell me then, if duty hadn't come into it, who would you have chosen to marry?'

Wilfred flushed and dropped his eyes to the wooden floor. He didn't reply at first, instead moving aside to let a couple of worse-for-wear junior officers past them who were puffing away on fat cigars and slopping whiskey on their uniforms.

Edward was not put off. 'There was someone, wasn't there! I can't believe it. Alice wasn't your first choice, was she?'

'She is kind and sweet and I love her very much,' he interrupted.

'Yes, yes, I get that. But there was someone else and yet you picked the duty wife. You idiot. I hope you didn't mess it up and ten years down the line realise you made a mistake.'

'I didn't make a mistake, don't you listen to anything I said?' His brother snapped. 'Alice's father was in the Colonial Service. She knows what it's going to be like stationed abroad in some foreign land for half her adult life, separated from her children once they are old enough to be sent to boarding school back in England. She understands all that. Do you think for one second that Isobel would have settled for a life in some blistering back-water posting, with only other army wives for company and the stupefying social mores that go with it? No. She wouldn't.'

The confession hung in the air between the two brothers. Wilfred flushed beetroot to the tips of his ears. Edward's mouth hung open, questioning what he'd just heard. He was the first to speak.

'Isobel? You don't even like Isobel!'

Wilfred pinched the bridge of his nose, exhaling before he answered. 'I do, alright. But this stays between us, you understand.'

Edward shook his head in disbelief. 'I need a drink.'

'Just don't trifle with her affections, she doesn't deserve to get hurt, that's all.' Wilfred stood nose to nose with him, driving home each point with a steely determination. 'Either of their affections. No kissing or standing too close or dancing too often with either until you have made up your mind. You need to be a complete gentleman about this and not an utter ass, which is what you were tonight. Make a decision and stick with it. Agreed?'

Edward's guts twisted inside him. He nodded, guilt worming its way through him. He never wanted to hurt Isobel, not for one second, but his family asked so much of him. He'd let them down before, could he do it again? His brother and Isobel though? It was ludicrous to imagine that Isobel would have even looked at Wilfred, but that didn't solve his own problem did it? He had to make a decision one way or the other. Isobel or Lucy? Heart or duty? How would he ever decide?

Chapter Eight

Isobel and Cecily's first few days were filled with trips and excursions to all that Cairo had to offer. They set off one afternoon to the Zoological gardens and marvelled at the animals they saw there including three newborn elephant calves. They sat relaxing in the Tea Garden and were fascinated watching the Pont des Anglais swing bridge lifting up to let boats of all kinds sail through and continue on their way up the Nile; small private steam ships taking tourists out to Luxor, houseboats moving up or down river, and an abundance of the single sailed felluccas, trading their goods back and forth across the river. Isobel thought she would never tire of watching them all.

One evening they attended a lively opera in the Opera House finishing up with a midnight stroll along the banks of the Nile. Tom had started to join their group now, and frequently brought them out to the Gezirah Sporting Club to watch the polo matches there, or a fun afternoon when the gymkhana was on.

More 'at home' cards arrived daily as people made their acquaintance and they were invited to bridge parties, evening soirees and dances. Cecily squealed with excitement when an invitation arrived for the four of them to dine at The Residency. 'Just imagine, Isobel! An invitation from Lord Kitchener, the British Consul-General in Egypt. Mother will be jealous she missed it. Mr Finch said he bumped into old friends of his who were on Kitchener's staff from when he'd been out in India.'

Isobel laughed at her younger sister. They were out most evenings with Edward and sightseeing every day with Cecily and the Finches. Not that Edward had kissed her again, or even brushed past her hand. He was still kind and politely attentive, but it was as though a distance had slipped between them, and always at the back of her mind was the possibility of him proposing to Lucy, and not her. Her heart ached, but she knew she was right to have set that boundary whilst she still had a modicum of pride left. It was up to Edward now.

It was hard saying goodbye to Alice and Wilfred as they set off on their final leg back to Aden. Wilfred hadn't seemed quite so frosty towards her in the last few days, in fact he'd been warm and friendly and had even sought her opinion on things – perhaps Alice had put in a good word or two. Edward was also leaving for a few days to travel part of the way with them and to follow up a business lead he had. Mrs Dunwoody had joined their picnics and excursions whenever she could, on a few occasions even extending the invitation to Lucy Hartington, but Edward had been the perfect gentleman and favoured neither lady above the other. Isobel was frustrated beyond belief but tried to follow her sister's advice and didn't let her emotions show or let it spoil her time abroad.

The first evening without the three of them was odd. Their presence was sorely felt, but Tom arrived with more of his friends and swept Cecily and Isobel off to dance again and again, so it was hard to stay glum.

'Cecily, I must get back to some sketching. You won't mind if I don't join you?' Isobel said one morning. Cecily was going to spend the day at the Gezirah Club again. They had met so many other young people by now that they were never short of company. It was hard to believe that they'd been in Cairo nearly a fortnight already, but Isobel was frustrated at not having more time to paint.

'Of course not, silly. I'll have plenty of company. Jane Fairweather and Annabel Crawford were planning on joining us too. I shall be quite all right. Where shall you be?'

'Well, here to start with, I expect, or not too far, the gardens opposite perhaps. I might take a trip to the Egyptian Museum tomorrow as I wish to take a closer look at the artefacts there and of course I intend to set up my easel in the front of the New Khedivial Hotel. Such fascinating architectural details, I must try and capture them.'

'That sounds lovely, Isobel, but please, don't sit out in the sun too long, will you? The temperatures are beginning to rise now.'

'I shall be perfectly fine, Cecily. You go off and enjoy yourself. I intend to take several trips out whilst Edward is away. But if I'm not back for lunch I will leave a note where to find me, or when I expect to return. You won't be lonely, will you?'

Cecily leant over and kissed her sister on the cheek. 'Of course not. Just be sensible, please. You remember what Edward said about being out alone, and also not drinking the water. We don't want you catching typhoid fever.'

'Yes of course I remember. I have no plans to go far. Now, off you go and enjoy yourself.'

Isobel waited impatiently for her sister to depart before setting off with her portable easel and folding seat and a new sketch book that she had purchased in a large store one morning the previous week. For the first few days she kept strictly to the times she told Cecily she'd be away and didn't wander too far from the hotel. The streets opposite the hotel and past the Ezbekiyah Gardens contained older streets and she grabbed the opportunity to capture on paper the stalls in the bazaar, the craftsmen sitting next to their goods and local Arabs.

Once Cecily had settled into their new routine of spending the day separately, Isobel got up early and pulled out a bag which she'd already packed and took a cab from outside the hotel across the city to the Pont des Anglais and caught a tram out to the Mena House Hotel. She was confident of the route this time, since the electric tram ran parallel with the road they had driven up the first time they'd been out with Wilfred and Alice. There was a small lake on the right-hand side which sparkled in the sunlight and she watched locals going about their normal daily routines, walking beside the road, or leading camels and donkeys laden with all kinds of wares. She had bought a new riding outfit and extra paints. She arranged to leave her belongings at the hotel for a few piastres and return every day.

Arriving early in the morning, she changed her clothes and started to climb the ancient blocks of the pyramid. She had a small bag strapped to her back and a canteen of water and her sketch pad. When she returned home late afternoon, her arms and legs ached, but she was determined to practice climbing the stones. When Edward returned, she would be ready to climb right to the top with him. After her climb and a few refreshments, she always got her easel out and spent the rest of her time sketching and painting.

'You're rather good, you know.' A man's voice floated across the terrace to her one afternoon. 'My girls and I have been watching you.'

Isobel turned to see who was speaking to her. An elderly gentleman with bushy eyebrows and a matching moustache was sipping tea not far behind her. 'That's very kind of you.' His four daughters, so similar with rosy cheeks, jet black curls and cornflower blue eyes invited Isobel to join them for some tea. They were very pleasant and so interested that she opened her sketch book and showed them her work. They offered to bring out more supplies if she needed, as they were on a touring holiday and had their own motor, having driven down from Alexandria. She jumped at the chance and returned early one afternoon to Cairo with them and bought a large canvas and some oil paints to be transported back to the Mena House Hotel. She was determined to capture the light of the sun as it bounced off the pyramids and the desert scene with a small camel train in the foreground.

One week moved into two, and a message came back from Edward. 'Oh, Cecily. He's been delayed again.' Isobel walked through to her sister's bedroom, clutching the letter to her chest.

'You must miss him dreadfully.'

'I do, naturally, but I'm trying to get a painting finished before he returns. What about Mother? I see you have a letter too.'

Cecily rolled her eyes. She wafted the pages at Isobel. 'They are filled with all the people she has met, and what clothes they have bought for Rosalie and how rich everyone is. She seems particularly enamoured with a family who own a string of hotels in America. A Mr and Mrs Chesters, their daughter Felicity and a son John-Charles. She has three paragraphs about John-Charles!'

Isobel snorted. 'I presume he is single. Come in, Mrs Finch,' she called as their friend tapped on the bedroom door which she'd left ajar.

Cecily raised her eyebrows. 'Mother seems to have her eyes set on the heir to a hotel chain for Rosalie,' she said, smirking at the thought of it.

'I wonder if Rosalie thinks the same or did Mother make up her mind for her?' Isobel retorted.

'Now, now, my dears.' Mrs Finch chided them when she heard what they were discussing. 'Your mother will do what she thinks is best.'

'Best for whom, Mrs Finch?' Isobel quipped. 'Because in my experience it was never in my best interests, only what Mother wanted.' She said not another word however, anxious not to earn the censure of her dear friend Mrs Finch. Another few days passed, and Edward was expected soon.

★ ★ ★

'Cecily!'

'Edward! You're back. We weren't expecting you until at least tomorrow at the earliest. Isobel will be disappointed to have missed you. She has already gone out for the day.' They moved aside to make way for hotel guests walking up the steps from the street. 'Do come and have a drink, won't you? I'm meeting friends on the terrace before we go shopping.' Cecily saw the way his face had fallen.

'I hoped to surprise her by arriving a day before I was due you see.' Moving aside to allow her to go before him, they made their way to a vacant table where Cecily ordered drinks for them both.

'You're looking very well, Edward, if a little sunburnt.'

'The time was well spent I must say, but I have missed you both. Especially Isobel. She does keep me on my toes.'

Cecily laughed. 'Indeed. My sister has an abundance of energy and an equal measure of ability to get herself into trouble.'

Edward batted away a fly. 'So where is she?'

'I just glanced at her note. Possibly sketching outside one

61

of the palaces. I haven't bothered checking much. I've got so used to her entertaining herself, rather selfish of me, I'm afraid. She gets bored at the Bridge parties or playing croquet or watching Tom train on the polo fields. We've been spending time apart during the day.' The waiter appeared silently at their side and placed the amber-coloured drink down in front of Edward and poured Cecily's tea into the china cup.

'Please tell me you have verified that she is telling you the truth.'

'Gracious, Edward. Why wouldn't she be?' But instantly they both knew that it was a distinct possibility. Edward threw his drink down his throat in one go. 'Hurry up, Cecily please, I want to see that note. I'll go and find her. I hope I'm mistaken.' Throwing some coins onto the table Edward pushed back his seat and waited for Cecily to rise.

'I'm waiting for friends. Why don't you take my key and pop up to our room yourself? The note is on the dressing table. I haven't even started my tea.'

'Fine. I hope I'm wrong, Cecily, but I can't wait another minute.' She opened her purse and passed him the key while he tore off through the lobby taking the stairs two at a time. When he opened the door, the note was exactly where Cecily said it would be.

Dearest One, I shall be sketching in the New Khedivial Hotel gardens. I shall take some refreshment there and be back in time for dinner as usual. Your loving sister, Isobel.

The New Khedivial Hotel was only a short distance away, past Thomas Cook & Sons travel office and on towards the railway station. He felt relieved, and somewhat foolish. Of course she would spend her time drawing, she was so talented. He should have trusted her more. His eyes fell on her sketch book lying on top of a dresser and opened it up to see what had captured her attention. The first few drawings were buildings and views around the city. The next few were astonishing; he recognised the streets of the bazaars and the people who lived there. Her ability to capture their likenesses was astounding. But he chided himself now for thinking she might have been doing something other than what she'd said, except he had a darn good feeling that she'd gone to those places alone. She must have spent the entirety of the time he'd been away working hard. Lifting his helmet, he returned to the front terrace where Cecily was fanning herself in the heat and chatting to some ladies he didn't know. After introductions had been made, he waved Cecily and her friends off and walked in the opposite direction to meet up with Isobel in the hotel gardens.

He expected to see her familiar figure, perched somewhere on a seat, sketchbook in hand. But although there were plenty of young ladies around, Isobel wasn't with them. *Where on earth are you, Isobel?* He returned inside to look around the tearoom thinking perhaps he had missed her. He asked at the front desk and he asked any of the porters he could see, but no one had seen a young lady carrying a sketching book today. Or the day before.

The vein on his neck pulsed as he took a cab back to the front of Shepheard's and asked the porters and cab drivers there if they'd seen her.

'Yes, yes, sir. Miss Harris. She carries large paper always,' one cab driver exclaimed. 'Yes, we know Miss Harris. I take her every morning to the tram station across the bridge.'

Sweat was trickling under the rim of Edward's collar. 'But today, did you take her anywhere this morning?'

'Yes yes. I told you. The tram stop this morning.'

'But she was supposed to be ...' he began and then, furious

with Isobel, he stopped. He cracked his knuckles on his left hand, something his mother had always deplored. 'But have you any idea where she went after that?'

'Yes, yes, sir. She go to the pyramids to draw. Every day.'

'Every day?' His voice rose a bit higher. 'You are sure of this?'

'Yes yes, you get in, I take you there.' The cab driver held his hand out looking money in exchange for his services. Frustrated, Edward thrust some piastres into his hand. 'How do you know she goes to the pyramids?'

'Because she comes back every night covered in yellow dust, all over her boots. She laughs every day, stamping her feet and dusting off her clothes. Every day I ask her how she gets on and she tells me she climb higher each day. She is very strong, is Miss Harris.'

'Right, take me there now,' he shouted, jumping back in and slamming the door.

'The pyramids?'

'No, the tram station.'

The journey was infuriatingly slow. They got caught up in a wedding procession as they turned into the next street, crowded with families and a band beating their drums. The women were carried in a screened box on the back of a cart and the overall noise was a cacophony giving Edward a blinding headache. 'Can't you go a different route?' he pleaded several times before they took another street and the sounds disappeared behind them as they arrived at the tram stop.

He checked his watch several times as he paced the pavement, his mouth dry as desert sand and his back damp with sweat, which did not improve his mood. Many times he removed his handkerchief to wipe droplets from his brow. When he found Isobel, she'd have a lot of explaining to do.

The sun was blazing high in the sky in the early afternoon when Edward reached the grounds of the Mena House Hotel. He presumed she'd have walked straight through the hotel and be outside the grounds on the far side. Blood pounding in his temples, he halted just across the desert track. His eyes were drawn to a figure on the lower stones of the pyramid. Agile, they let themselves drop down onto the last block. It was her, he would have recognised her anywhere.

Breathing heavily, he tried to calm himself. 'Isobel.' She didn't hear him. 'Isobel!' Still no answer. He walked towards her but it wasn't until he stood right by her feet that she noticed him.

'Edward, what are you doing here?' Her face lit up at him, then fell almost as immediately.

'I might ask you the same thing, since according to your note you should be sketching in the New Khedivial gardens today. But you're not because I've already been there looking for you.'

'Oh.'

He cracked his knuckles several times. 'I asked you not to go out by yourself and yet here you are. Do you know how worried I've been?'

Shifting her weight from her feet, she dropped down to her haunches, to look at him better. 'You look very hot. You should go inside and get a cold drink.'

'Isobel!' he exclaimed, his brows furrowed in frustration. 'Don't you care how worried I've been? You're not at home anymore. Anything could have happened.'

'But it hasn't, has it?'

'But it might have, and don't tell me it couldn't. I assume you've been climbing up the stones here alone. What about poisonous snakes, for example, or scorpions?'

Right at that moment a skinny brown snake slithered out from underneath the block of stone that Isobel was crouched on. She looked quickly at Edward before efficiently despatching it with her sketch book. It tumbled harmlessly to the sand, a few feet from where Edward stood and disappeared out of sight.

'I'm not scared of snakes as you have just seen, and I have boots on. I can look after myself and I have every intention of carrying on doing this.'

'I hope you feel the tiniest bit of guilt because I was concerned when I couldn't find you, and I have something important I wanted to tell you. Never mind that you lied to your sister.'

'I ...' she faltered. 'I'm sorry if I have deceived Cecily, but she would only have worried. But you weren't here anyway, so it's your own fault for coming back a day early. I'm only trying to finish a painting for you. I was going to surprise you. I thought it would look nice in your office. In between climbing, of course.'

'Thank you.' He stepped towards her, where she was now sitting on the stone block. His arms reached out and rested on her waist. 'I was looking forward to seeing you and then you weren't there. I missed you. I'd like to think you missed me too.'

'Of course I did,' she replied, pleased now at his being so close. He hadn't been like this with her since that first kiss at the Continental. 'I just can't bear too many of these social outings that Cecily is so fond of. I needed to get back to my painting.'

'I was scared something had happened to you, especially now that I'd made a decision.' He took a quick glance back down at the sand. 'Maybe we should move, I don't want to chance meeting that snake a second time, do you?' He held her firmly now, hands around her waist and lifted her down beside him. 'Perhaps you could get washed and come inside the hotel, there really is something I want to tell you.'

Her insides tumbled over. 'Honestly, Edward. I'm not like other young women who you see at the dances or sitting on the verandas who gaze adoringly at you. I like exploring and climbing and painting. If you'd rather someone who was as pretty as a picture and agrees with everything you say, then I'm sorry, but we're just not suited to be friends.'

'Of course I don't, Izzy. You are headstrong and infuriating all at the same time, and because of that I believe we are *perfectly* matched. I would be bored with anyone else.' He stepped in closer, pulling her into his arms, one hand reaching up to the nape of her neck and inhaling her fragrance before kissing her deeply, her mouth falling open in surprise. Releasing her gently from his arms they stood facing each other, breathless at what had just happened. Around them the wind swept trails of dust over their feet, other tourist voices could be heard in the background and the sound of several camels braying filtered across the desert. The scene was the same, but they were changed.

'I'm going inside for a drink to calm down. I know you're not like other women, that's why I'm attracted to you. But please, Isobel, don't scare me like that again.' Turning, he marched back to the safety of the public bar in the hotel there would be plenty of people, otherwise he couldn't account for not wanting to kiss her like that again.

'Heavens!' Isobel muttered as she watched his back disappear into the hotel. She couldn't concentrate any longer after the way he had kissed her. She didn't know if her tummy was doing cartwheels from the touch of his lips or what he'd just implied, but she couldn't leave it like this.

She paced up and down for a time trying to work through

her feelings before returning inside. 'Edward,' she'd whispered, coming up to his elbow where he sat at the bar. 'I'm sorry for upsetting you.' The distress in his eyes upset her so much more than she expected. 'But I can't promise to stop wanting to find an adventure, you understand. I'm not the sitting at home type. I must be clear about that and I must be free to make my own decisions; I'm not changing my mind over that. Not for anyone. I don't see why you are able to make better decisions for me, just because you are a man. Women are perfectly capable, you know – we're just not given the chance.'

He let out an enormous sigh before answering. 'No, I'm sorry. I was so scared I'd lost you after I'd taken so long to make up my mind, and I had no reason to put such expectations on you. I was upset because I'd imagined all sorts of terrible things had happened to you and I know I couldn't bear to live without you anymore. The thing is,' he took her hands in his, 'I took these few weeks away to think about my future … and about you.' The barman coughed discreetly just then. 'Come on, let's find a more secluded table somewhere. Drink?'

'Please.'

Taking her hand, he led them to a table right in the corner of the veranda, looking out at the majestic pyramids. 'I've fallen in love with you, Izzy, please tell me you feel the same?'

'Oh, Edward.' Their lips gently grazed the other's before pulling rapidly apart when the uniformed waiter arrived with her gin and tonic.

'I'll make it clear to Mother and Lucy that I have made my choice. I can't live without you by my side, and I wanted to ask if you felt the same way?'

'Yes. I do.' Her eyes filled with tears. 'I'm just glad I know how you feel now. We've always been friends, and that will never change, but yes, I want you right by my side too.'

They spent another hour or so discreetly holding hands and catching up on each other's news before reluctantly returning to the tram and dinner that was scheduled with the Finches, Cecily and Tom.

Chapter Nine

The six of them sat around a circular table in the centre of the dining room and Isobel couldn't stop smiling. The bottle of champagne popped open and fizzed satisfyingly into the crystal glasses.

'My my, Edward, champagne in the middle of the week. You must be pleased to be back,' Mr Finch said, beaming across the table at Isobel.

'Indeed. I missed you all terribly. Some more than others of course,' he declared, his eyes landing on Isobel, making her cheeks flare up with embarrassment. They had returned to the city late that afternoon from the pyramids after leaving her canvas at the hotel. She hadn't had time to finish it yet, but she planned to return the next day regardless.

'What do you make of the news in the papers, Tom?' Mr Finch asked. 'All this ongoing kerfuffle in Bosnia, these demonstrations. I read about it today. They don't like being under Austro-Hungarian rule, you know. Will it come to anything, do you think?'

'Unlikely, Mr Finch. If anything untoward was going to happen it would be in Ireland with the hot-headed Nationalists there. But don't worry, ladies, if anything started it would be quickly stamped out. The authorities would take a very dim view of it,' Tom said.

'But Russia is as hot-headed as anyone, don't you think?

Are they behind these demonstrations? You know how much they support the Slav people,' Edward asked.

'I don't think so. I understand it's just a small student group who like making a fuss.'

Isobel interrupted. 'Well, I understand their point, Tom, don't you? The Serbians and the Irish. Why does anyone like being told what to do by someone else?'

'Isobel, I'm shocked you would think that. One can't upset law and order. Of course we know what's best for them. It's the same for all these small under-developed nations. Where would they be unless they had the guiding hand of the bigger powers to help them?' Tom frowned at her.

'Quite so,' Mr Finch agreed.

'That's very arrogant of them, though. You wouldn't like Russia to meddle in our affairs. Perhaps they do know what's best for their own country after all, especially if you asked them!'

'Just stick to your painting and other hobbies, Isobel. That's what ladies are best at,' Tom replied.

She was going to make a stiff retort to that, but a sharp kick from Cecily and she had to bite her lip.

'That's not kind, Tom. Isobel is very talented and, besides, why can't women form their own opinions? Isobel is very well read and Cecily is too, I'm sure.' Edward defended her.

Tom's moustache twitched. 'I do apologise, Isobel, if I came across ungentlemanly, but as for politics, I do think we men have a clearer understanding of what is important.'

Isobel bit her lip but forced herself to smile and look agreeable. She didn't want any bad feeling on what was her and Edward's first night together. Nor did she want to appear ungracious in front of the dear Finches and her sister, but Tom was not quite the person she thought he was and she had hoped better for her sister.

'Now, my dears, I don't mean to bring anyone back down to earth, but I've had a letter from your mother,' Mrs Finch said to the sisters, discreetly re-directing the conversation. They sat up sharply, neither of them pleased. 'She tells me to expect her and Rosalie in less than a week.' Isobel groaned and got another dig on the ankle from her sister. 'Had either of you heard from her?'

'A little. Mother finds it difficult to keep up correspondence with us. Must be all that gaiety she's having.'

'Isobel!'

'Sorry, Mrs Finch. No, we hadn't heard anything in the last few days, but it will be lovely seeing our family again.'

'Well, since that is the case, Mr Finch and I thought we might take a week or two down the Nile. Your Mother will need the rooms in our adjoining suites, and we'll not be far away. You and Cecily are both well settled here, so I think we might depart in a day or two, returning before the end of May. It'll be getting so hot that we plan to travel back to France after that. If you would care to join us, we'd be very happy to have your company, Isobel.'

'Thank you, Mrs Finch. That's very kind of you. I'm sure we will be perfectly fine here by ourselves for a couple of days. We have a great many friends, don't we, Cecily? Although we will look forward to your return and I would be delighted to join you if Mother says I may.'

'Oh yes, we'll be perfectly fine.' Cecily agreed.

'Actually, I'd like to take a few days and stay up at the pyramids. Now would be ideal. Painting is such a selfish hobby, so many hours by myself. I'd better get my painting finished before Mother arrives. Cecily, would you come with me?'

Cecily looked a little downcast. 'But, Izzy, I'm having such fun with my friends. We've got croquet matches and tennis planned for the next couple of days. Couldn't you go now, before the Finches leave? I'd be perfectly fine on my own when they are next door.'

'Why yes, of course I could. If you're sure.' Her sister nodded her agreement.

'Isobel, you can't go by yourself, it's not proper.'

'But I won't be seen out and about. Think of it as work.'

'That's settled then,' Mr Finch said. 'What about Edward, what will you do until we leave?'

'I'm afraid I'll be terribly busy getting caught up in the office, putting my new orders through. I've decided to invest in cotton. The Egyptian cotton is much finer than American. I believe I can export it if I find the right contacts in Europe. I doubt I'll have time to see anyone for the next week or so, but I'll call in now and again to check up on you, Cecily, if you'd like.'

'Only if you can spare the time, but who's going to check on Isobel?'

'I'll not be socialising, Cecily. I shall have all my meals in my room if that makes you feel better and I'll bring a good book to occupy me in the evenings. I shan't be lonely, not when my head is full of what I'm trying to paint. The less distractions, the better.'

'Splendid, I think we're all settled then. But do enjoy your time away,' Edward said, to the Finches. 'And you are right about the heat. It's getting hotter every day now.'

'Indeed. Well that's agreed then. We'll enquire about a boat leaving towards the end of the week. Now, cheers, everyone! Let's enjoy tonight.'

'Cheers.'

The Finches retired to bed early leaving the others to enjoy the dance in the hotel that evening. Edward didn't let Isobel out of his arms if he could manage it, and Isobel whispered her plans in his ear.

73

Chapter Ten

The next evening, light was fading from the sky, and the first stars of the evening were just beginning to twinkle when Edward arrived at the front desk of the Mena House Hotel and booked himself in for a few days. He requested a quiet room away from any noise. Taking his room key, he went straight up to change and arrived back down in the bar. Isobel was waiting for him.

'Imagine seeing you here, Edward,' she said gaily. 'What a coincidence. Are you staying for a few days?'

'I might be.' He winked at her, ordering them both a drink before escorting her to a table in the dining room. Isobel felt very bold and grown up. A small band played just after dinner giving them the chance to dance again. It was glorious to be together without being interrupted. Edward said goodnight to her at the bottom of the staircase, kissing her quickly on the lips again and she skipped most of the way back to her room. A little later there was a discreet knock on her door and a note slipped underneath.

Early morning ride? Meet me at the stables at five.
Yours E xx

She should have been sleeping, but her mind wouldn't switch off. She went over and over their time together. What he said, the way he looked at her, the feel of his touch upon her skin. She never wanted this little interlude to end. Just the two of them, together beside the pyramids; as though the Gods of old and Kings of the Ancient World were looking over them and raining gifts on them. How did anyone manage to live when you were in love; to carry on living a normal life, knowing even the touch, or a look from your other half would make your skin feel like burnished gold and your veins feel like molten fire?

She didn't think she had slept even a few minutes before her door was tapped again and a servant was arriving with a pot of tea that Edward had thoughtfully sent up for her. Dressing quickly, she was ready and waiting for him. Edward was already at the stables, checking over the two horses he had selected. 'Ready?' he asked her.

'Yes. Thank you, I've wanted to do this since we arrived that first day out here. It seems hard to believe that was over a month ago.'

'I know. Jump up then.' He cupped his hands for her to step into and she pulled herself up into the saddle.

'Where are we going?'

'The dragoman has shown me a circuitous route, around the far side of the pyramids; it will leave us back here in an hour or so. If you find it pleasant, we could go further another morning.'

Isobel's inside flickered at the thought of 'another morning'. The two of them together was bliss, no one interfering, telling them what to do or how to behave or that things weren't suitable. 'Come on then.' Tapping her whip gently against the flank of her horse, she led the way out of the yard until Edward fell in beside her as they joined the desert road. The track wove out of sight behind the pyramids, leading them on, around the side of the majestic structures. No matter how many times she saw them, she couldn't fail to be filled with genuine awe at their existence.

During that short hour as the sun chased the moon away, the colours crept across the land, changing from tones of blue greys, warming into honey yellows, and a rose-blushed sky. They were alone except for a few camels to the west, and an early morning bird of prey circling far overhead, its eerie cry sending chills down Isobel's spine. As the sun crept up the side of the Great Pyramid, Edward reached over and pulled gently on the halter of her horse. 'Whoa there.' His voice was hushed in the echoing landscape. Slipping out of his own saddle, he came around, waiting by Isobel's side. He reached his arms up to her, indicating for her to climb down. She slipped out of the saddle into his arms.

'There's no one here, my darling, well except perhaps the ghosts of several centuries past.' They paused, looking around them again. The sky was filling in to turquoise blue now as the sun rose, spreading outwards from the molten ball of light, deep pinks fading to salmon then peach and finally to the blue sky. 'I didn't ask you before, but I want to be sure today. May I kiss you, Isobel?'

His amber eyes, dark as a peat-bog in the half-light, bore into her own. Reaching out, she touched his face, tracing her finger round the curve of his suntanned face, down the hairline, finishing at the corner of his lip. He moved his head to catch her finger in his mouth, her insides jumping as though she had been struck by lightning.

'Please do,' she whispered, her voice catching in her throat it was so beautiful. Slowly he traced the contours of her lips before leaning in close, lingering over this new kiss, nose to nose, barely touching, yet every single one of her senses burnt as if on fire. Slowly he met her lips, and involuntarily they parted, as though their two souls would be entwined for ever. Breathless, they separated briefly, gazing at the other in wonder, before kissing once more.

'Edward,' Isobel gasped, as they stepped back once again. 'My knees feel a little shaky, is this how it always is when you kiss someone?'

'I swear I have never kissed anyone like that, Isobel, you are the only one. You do things to me I never imagined. I am falling so badly in love with you. I can't believe we get to spend a few days alone.'

'I know. I feel the same way.'

'Will we ride out tomorrow morning?'

'Yes. I do want to climb right to the top of the Great Pyramid though; wouldn't it be better to start early? Could you spare a day to join me?'

'Yes, Izzy. Just you and me. Are you up to it?'

She laughed. 'I will be so long as you don't keep kissing me. My legs feel totally useless right now and I don't think I could even climb the stairs back to my room.' He leant in for one more kiss before reluctantly pulling back.

'Isobel, you make me feel things I can hardly control. Let's return for breakfast and then I must head back into Cairo and be respectable for the day. I'll call on your sister before I leave town this evening.'

'You'll have to help me up though.'

Still holding the reins with one hand, Edward held his hand out for her to step lightly into and she pushed up, back onto her saddle. They trotted back, side by side, marvelling how fortunate they both were to have found each other and making plans for the evening ahead.

Edward returned that evening with a present for her. She waited downstairs while he dressed for dinner. 'Here you go. I'm amazed you don't own one already, but I saw Cecily this afternoon and asked her advice.' He placed a small beige cardboard box on the table in front of her.

'Thank you. What is it?'

'Open it, Izzy.'

Grinning, she carefully lifted the lid off the square box. 'Oh,' she exclaimed. 'A camera! Oh, thank you, Edward. I've always meant to buy one.'

'I thought you'd like it. You can capture the scenes outside while we're here and then paint them when you get home.'

'Truly, Edward, I'm ecstatic. It's hard to remember the last time I was surprised by anyone. Well,' she felt her cheeks burning up remembering their kisses from the early morning ride, 'apart from today.' He joined in laughing at her evident delight.

'When you finish your roll of film you can get them developed in the shop in Shepheard's before you go home.'

'It's hard to think about going home. It's so perfect here.'

'Do you think you'd be happy staying here long term? I mean, the climate doesn't bother you?'

'No. I seem to have survived so far. I would like to travel further sometime. Down the Nile, into Africa. India, oh, so many places I want to see.'

'I thought as much but I just wanted to be sure. Now, how about a drink?' He lifted his hand and a waiter appeared by his side. 'Champagne, please. We're celebrating.'

'We are?' asked Isobel.

'We are. Being together, your new camera and tomorrow we are going to climb the Great Pyramid.'

Almost immediately the waiter was back at his side with a bottle and glasses for two. 'To us, Isobel,' he said.

'To us,' she echoed.

★ ★ ★

A gentle tap on her bedroom door woke Isobel and a servant appeared with her morning cup of tea. She had packed her satchel the night before and laid out her clothes ready for an early start. Edward was waiting for her on the terrace when she went down.

'Ready?' he asked.

'More than ready.' And she was. She felt like this morning was the culmination of all her dreams and daydreams since she'd been old enough to be aware of the wider world. And she was doing it with Edward.

It was still cool as they strode over the shifting desert sand and stumbled on the hard stony path, well-trodden by tourists for the last hundred years. Edward carried a lantern for the start of their walk but left it at the bottom once they started climbing. A chill had crept through Isobel's body to start with – be it from the still night air or purely in anticipation at being a part of a man-made monument that had stood the test of time, it was hard to tell. This was it. Her moment in time to climb it. She said a silent prayer to all those who had toiled and strived and ultimately died building this huge edifice to the Egyptian monarchs from over 3,000 years before. Some might call it an unnecessary folly and waste of life, yet here it still stood.

Her stout boots echoed off the rocks as she and Edward helped each other up the huge stones and her body soon warmed up. 'Happy?' he asked at one point as they paused half-way up, breathless from the exertion.

'Of course. So long as I can be with you, I'd be happy anywhere.'

'I feel the same.' He pulled her close to his chest and kissed that spot at her hairline, just resting his lips and stubbly chin against her soft skin. 'Come on. I wanted to make it to the top before the sun rose.'

They pushed on, aware they were chasing the molten glow of light bulging up from the skyline. Where half an hour ago shadows had chased ghosts away, now a mellow glow was creeping stone by stone up the Great Pyramid. Pausing only briefly to take in the shifting light and experience the beauty of the morning, they persevered, Isobel climbing side by side with Edward. As strong and as capable as he was.

'Last block, Izzy. Are you ready now?'

'I am. Hurry, though. I just want to stand and stare and drink it all up.'

Their arms and legs ached with the effort, but the magical qualities of the occasion made it more than worthwhile. 'Look!' Isobel breathed heavily, catching her breath. 'Just look, Edward.'

Dawn had broken now, the sun, one huge ball of fire, had just risen on the far side of the pyramid. Shadows still chased across the undulating plain of desert sands, but above them, cool, clear turquoise blue sky sparkled with the stubborn remains of the last of the night's stars. Edward stood by her side, his shirt sleeve touching hers, his fingers sneaking out and entwining themselves with hers. They watched the sunrise, their hearts beating as one.

'It is truly beautiful up here. Nothing else anywhere in the world can surely compare with this.'

'No, you are beautiful. This is simply stunning. I know I would rather have a beauty all the way through.' Leaning in towards her, his voice low and husky, he continued, 'And I have found that with you, Isobel.' They turned to face each other, their eyes locked for the longest time when he lifted his head, noses almost touching. 'I love you, Izzy.'

Heat exploded inside her. It was something so ferocious she couldn't explain its beginning, but when he looked at her like that, she only knew she wanted to touch his skin, to devour him in kisses, to run her hands up and down his chest and more, much more. He bent down on one knee.

'Will you do me the honour of spending the rest of your life with me, Isobel? Will you marry me? I couldn't bear to be apart from you for another hour, a minute, even a second, I love you so much.'

'Edward! Yes! I love you too, my darling.'

'I love you more than anything in the whole world,' he replied, getting back up to his feet.

With the skies above lit up like the most brilliant painting, Edward leant closer to Isobel and kissed her long and passionately. Nothing could take away the joy of that morning, nothing.

Chapter Eleven

Mrs Dunwoody was fussing about having to arrange Edward's wedding and laying out on the chaise longue in her suite, calling for iced tea.

'Really, Mother, if you thought it would be too much for you, you should just leave it all to Isobel and her family.'

'Sarcastic remarks are not becoming in a gentleman, Edward. You'd do well to remember that. Your father and I have suffered enough after you refused to join the regiment and came out here instead. And now you insist on marrying that insufferably common girl. Is she pregnant? Is that the reason why? Because there are ways to deal with that you know. Arrangements can be made. Your father had a mistress for many a year until his stamina left him.'

A rage burnt deep within Edward. Isobel was worth so much more than his family could ever see, blinded as they were by rank and position. 'I love her and I chose her. I'm not giving her up. Push me too far and you'll not see me either.'

His mother sniffed, turning her face away.

Edward was not put off by the act, though. He loved Isobel with all of his heart, and as soon as the wedding happened, then he and Izzy could return to Cairo and never see his parents for months on end. 'Mother, the simple question is this: do you want me married or not? I only ask because I seem to displease you no matter what I do. But I'm happy to arrange my own wedding for next week if that would be simpler.'

'Not at all,' she said with a wide smile on her face. 'I have already sent off the notice for *The Times*, I have also sent my dear sisters letters, even though November makes it such a rush. But it will be in London. I will not be outdone. I want a society wedding in London. You can be married from your uncle's house; as he has the title it will sound so much better. Mrs Harris and I have already been exchanging letters.'

Edward sighed. It had gone badly with his mother from the moment he had told her he'd proposed, but it was done now and he'd stood firm. It was Isobel he felt sorry for.

Isobel was hiding in her hotel room with Cecily. Mother had written again to say she wouldn't be coming, but sent her congratulations on the event of Isobel's engagement.

I don't know how you convinced that young man to marry you, but I'm thrilled. He's a far better catch than I could have ever hoped for you. Bravo. Don't do anything to let me down. I insist on a society wedding in London. It's the only way. November will be time enough.

A tap on the door revealed one of the hotel staff bearing a card on a silver tray.

'For Miss Isobel Harris,' the porter said, as she took it from him.

'Oh, Mr and Mrs Finch have arrived. They will be waiting for me downstairs. Cecily, would you join us on the terrace, or perhaps you would like me to bring them up? Maybe your headache is too much to receive visitors right now?'

'Not at all, not at all. I feel quite refreshed and a little walk downstairs would do me no end of good. Tell Mr and Mrs Finch I will join them downstairs shortly.'

Isobel had to bite her tongue. She was worried about her sister. Cecily had also been proposed to, by Lieutenant Tom Fitzsimmons, but from the moment she'd accepted, she'd suffered from such dreadful headaches. 'Well as long as you feel well enough. The Palm Room might suit us best, I'm expecting Edward's mother to call as well. I shall secure a table for us all. If you're sure.'

'Of course. Mrs Finch will be delighted to hear my news, Isobel.'

'Splendid, well take your time, Cecily. I'll see you soon.'

Isobel took the lift to the ground floor and looked around for her dear friends. She spied them resting in the armchairs in the lobby, not too far from the half-naked gold lamp stands. It was curious, in her opinion, when society spent so much energy covering women up, why then, did great artists always paint or sculpt them nude? She hadn't voiced this opinion out loud as she was sure Mrs Dunwoody would take a seizure if she did.

'Mr Finch, Mrs Finch, how lovely to see you again.'

'Oh, Isobel, we have missed you so much, my dear.' Mrs Finch swept her into a warm embrace, kissing her on both cheeks. 'How well you look and engaged too! We were so happy to hear that. So happy indeed. That makes us practically family already.'

'Come, let's find a table. Mrs Dunwoody and Cecily might join us. Did you hear Mother didn't arrive after all? It seems she and Rosalie have made friends with the Chesters family, the family who own a huge chain of hotels in America, and Mother believes that Rosalie might make a good match.'

'I see. And what does Rosalie think of that?'

'She just talks about how rich John-Charles is. Frankly it makes me nervous.'

'Just remember that your ways are not their ways. Lots of people get married for the advantages it will bring them, *not for love.*'

Isobel grimaced with horror. It would be her worst nightmare but, she reminded herself quickly, she was one of the lucky ones. She had found her soul mate. 'Oh, it is lovely to have you around again.'

'We feel exactly the same.' The older couple exchanged glances. 'Now, before Mrs Dunwoody arrives, we have a little favour to ask of you.'

Mrs Dunwoody walked stiffly into the dining room, with Edward by her side. Isobel remembered her manners and got up immediately to greet her future mother-in-law. Should she offer to kiss her? Glad that her dress covered her knees which wobbled under her linen dress, Isobel stepped forward with her hand out. She watched Mrs Dunwoody's eyes focus on her hand and then immediately turn her head and go straight towards Mrs Finch and gush warmly over her instead.

Isobel exchanged a quick glance with Edward. Oh, they both saw it clearly. His mother was not pleased, not in the slightest, but since Isobel knew Edward loved her she could smile pleasantly for the people gathered around them and she would bear anything if it helped Edward. Mrs Dunwoody appeared to be delighted with the large table Isobel had secured near the middle of the room. Regardless of her obvious dislike of her, her future mother-in-law liked being the centre of attention, and the engagement had been the talk of the hotel. She never tired of receiving praise and admiration.

'Mrs Dunwoody, we wonder if we might beg a favour from you.' Mrs Finch smiled warmly across the table. 'We have grown very fond of Isobel, and right now we are feeling the separation from our own daughter quite keenly. We wondered whether you would mind if Isobel, and Cecily too should she wish, spend a couple more months with us at our lodgings on the Riviera? Just until the end of July, when we will return to our Norfolk home. We like to feel we are close to Alice, even if it is still five days by boat. It feels closer than if we returned straight home.'

'Certainly, you may have Isobel, have both in fact. Just as long as she returns to London in time for her dress fittings.' She looked at Isobel. 'I'll need to meet up with your mother, Isobel, this wedding won't arrange itself, you know.' Isobel tried to smile, but inwardly she was a knot of hatred. Mrs Dunwoody's tongue cut Isobel just as badly as a knife. And she had no idea why the Finches had looked to Mrs Dunwoody for permission.

'Thank you, Mr and Mrs Finch, for asking me. I shall look forward to being company for you.'

'And painting, I hope you can have some time for improving your painting skills. Alice was very pleased with the landscape of the pyramids you sent her. She said many people have remarked on it already, most unusual it seems.'

'Have you had the pleasure to be introduced to my close friend, Mrs Finch? I see she has just arrived.' Mrs Dunwoody swiftly changed the subject from Isobel's paintings, which she disliked, to people whom she did like.

The last few days of their visit passed by pleasantly for everyone. Isobel and Edward spent as much time together as was possible, usually in the presence of Mr and Mrs Finch, as they were the most amiable of the party. Mrs Dunwoody remained cool with Isobel but announced her decision to leave for Italy imminently.

There were trips planned to visit the pyramids for the last time. 'Although only for now,' Edward reminded her. 'You will be returning as my wife in December.'

A picnic was arranged for the Ezbekiya gardens, and a boat trip on the Nile to picnic at the barrage and see the locks. Naturally Mrs Dunwoody insisted on renting the biggest boat possible and ordering the most lavish food. When possible, Isobel stuck with the Finches or Edward as they all seemed to have a calming influence on her; left to her own devices she was apt to unleash remarks which were unsuitable for ladies. Now that she had a ring on her finger, Mrs Dunwoody appeared to have relaxed a little – it seemed Isobel was invisible now, instead of at the end of cutting remarks. She thought she'd got away remarkably lightly with Mrs Dunwoody until the lady neatly claimed the seat beside her on the boat as they sailed down the Nile. Isobel's immediate reaction was to get up and look for a better seat.

'Sit down, Miss Harris.'

From her standing position, she looked wildly around for a reason to ignore her future mother-in-law, or at least make a reasonable excuse to leave. There wasn't one. She sat down.

'Now, you and I need to have a little talk so that we understand each other,' Mrs Dunwoody said in the pleasantest tone. If Isobel had closed her eyes, she could have mistaken the tone for real warmth. But her eyes were wide open and the expression on Mrs Dunwoody's face was one of contempt. Be brave, Izzy, she scolded herself. You are her equal.

'I shall be blunt, Miss Harris. You are not my first choice as a daughter-in law.'

'I know. I heard you discussing myself and my sisters in the ballroom at Shepheard's.'

'My my, worse than I thought. Not even good-mannered enough to pretend you didn't hear me.'

'What do you want, Mrs Dunwoody? I'm marrying Edward, not you. We'll be living in Cairo, not Mayfair or Belfast. What we do, what I do, is none of your business.'

'Quite the tongue on you. I wish I could say I admired a woman who can hold her own, but I don't. I'm the one in charge, not you, and I have no desire for you to ruin our family name with all this creative paraphernalia. If you want to be a part of the family, then you need to knuckle down and take your place in society.'

'No.'

'I beg your pardon?'

'I said no. I am an artist. Edward loves me because of it – not despite it. I fully intend to carry on painting and not as a sweet little hobby either, but as a career. I suggest you get used to that.' Her stomach lurched painfully and her pulse throbbed in her temples. She was afraid of this woman, but she wasn't going to let her order her around.

The expression on Mrs Dunwoody's face warned Isobel to be careful. Her dark brown eyes, similar to Edward's amber ones, reminded Isobel of the lakes high up in the Mournes – deep and foreboding. A steeliness flooded the woman's features; she was not used to being thwarted, and it showed. Small circles of magenta lit up her cheeks. Isobel swallowed, holding her gaze.

'No woman in our family puts their own needs first. No one,' she snapped. 'We are there to serve them, not the other way around.'

'Why? That makes us on a par with the servants. Edward and I consider ourselves as equals.'

'I cannot believe I am hearing this! What you need to remember, young lady, is that you are joining a family that can trace their roots back four hundred years. We served the king through many a conquest at home and abroad, and you ... you!' Her lips turned a mottled purple with rage. 'You are ready to usurp all that – you, the daughter of a shop owner and grand-daughter of a tailor. Just be mindful that Edward doesn't wake up one day and realise he's made a mistake. It's a long time until November, you know.'

Isobel spoke with more calmness than she felt. 'What is your point? That I'm not good enough for your son? Is that it? Because, luckily, it's not your choice, is it? It's his.' She stood immediately, erect in her stature, towering over her. 'He picked me, Mrs Dunwoody, and you better get used to the idea. Good day.' She swept away from the woman with more bluster than she felt deep inside. She wasn't good enough, yet again. She would always be found wanting by Mrs Dunwoody and her own mother. *Always. Well,* she thought, *I shan't even try.* Storming the length of the small steamer that had been rented for the day, she went straight to the first waiter she spotted and lifted a glass of champagne off the silver salver. Chin firm, chest out, she made eye contact again with Mrs Dunwoody who had followed her, and Isobel downed the glass in one. She would not let the woman talk down to her. She would not!

If only Alice was still here, she thought later. Alice would have supported her and been the balance between them both. But she was miles away in Aden. She tossed and turned in her bed that night, sleep an impossible accomplishment. She hadn't backed down in the slightest, but more than anything she knew she'd made an enemy of Mrs Dunwoody now. An enemy, and there was no one able to soothe the troubled waters.

A party was arranged for their last night, under the stars out at Mena House. Tom Fitzsimmons had brought a few of his fellow officers from the Devonshire regiment, and

Cecily had invited extra friends. Torches lit up the garden and a band were playing music just inside the dining room. Waiters moved about on soft-soled feet, unobtrusively filling glasses and bringing around plates of food. The night air was filled once again with the sound of insects and birds calling as the light faded, and the moon rose high into the sky. Preferring to sit slightly away from the main throng, Edward held Isobel's hand. 'Remember, Isobel, no matter where you travel, wherever you are, my darling, know that I am forever thinking of you, my sweet. It will be the same moon that we see, and the same stars that light our way. You have lit up my life more than I can say through these last few months.'

'Edward, I think you saved me from myself. I was so sure I would never be happy in marriage that I had refused to even consider it. You love all of me, all of my awkwardness and un-ladylikeness that positively sets Mother's teeth on edge; yet you still love me despite that.'

'Because of that, Isobel.' He gently circled the back of her hand with his thumb. 'You are unique, in my eyes. Why would I want a copy of an old master, when I could have the real canvas of a brand-new work of art. Always be you, Isobel. And know that you make me so happy, my darling. I will be counting down the days until I see you at the altar in November.'

'And I you, Edward.' The tears threatened to spill onto her cheeks at the thought of being separated from him. She had been having nightmares recently where she woke, drenched in sweat in the early hours of the morning, because she felt Edward slipping away from her. In some of her nightmares, their fingertips were touching, but nothing could be done to stop them being swept away from each other. Cecily would wake her, gently rubbing her arm, and then soothing her until she could sleep again. When Cecily asked her about it in more detail, she couldn't explain. Her chest was so tight, as though the air was sucked out of her. She imagined it was how drowning would feel, if that ever happened to her. Was she just so happy she didn't trust her good fortune to last? Or was it a bad omen for the future, a warning of what might be?

But her last evening was now, and she was determined to enjoy her last few hours with Edward. The soft warm breeze tugged at the unruly locks that threatened to escape Isobel's elaborate hairdressing. Her evening dress was salmon pink with a sheer layer embroidered with a profusion of pink, crimson, magenta and gold flowers, the spring green of their leaves helping to soften the overall dazzling effect, for which Isobel had been glad. Clashing colours were perfectly at place in her new-found boldness when she painted, but not adorning her gowns.

One of the young men had brought out a gramophone and was proceeding to put on one of the new rag time songs. 'Come on, Isobel, let's dance too,' Edward said, pulling her out of her seat and into his light embrace. Music spilled out of the gramophone as nearly a dozen young couples danced the evening away.

'Whatever happens from now on, Isobel, our fortunes will be forever entwined. I can't ever imagine a world without you in it, or me not being by your side.'

'I love you so badly it hurts.' Her stomach ached for him in a way she had never experienced before.

'I love you too, Isobel. For ever.'

She pulled him by the arm off the dance floor. 'Let's slip away, Edward, I want to be alone with you.' His eyes locked with hers. He felt it too, she just knew it. Without a second glance at her sister, they slipped out onto the veranda, lit by hundreds of flickering lamps, then they threaded their way through the gardens until they found a space to be alone.

Chapter Twelve

Isobel spent a few quiet weeks on the Riviera with Mr and Mrs Finch; she missed Edward desperately and for some reason felt nervous about their separation. They chose a small house in the fishing village of Juan Les Pins, which was quiet out of season; the fashionable set had moved north to get away from the intense heat. Cecily had travelled on by train along the coast with Minnie as a chaperone, meeting up with their mother and Rosalie in Rome.

Reports of the shocking assassination of Franz Ferdinand and his wife filled the papers. One paper described it as 'an ultimate explosion', and editors discussed the prognosis if Russia stepped in and took advantage in Europe now that Franz Joseph, the Emperor of Austro-Hungary no longer had an heir. Mr and Mrs Finch and Isobel felt uneasy, and none of them felt like entertaining or going to the Casino in Monte Carlo. They limited themselves to picnics and small pleasure cruises in the bay or taking the tram along the coast.

Now and again they would join a small party of friends and head up into the mountains for a change of scenery and to escape the summer heat that was starting to intensify. But many days they were happy to breakfast on the terrace, and wander around the village in the morning leaving Isobel free to attend to her painting. In the afternoons they would go out together or meet on the terrace in the shady part for tea and refreshments.

Letters arrived almost daily from Edward, and twice weekly from Alice, Cecily and now and again from Isobel's mother. Cecily, Rosalie and her mother were cruising up the Mediterranean Sea, had stopped at many islands, and were now spending a week in Malta, before heading on to Gibraltar and then back to England. Mother had had to send her apologies, Cecily wrote, to her future parents-in-law, to explain that they had got delayed in southern Europe on their cruise, and she hoped to be back in England before much longer. Cecily was most annoyed, but was unable to do anything about it. She wrote to Isobel to complain about the unfairness of it, making her look bad in front of her future family. Mother, it seemed, only had eyes on the Americans, and Cecily observed that it was a pity Rosalie's fiancé couldn't just have eyes for Rosalie.

Cairo
4 July 1914

My Dearest Isobel,
Every time I think of you, I think of that last night in the desert, dancing in my arms, with the stars above our heads. Oh my darling, darling girl, November seems like such a long time to be away from you, I can hardly bear it. What wouldn't I give to hold you in my arms once more, and smell that perfume you wear?
We have so much to look forward to, Isobel, you and I. Just think, this time next year, we will be waking up every day in each other's arms, and breakfasting together, oh how I shall enjoy that. We will have lots of picnics and excursions to the parks, and we must go back to Mena House. Whenever I think of you, it is always with the pyramids at Giza as the backdrop. We were so happy there, and I

promise you we will meet again at Mena. We will always think of it as our special place.

I see Alice is due to arrive in the next few days. The heat is unbearable in Aden. She sent me a letter to say she is to accompany a friend of hers with several small children to spend the summer months in Alexandria. The breeze there is quite delightful. Perhaps Mr and Mrs Finch might reconsider returning to England quite so soon, and return across the sea to visit one last time?

Oh, my dear, think how marvellous that would be?

I must rush now, more work to be done. I'm not sure what to make of the assassination in Bosnia, but I doubt it will have any effect out here.

Good night, my sweet darling, remember to look up and see the same stars that I see. Then we shall each know we are still together.

My darling, my heart is always yours,
Edward.

Isobel re-read her letter which was already over a week old, several times more, whilst lounging on the terrace. She had a large box of them now, and frequently lifted a few out each evening to re-read and daydream. The wooden beams above her head were covered in crimson bougainvillea flowers, shading her face from the sun, but the heat still penetrated, even through her white muslin dress, and she fanned her face with the envelope.

'Isobel! Isobel! Hurry, where are you? Isobel!'

She was roused from her daydream by Mrs Finch, running through the small villa. 'Here, Mrs Finch, here I am.' Staggering to her feet, she was alarmed by Mrs Finch's expression. The older lady's features were stretched and pale, her hand half covering her mouth, the other clasping a small brown envelope to her chest.

'Mrs Finch, quickly, sit down, I'll get you water, or smelling salts. *Allez vite!*' She called for help. 'What is it, my dear? Has something dreadful happened?'

'Oh, my dear girl, I can barely say it out loud, for that would make it true. Here, read it yourself. I cannot, oh—'

The poor woman collapsed onto the seat, losing all ability to stem the tide of tears that now engulfed her.

Isobel scanned the wire that had just arrived. It was from Edward.

Alice very ill. Stop. Come immediately to Cairo. Stop.
E Dunwoody.

'We must go immediately, oh my poor girl. My poor girl.'

'Please, Mrs Finch. We have no way of telling what this is. Please. Rest yourself. We shall get packed up immediately, where is Mr Finch? I need him now.'

'He has already gone down to enquire about the quickest form of transport for us. I can't bear this. What if we are too late? I can't bear the thought. Oh, poor Alice. Poor Alice.'

The rest of the day was all confusion and panic. Bags were packed and travel arrangements made. They were to leave at dawn for the train to Naples and then board the *Oceana* again. But whether they liked it or not, the journey would still take four days. Four whole days, and as they all knew, a lot could happen in four days. That Isobel would get to see Edward again was small compensation for the distress that her dear friends Mr and Mrs Finch were feeling. Oh, poor Alice. She knelt by her bed that evening and prayed so hard for her close friend. But out in the eastern Mediterranean, they all knew that certain illnesses could take hold within hours and could kill you before the sun set again.

Mr Finch sent a wire to Edward just before they boarded their ship. There was nothing they could do now but wait. And pray. The weather was interminably hot, and the miserable party spent the days intermittently walking on the promenade deck or lying prostrate in their bunks. Some moments they felt Alice was safely recovered and they had hope, and at other moments as though all hope had gone, and she was fading away, about to breathe her last.

As they docked in Alexandria, a wire awaited them from Edward.

Hurry. Stop. She is unlikely to recover. Stop.
E Dunwoody.

Mr Finch screwed it into a tight ball and never showed his wife.

They went straight to the Victoria Hospital in Cairo. Edward had appointed a friend to meet them as they disembarked, a Mr Thompson, to usher them as speedily as possible to Alice's bedside, the minute they arrived.

They saw Edward first, hunched over, head resting on his folded arms; Isobel knew in an instant they were too late. This was the repose of a defeated man. The body on the bed lay with arms folded neatly, one across the other resting on her chest, eyes closed, skin as white as porcelain. The stubble on Edward's chin, and lines etched deeper into his face, showed more testament to Alice's suffering during the last few days than the angelic pose with which she now rested, eternally safe.

Mr Thompson caught Isobel just as her knees gave way

beneath her. Edward was unable to move from his seat, his body stiff from his permanent position by her bedside all this while. Mr Finch couldn't restrain his wife and let her throw herself over her dear Alice. She was breathing no longer, yet her skin still held a gentle warmth to it.

They had missed her departure from this life to the next by not even two hours. She was gone, and there was not a single thing anyone of them could have done to have stopped it.

Edward raised his head, his shoulders stiff and painful, unable to look directly at Mr and Mrs Finch keening over the body of their only child.

Pulling out a silver hip flask, Mr Thompson passed it to his friend. Edward slugged back two mouthfuls.

'My brother Wilfred will be here by six tomorrow evening. He was on operations up country before word came. He was unable to get here sooner.' He took another swig, his head jerking back, his movements slow and stiff.

'Edward?' Isobel was alarmed. Her fiancé, dishevelled and bleary-eyed, lifted his head towards her, but stopped short of meeting her gaze.

Still supported in part by Thompson, she made a small step towards Edward. 'Miss Harris, Edward has not slept more than three hours, I would say, during the last three days. Not since Mrs Dunwoody became critically ill.'

'Edward, Edward, it's me, Isobel. Come now, it's time to go home. Edward, can you hear me?'

Slowly, as though his shoulders were in pain, he lifted his head towards her, bags under his eyes as though he had kept his eyes open by sheer force of will. 'Isobel?'

'Shh, shh, Edward. It's over, you can go home now. It's over. Come on now.'

★

'We're bringing you back to a family home, Miss Harris. Friends of Edward and mine, Mr and Mrs McMurty, from Edinburgh, are renting a very peaceful villa,' Mr Thompson explained a few hours later. 'It has plenty of rooms, and a garden. They have offered for you all to stay there, together with Alice's husband Wilfred, when he arrives. Their servants will be on hand to assist with everything.'

Isobel couldn't make her legs do as they were told, and neither could Mr and Mrs Finch. They hovered, unwilling to move away from the body, knowing it would be the last time.

'Please, Mr Finch, the undertakers have arrived,' Mr Honeywell, the minister said. 'We will take the very best care of your daughter, but we need a few hours now. I will call at the house, I'm sure someone will still be up. We will talk then. Now, please. Go with Mr Thompson.'

Isobel was supported by Mr Thompson and Mrs Finch by her husband and they staggered down the corridor, handkerchiefs pressed against their mouths, lest a great wail erupt.

The party made it to the front steps and were surprised to see night had fallen and the stars were now out.

'How bizarre,' remarked Mr Finch. 'When the sun last set, our darling daughter was still alive, but now, now she is among the angels.' They all peered up into the purple ink, that hung heavy with twinkling stars.

'Is she there, do you suppose?' Mrs Finch asked.

'Oh yes, yes she is. I can feel it, Mrs Finch. Can't you? She feels so close, in the humid air and the soft twilight, I believe she is, and always will be. I feel more connected to her now, than all those weeks we were separated,' Isobel said.

Nodding through her tears, Mrs Finch attempted to move her lips into a smile, but it was far too early for that. The grief was overwhelming, and nothing would bring comfort tonight.

'Here now, ladies. These are our carriages. Let's get you back.'

Once they arrived at the home of the McMurty's they were swept in by hushed servants, who calmly and gently ushered the ladies away to bedrooms with baths already drawn. Clothes were gently pulled off them, and caring maids stood by to soak them and rinse away the dust and dirt of the last few days. But nothing could be done with the painful memories of the last few hours. They could not be erased.

'Please,' Isobel asked, when she was dressed again in a nightgown and silk dressing gown, which must have belonged to Mrs McMurty, for it was not hers, 'please tell me where are the others? Mr and Mrs Finch?'

'Please, lady, the Finches have retired. Mrs Finch is now sleeping; a doctor arrived to administer a sleeping draught. She will not rise until the morning. The other gentlemen are also sleeping, except Mr Dunwoody. He has arrived and asked for you. Are you hungry? We have food laid out downstairs, he is waiting for you.'

'But I can't see him like this?' she replied in dismay.

'No one will see you, I promise. Just for some food and then back to bed. I have shown Mr Dunwoody where his room is for the night. Mr and Mrs McMurty will be away for a few days, and you are all to stay here. Whatever you need, miss, consider it done.'

Isobel gave up worrying whether it was proper or not and followed her down the stairs. As she said, no one was about. The maid showed her into a little sitting room, where a small table had been laid out with a supper. And there stood Edward, like a ghost of his former self. Her heart broke for her fiancé, and she held open her arms, not knowing whether he would come to her or not but feeling instinctively that she needed a human touch, to be held by him tonight.

'Isobel, my darling. Darling girl.' A split second was all it took as he swept her up into his arms. He kissed her hair, still damp around her forehead from the bath, then, her temples, her ears and then he found her mouth.

For a little while, time stood still, as if the air no longer belonged in her body. The kiss was as deep as the deepest ocean, yet as light as the most jeweled stars in the night sky.

'Edward,' her breath was husky, as his lips devoured hers and she thought she would faint.

'Edward, my love, I'm here. I'm here, my darling, I'm right with you.' His kisses shook her to her core, not because she didn't know what she was doing, but because her body seemed to know instinctively what it was he was doing, and what she wanted. Stretching up into his body, her curves pressed tight against his body, his chest, his thighs. He groaned.

'Are you ill? Do you need a doctor?'

Pushing her away from him he shook his head. 'You are irresistible, Isobel my darling, but I need food. Come, sit down and we shall eat.'

Reluctantly she sat down, but her legs still quivered, and her temples throbbed as though she had taken too much drink. 'Edward …'

'Shh. Just eat, Isobel. There is too much to say, and I can't find the right words. Not for Alice, and not to explain how you make me feel. Here.'

He poured her a glass of wine and placed small portions of food on her plate, then did the same for himself. Neither of them tasted the food as it passed their lips, but it filled a need from within their bodies. Edward had missed many a meal in his bedside vigil over the last few days.

When their hunger was satiated, the grief flooded back once more and Isobel burst into tears. 'Oh, poor poor Alice. She was such a dear friend to me; how swift and sudden it was. Oh, Edward darling, such an uncertain life we live. We do not know what each day shall bring, yet we treat each day as though we have thousands of them before us. How careless we are of time. Oh, my poor Alice.'

'Shush, darling girl. We must learn to appreciate what we have.' He let his breath out slowly. 'I understand that Alice might have been with child. She didn't stay more than two days in Alexandria before she caught the train back to Cairo to visit me and seek medical advice at the hospital. That was when she became unwell. I could do nothing except sit with her and wire her parents.'

Her sobs became louder and louder, deep angry sobs from within her. Abandoning his chair, he came and knelt on the elaborately woven rug beneath her feet, his head pushed into her belly, arms tightly encircling her soft yielding body. His own tears fell too, hidden because they soaked into the white embroidered negligée that she wore, barely separating her bare skin and his mouth. The miniscule second that teetered between grief and desire passed over and then he was covering her breast with his mouth, kissing her warm body. Gasping, she opened her knees to draw his body closer to hers, arching her back involuntarily as his thumb reached up to stroke her exposed skin across her chest. 'Please, Edward,' she breathed, 'whatever this is, don't stop. I want you with me all night. I want your body next to mine all night long.'

Lifting his face to meet hers, he whispered back. 'Are you sure, Isobel? I want to make love to you too, but if we do it there is no going back. We can't undo it.'

'I am sure, Edward. I am not going to waste a single precious moment of the life that I have. I am sure. Make love to me please.'

'Very well.' He got to his feet before scooping her up into his arms and carried her back up to her bedroom. It was Alice's death yes, but there was something else. An urgency, a feeling, something agonising in the night air or in his dreams. Life was precious, and they could not waste even a second of it.

Chapter Thirteen

There was a deathly silence in the carriage. Nothing anyone could say would make it any better, so they kept their faces turned away from each other, desperately trying to hold back the tears. Perfectly matched Arab horses pulled their carriage, trotting past The Residency, following another which carried Alice's coffin. Black feathers on the horses' bridles fluttered in the breeze and Isobel had to clench her fists not to throw herself out and onto the road. Alice was only dead a day and yet here they were, driving her to her final resting place. It shouldn't be so. She wanted to scream and shout and rage at the sun, tear her clothes and disturb her nicely dressed hair and let it blow ragged and wild in the wind.

Several times she'd seen a funeral procession proceeding past Shepheard's, all bustle and clamour and wailing; she'd often remarked how much more civilised it seemed to allow the mourners to shout and cry and beat their breasts like that and let it all out. And yet here she was instead with a carriage full of Alice's loved ones and not a single sound among them.

There had been a funeral service in the protestant All Saints church just off Opera Square. Three of Alice's favourite hymns had been chosen and barely one of their close party had been able to sing a note.

The first view of the gaping hole in the sandy earth was Mrs Finch's undoing. She staggered as though to faint. Mr Finch caught her by one elbow and Edward the other. Isobel knew she wouldn't swoon, but if one single soul was kind to her right this moment it would likely unleash a tidal wave of emotion. She balled her fists hard, nails biting into flesh, and kept her eyes to the ground; only discovering how disturbing it was to see the Cairo dust covering everyone's shoes and thinking how Alice would surely hate to be covered so inside her coffin. In a handful of dust flung down onto the coffin, and a bouquet of palest pink spray roses placed at the side, it was over. Nothing could ever change the fact that poor Alice was now lying for eternity in a cemetery far from her home. *But I will be here*, she reminded herself. When Edward and I are married, I will come and share my news and keep her company and she will be a friend for me too.

A stream of mourners came, one by one to clutch the hands of Mr and Mrs Finch and wring their handkerchiefs in despair and exclaim about the dreadful climate they lived amongst, and how that must have played a part in it all. Isobel turned her head away; she couldn't bear to hear the 'if onlys' and the 'what might have beens'. And then it was over, and the final wreath was placed on the grave and Edward, always hovering by her elbow directed her back to the carriage and they drove back to the McMurty's house where strong drinks were poured.

'Say something,' Edward whispered when they were perched on a gold stuffed sofa in the corner of the drawing room. She shook her head, no.

'Please. Just one word to let me know you are still in there somewhere.'

Dragging her eyes from the safety of investigating the minutiae of the handcrafted Persian rug, she followed the outline of his leg, up past his knees, his thighs, his hands, his body, his chest and finally up to meet his gaze. 'Last night,' he mouthed, 'are we, *are you*, happy?'

There was an almost imperceptible curve to the corner of her lip, and her hand reached out towards his, the fragile touch of her baby finger slowly caressed the tip of his. Her eyes dropped slowly down the extent of his body again, seeing more than just his suit. She was torn; a part of her wanted to curl up and never face the world again now it had dragged her beloved friend from her; but yet, if that hadn't happened, she wouldn't have had the night and the joyous experience that she had had with Edward. 'Later,' she whispered before shooing away another servant who hovered with a plate of cucumber sandwiches and slices of tongue and beef. Nothing would induce her appetite today.

Daylight faded slowly through the afternoon, the curtains were drawn, and they perched, like sad little ducks on chairs and sofas in a hazy half-light until it was acceptable to retire to bed. Dinner had been more cold meats laid out in the dining room, but Isobel could hardly register she was hungry. Edward left for a short time to return to his lodgings before returning after dinner carrying a small box which he passed to a servant to have delivered up to Isobel's room along with a request to pass on a note.

Some sweetmeats to tempt your appetite. I'll be waiting in the garden. E x

Isobel sniffed the small pastries, inhaling a delicious fruity concoction mixed with spices. Now her stomach rumbled. Pushing her feet into a light pair of slippers, she returned to the downstairs rooms. When a servant appeared, she flipped open her box of pastries. 'What would you recommend drinking with these please? Tea? A cocktail?'

'I shall pick for you, Miss Harris, please, I bring you.'

'Thank you, I'll be outside.' He bowed before silently

slipping away, leaving Isobel on her own again. The house was deathly still; the Finches had retired to their bedroom. Finding her way in the dim gloom, she padded towards the garden room, a loggia of Italian columns at odds with the Arabian-styled tiled fountain in the centre of the garden. The glow of his cigarette gave away Edward's position, the moon and stars not giving enough light into this sheltered courtyard. He reclined in a basket chair, and there was another pulled up close to it, a small octangle table decorated with colourful tiles and inlaid with mother of pearl sat on his right side and he intermittently swigged from his glass or blew puffs of pungent smoke into the sooty darkness.

'Isobel.'

'Thank you, they look exquisite. Why did you buy them?'

'Sit.' He patted the chair next to him. 'You needed something different, a new experience. I think you'll like them.' The servant returned with a tray with a silver plate with the treats and a pot of tea. The smell was unusual, something she couldn't place.

'Rose petals perhaps, and fruit. Fragrant, you'll like it.'

'Thank you.' And then it became just the two of them again. As her tea cooled, Edward caressed her hand with his spare one. 'I believe I'm dreaming, Isobel, and when I wake up, you'll be gone.'

'I feel that too, though right now it feels like a nightmare, yet, with us, it is a dream. How could I ever have known that could exist between us. It is so special.'

'Magical, Isobel. Magical. To think, all those years ago when we slept out under the stars in Summer Hill, that one day we'd be together like this in Egypt. The same stars, but everything has changed.'

'Not everything, Edward. We were friends back then, and I believe, we are still friends now.'

'True. We are, and we will still be friends even though we will be married. I love you, my darling, you make me so immeasurably happy. I just regret that Alice's life was the knife on which we found our happiness.'

'Shh, please. I can't even think of it. Being together right now, that is what is so special.'

They stayed where they were for a while, Isobel sipping her fragrant tea, and nibbling at the pastries and sharing a cigarette; their eyes becoming accustomed to the darkness. The heavy scent of jasmine and lilies perfumed the air and above it all the sounds of the city drifted leisurely over the walls of the garden, and the occasional door closing within. They were essentially alone. When the time came for Edward to depart, she held firmly onto his hand and led him quietly back up to her room.

Chapter Fourteen

Wilfred joined them at the McMurty's house. The day he returned in a sweaty, dust-covered, grief-stricken state, Isobel had sat by his side in the carriage as he paid his last respects to Alice. On the way home he'd simply held her hand tightly while tears wet his face. He was as silent as the mummies inside the pyramids.

The household was still observing the mourning period, and they weren't accepting visitors. Wilfred walked out every day to meet with old friends at the barracks and drink too much. He brought news of disturbances in Bosnia, and tales of what retaliation Emperor Franz Joseph might impose on Bosnia after the Serbian nationalist had murdered his nephew and heir. Indeed, he talked more of it than he spoke of Alice.

'What should we do?' Mr Finch looked to Edward and Wilfred for advice. Neither he nor Mrs Finch wanted to leave Cairo so soon. 'Are we in danger, do you think?' He had aged over the last ten days, wrinkles deepening around his eyes. 'Will it end up in a war?'

'Mr Finch, please don't concern yourself. If there is any trouble it is still a long way from here, and I imagine will be dealt with quickly. None of the other European powers want to go to battle. It is all just talk. Please don't alarm yourself,' Wilfred said, one night, holding yet another whiskey glass in his hand. The bags under his eyes now matched Edward's and the Finches.

Every day the Finches took a carriage ride in the early morning to visit Alice's grave and when they returned, they cloistered themselves in the dimness of the drawing room with only Isobel for company.

Isobel thought she would scream if she couldn't get out and get air into her lungs. Slowly she increased the time she spent outside as the dim light was no good for her usual pursuits. She couldn't draw, she couldn't write, she couldn't even read.

A message arrived from the McMurtys; they'd be returning in a week. Wilfred was leaving too. 'I was wrong. Apologies. I've been summoned back immediately,' he announced that morning over breakfast. He arrived downstairs with blood-shot eyes and the stale smell of alcohol on his breath. 'There is news of the countries calling up their reserves. I think you should go home to England, *now*.'

'I want to spend a few days back at Mena House before we go. Would you mind?' Isobel said, looking at Mr and Mrs Finch, her insides twisting themselves into a sharp knot with panic at the thought of leaving Edward so soon. Her two friends barely lifted their heads, but Wilfred sighed loudly over his breakfast eggs and looked at her.

'I can't imagine returning to the normal world without Alice.' Mrs Finch picked over the fruit on her plate.

'But we must. We have to face people again. We have to move back into daylight and people and conversations. Take a few days there before we leave.'

'I don't think I...' Mrs Finch mumbled.

'We won't stay there, dear. But we will drive out there once a day. After stopping by Alice's grave. And take tea. We must start. I will ask Edward to enquire about berths back to

France. Marseilles, I think this time. I don't believe I could do the same journey we undertook on our way out. My heart would fracture,' Mr Finch said. 'If we get a sailing in the next week, that would seem time enough?'

Wilfred shook out his newspaper with such force across the table and glared at Isobel. 'How you can possibly think of enjoying yourself at a time like this, is inconceivable.'

She wanted to say something back, but she couldn't. Anything at all would seem callous and insensitive, so she cast her guilty eyes into her napkin instead and prayed he couldn't read her mind. She hung around downstairs until he reappeared with his bags packed. Edward had been sent a message and he was also waiting to say goodbye to his brother. Isobel leant closer, trying to hear what they said.

'Send them home now! I insist.' Wilfred seemed very agitated. 'You don't know what could happen ...' Their conversation finished, Wilfred gently took his leave of the Finches, all of them holding back tears, before he stood in front of Isobel. His brows furrowed as he squinted in the late morning sunshine, making him seem more annoyed than perhaps he was.

'I can't speak as freely as I would like, Isobel, or explain why, but go home. Please!' She thrust her chin out, holding her ground. 'I mean it. I've given Edward orders to send you home. And it's not because I don't care, but because I do. If Alice was still alive, I'd make her go with you.'

Isobel couldn't say a word, her throat ached. Instead, Wilfred closed the distance between them and pulled her into his arms, hugging her tight.

'Listen to me, please. Edward and I can't fight a war if we are worrying about you and the Finches. Cecily and your mother too. You must all get home now. If you leave it too late, the whole of Europe will be on the move and fighting each other for space on any available train and boat home. Trust me.' He held her closer now, his cheek pressed into her hair, his voice gentle. 'Write to me, won't you, if it comes to war.' His voice was as thick and throaty as hers felt. 'I don't have Alice any longer to keep me entertained with letters from home. I need you instead. Stay safe, whatever happens.' He hugged her so tightly she thought he wouldn't let go, but then he broke away and without much more than a firm handshake and a slap on the back for Edward, he was gone, jumping into the motor that was waiting for him. The vehicle kicked up dust as he sped out the driveway and disappeared down the road.

'The papers have arrived,' Edward said later that day. He'd been to the Thomas Cook office and booked their berths home. 'The emperor has issued an ultimatum to the Serbians. I can't see that they will agree to it. Dreadful business.' Edward threw the Egyptian Gazette down onto the coffee table.

'Is it serious?' Mrs Finch gazed at him with sorrowful eyes. She was half the woman she had been when they had arrived in Egypt just a few months before. 'Wilfred said it was.'

'It's hard to tell, Mrs Finch. All the European states have these agreements with each other, but I can't see how it will escalate, not unless Russia decides to mobilise its troops.'

'I feel uneasy though, don't you? Russia is already backing Serbia. They said so, I read it in the paper.' Mr Finch joined in the conversation.

'I should feel safer if you came back with us, Edward.' Isobel cast a worried glance towards him across the small table.

'My dear, I shall be fine. Nothing will happen, and besides, we're far away from any trouble. On the contrary, your passage is direct to France. I would have been uneasy had you been delayed in Naples.'

No one was satisfied, though. Whether it was Alice's death, or the news coming from Vienna, there was a nervous tension between them all. A discreet knock at the door and one of the Nubian servants padded in so silently he could barely be heard. He held a silver salver out for Mr Finch with a letter on it.

'Who is it from, dear?' Mrs Finch enquired. All of them watched his expression change as he read the letter. 'It's from Tom. He sends his apologies that he can't visit, but he also sends his express wish that we return home immediately, not stopping. He says he will only feel reassured when he hears we are safely back in Norfolk. He has written the same to Cecily.'

Isobel snorted. 'Mother will hardly listen to him, I'm sure. She only has eyes and ears for her new American friends, according to Cecily.'

'Your boat doesn't sail for four days. Perhaps I can meet you out at the hotel again, Isobel. You still have a few days for taking photographs and working on new sketches, if you like,' Edward said.

'Yes, do, Isobel.' Mr Finch encouraged her. 'Why don't you pack a bag and spend your last few days there? Mrs Finch and I will drive you out tomorrow.'

Looking across at Edward, she saw his mouth smile and the slight nod of his head. They could be together. 'Thank you, I shall if you don't mind. I shall pack my trunk today, so that everything is ready.'

'Good. I know you are a sensible girl.' Mrs Finch leaned over and clutched her hand, eyes full of tears again. Leaving without Alice was going to be excruciating.

'Come, Isobel,' Edward said. 'Drink your coffee and start

your packing. We shall have our last few days together. Let's not think about what's happening in Europe. With any luck these peace talks will prevail, and this will all come to nothing.'

26 July 1914

'Sit still, Edward, do.'

'My arm is nearly asleep, Izzy. Honestly, I cannot hold onto this book any longer. I must set it down.'

Isobel smiled. They were upstairs in her bedroom, they had made love only hours before and Edward was reclined in a basket chair while she rushed as best she could to preserve his features on paper. The sun blazed outside, and her room was only marginally cooler. She had cast off her short corset, preferring to draw unrestricted. Edward's white linen shirt was crumpled and his sleeves rolled up to his elbows. She'd taken several photos of him, in different poses, trying to capture the way the sun cast shadows on his body and face.

'Come closer, won't you?' He reached forward, trying to catch hold of her delicate blouse which was only pulled across loosely and tucked into the waistband of her skirt. His strong hands worked the fabric loose, gently slipping his hands underneath and finding the gap between her chemise and her bare skin. Gasping at his touch, she allowed him to caress her, enjoying the sensation of his hands finding their way across her stomach and up to her breasts, before remembering her art work.

'Please, Edward, I have only a few hours left. I'm trying to draw you.'

'But I'm in love with you and love beats drawing, so I win. Come back to bed.'

Laughing, she skipped out of his embrace and carried on. 'One hour. I promise.'

Groaning he sat back in the chair, watching her every move. Neither of them wanted this day to end. Finally, as the silver clock on the side table chimed the hour, Edward could wait no longer. The sunlight was just beginning to fade outside and the squawk of birds in the garden was increasing as they galvanised themselves to feed before settling in for the night. Slipping out of his seat, Edward gently lifted Isobel's pencil out of her hand and laid it to one side. 'Now it's my turn, and I've been very patient.' He said. 'I love you so much, my darling girl. Come back to bed.'

27 July 1914

The sun had risen over the pyramids at the Mena House Hotel hours before. 'I'm scared, Edward, please come back to England with us.' They lounged in bed together, putting off the moment when they must get dressed and return to the Finches. A breakfast tray of fresh juice, dainty pastries and strong Turkish coffee sat on the table near the side of the bed. It was their last breakfast together.

'You know I can't, but I'm not in any danger.'

'I beg you, Edward. I feel so anxious. I will not rest until we are back together again.'

He held her in his arms, caressing her lower back. 'Listen to me, if anything should happen to you, write at once and I will come.'

'What do you mean?'

'I was always careful with you, but, if perhaps you should find…'

'Don't say that. I wish I could stay here instead.'

'Stay then. Marry me now and stay here.'

'But who will help the Finches get back to England? I can't abandon them and your mother and my mother would never let us hear the end of it if we got married now.' No, today was just too quick for her to consider. As much as she loved him, she still felt a frisson of fear about marriage itself – about losing herself. She breathed in his scent, drawing in closer to his smooth chest, nestling her cheek against his shoulder. 'If we could just stay like this.'

'I feel the same, but it's only a few months until we are together again. This is the end of July already. Three months, that is all. What could possibly go wrong in that time?'

'War! That is what might happen. Please, promise me you won't join up. I couldn't live if something happened to you.' Tears slipped down her cheeks and onto his bare chest. They lay side by side, every part of their bodies touching. He didn't answer her. 'Edward? Promise me!'

'I can't, Izzy. Remember that day when I was annoyed because you lied to Cecily? You told me you couldn't make any promises either. You had to be free to make your own decisions.' Gently he kissed the tip of every one of her fingers. 'I can't make you this promise either. Because if it comes to war, I will go. I was trained for years at school and university to do this. It's in my family's blood. It's my duty. I will go. I'm sorry.' Tenderly he kissed every single tear as it fell, but that didn't change facts. If war was declared, Edward would go.

There was a dead weight in her chest as she dressed later in the morning. Driving back to the city she feared she might suffocate, the anxiety coursed through her body so badly.

When the time came the next day to board the train to Alexandria, she felt an unnatural urge to fling herself from the carriage and return to Edward. Barely keeping her tears at bay, she mournfully waved goodbye, watching him get smaller and smaller on the train platform before he vanished completely. When would she see him again?

A newspaper lay discarded on the train as it rattled on to Alexandria. Isobel held a handkerchief against her mouth to stop herself crying out. The paper was full of the looming threat of war. The headlines claimed every country across Europe was getting ready to mobilise their troops. As the hot Egyptian sun blazed through the carriage windows, Isobel remembered Edward's words. 'I won't shirk my duty if I'm needed.' Edward would stick to his word, she knew without doubt. A chill ran through her body. If England went to war, then Edward would join up. Her few short months of happiness were evaporating right in front of her eyes. She had been greedy; she didn't deserve so much joy in such a short space of time. The sense of foreboding crippled every thought she had as all she could do was wait and watch.

The small party joined the steamship a few hours later and retired to their cabins for the main part of the voyage. When they docked briefly in Naples it was to hear that Germany had declared war on Russia. By the time they arrived in Marseilles two days later, it was to hear the news that all the major European countries had mobilised their armies. It was only a matter of hours until Britain did the same. Mr Finch enquired immediately about securing berths for the return passage to England on the same ship, and the Finches and Isobel continued their voyage home. Egypt was far behind them now and the armies were marching into battle.

Chapter Fifteen

Summer Hill, Ireland, 30 August 1914

Summer Hill was empty. Isobel wandered from room to room, dust sheets still covering the sofas and armchairs. No one was here except Mr and Mrs Cox. The house lay in that blurry summer sleep, like so many people take in a glorious summer afternoon – batting away flies, semi-conscious of your surroundings, and not quite truly awake. The spectre of war barely registering on this small place so far from the fighting.

Dust motes shimmered in the air because she disturbed it, meandering as she did, through the drawing room, the dining room and onto the breakfast room. Each of them with doors begging to be flung wide open, to breathe in the sea air, to live and not feel as though she was going to drown in an overwhelming mist of despair.

She had sent Edward several letters so far and gave Summer Hill as her new address. If she couldn't be with him, and she couldn't stay in France, then Summer Hill was the place she had to come home to. Not the house in Belfast. She tried to shut out early reports of casualties from the newspaper reports. Everyone said this war would be over by Christmas. She prayed with all her heart that Edward would come marching home in time for the New Year.

Shaking a few curtains open as she went, she felt an undeniable urge to run through the house screaming 'I'm alive', 'I'm here', 'this is me'. She was here, and she was going to live as she so wished. Fresh air was needed in the house, and people, laughter again. Last summer seemed so long ago. Hugging herself she paused, wondering which room she might use for herself, seeing as she was alone. The best one for painting, of course. Bounding up the stairs, she stopped for a moment to gather herself. Her head spun so. Surely the travel sickness would wear off soon. She had been plagued by it since they had stepped onto the boat at Marseilles and the long journey home by sea instead of overland. The French soldiers had commandeered all the trains. Steamships had been the only way.

Mr and Mrs Finch had been relieved to secure berths for themselves and Isobel, after all they had been through; Alice's death, then the declaration of war. Going home was the only option. But for some reason Isobel couldn't quite explain, she kept travelling on, not wishing to stay with them too long in Norfolk, or with her aunt in London, and most definitely not joining her mother, Cecily and Rosalie. She wanted to be alone, to feel free, and, more than anything, she needed to paint.

If only she didn't feel quite so queasy. Ignoring the latest nausea, she turned left at the top of the stairs and peeped into the room. It was the only room in the house to have windows facing both east and west. There were other rooms with bigger windows, but in here, with two small windows both tucked into the eaves, she could see the full expanse of Strangford Lough in the morning, and then in the evening, as the sun sank slowly into the west, she could peer out and watch the light change over the meadow and the pond and the smoke streaming over the countryside from the trains constantly passing. This was where she chose to be.

It opened onto a smaller room, which could be used for a maid, even though she had no maid, for Minnie had stayed with Cecily. She would keep her canvases in there. It also had a small cupboard in the back corner which stretched out under the eaves of the roof where this room met the main part of the house, which was half a storey lower. It would suffice to hide away her letters from Edward, should anyone come snooping.

'Miss Harris, Miss Isobel!' called a voice from down below in the hall.

'Up here, Mrs Cox. I shall come down, don't come up.'

Isobel retreated from her chosen rooms and returned down the stairs to the hall. Mrs Cox bobbed a curtsey at her.

'I do beg your pardon, miss. I had no notice at all you were coming. Your mother, Mrs Harris, had not alerted me.'

'Do not trouble yourself, Mrs Cox. Mother doesn't know and I'm quite sure she will be very vexed when she does find out. I travelled by myself and I managed fine. There is a war on, as you know. But for now, I shall be the only one here, so please don't get in a fluster.'

'I'm not sure Mrs Harris will be pleased.'

'I am quite sure Mother will be very displeased with me, but since she is in London right now, or Devon with Cecily, I forget which, there is no one to trouble us. Now, just bring my meals to the breakfast room, and pretend it's a summer picnic. We shall be terribly informal whilst it's just me and you. Air the place a little. Get rid of the dust covers, but don't worry about the dining room, I shall not need that. Does that seem to be everything?'

'Yes, Miss Isobel, as you say. Might Mr Harris come down?'

'Oh dear, yes, I suppose he might, but he shall have the large bedroom overlooking the drive as he normally does. Although he has hardly ever stayed here. The house is for holidays, isn't it? Father doesn't take holidays, so I shan't imagine he shall come. But I'll write to him immediately.'

'Thank you, miss. I would feel more reassured if he approves of this plan. Only ...'

'Only what, Mrs Cox?'

'Begging your pardon, miss, it's just without you having a maid, miss, it doesn't seem correct.'

'But you are here, Mrs Cox, and no one else is. And I am not planning on entertaining, so that will be perfectly suitable. Haven't you anyone local who you could hire to be my maid? Now, if you could bring me some tea to the breakfast room please. And my trunks have been left at the station. I walked the mile back myself. If Mr Cox could go and get them, please.'

'Yes, miss. As you say, miss. There's young Sarah Heaney. She's worked here lots of times. I'll send her mother word that we need her.'

Round one to me, Isobel thought gleefully. Give orders just as Mother would, and Mrs Cox will carry out my wishes. Settling herself in the cosiest armchair in the breakfast room, Isobel knew she could be happy here. Perhaps Cecily could join her for a few weeks before they needed to return to London. Mother hadn't given up on the November weddings despite the war and no doubt would expect dress fittings and plenty of excursions to buy household items, but Isobel was not in the slightest bit interested.

Whatever she needed when the war was over, she could order then. And, until the war did finish, she would not be setting up home anywhere, certainly not in Cairo. Summer Hill would be a perfect place to be for now. All she wanted was to marry Edward and make love to him whenever she was able.

Keep him safe, dear Lord, that is more important than anything else. Just keep him alive.

Chapter Sixteen

Summer Hill, Ireland, October 1914

'I am taking the train to Belfast. Are there any messages I can get for you?' Isobel asked when Mrs Cox brought her pot of tea to the breakfast table. Her face looked doubtful at Isobel's venture. Isobel felt the need to prop up her statement with reassurances. 'I shall be taking Sarah Heaney with me too, to help with the parcels. So, was there anything?'

'No, miss. Shall I get a basket for you though, for the parcels like? I suppose you want a picnic for the trip.'

'What an excellent idea. The basket, I mean. But no, not the food. I shall find a café or hotel and I will call on my father before I return.'

'Very good, Miss Isobel.'

Mrs Cox's face still looked unsure though. Isobel poured her own tea and stirred the milk vigorously, the spoon tapping off the side of the cup until it spilt. Honestly, she'd navigated the souks of Cairo, and caught trains and boats by herself to get back to Ireland. She was not completely incapable of looking after herself and she had been feeling so much better recently.

She had spent the last few weeks keeping busy with Edward's portrait, but she was very low on paint and felt invigorated by planning a trip into Belfast. Little Sarah Heaney had proved a worthy maid for her within the house, but there were supplies that she needed and she wanted to train her up so if she had to send her for more painting supplies in the future, then the girl would know where to go.

'Ready?' she asked the maid when she met her in the hallway after breakfast.

'Yes, miss. I ain't never been to Belfast before.'

'Good. Then let's go and enjoy ourselves!' Isobel whispered, conspiratorially. 'You've got Mrs Cox's basket, I see, so let's go.' Sarah bobbed a curtsey and held open the door for her.

The two of them were in good time for the train. Isobel purchased the two tickets and they sat on the wooden bench waiting for the train to come puffing and blowing into the station.

'Beg pardon, miss, what station are we getting off at? Just so I know where to get out?'

'Why, Sarah, you don't need to worry about that. You're sitting in First Class with me. You're my maid, aren't you?' She smiled down at the tall skinny girl beside her. Her eyes were wide open and a look of horror was on her face.

'But how will I know what to do, miss?' she whispered, her voice hoarse with fear.

'Just do what I do. Don't fidget though. Have you a clean handkerchief?' Sarah nodded.

'Me mam made sure of it.'

'Good girl. We're going out to have some fun, Sarah, only don't tell anyone!'

'Really?' Now her eyes lit up, Isobel was glad to see. The poor girl looked scared as a mouse most of the time, but she was clean and neatly turned out, even if she could do with better boots and a smarter maid's uniform. Particularly if Isobel intended to be going out more places and the girl would easily do as a chaperone. Besides, she looked like she could do with a bit of excitement, or relaxation. Perhaps both. The family lived in a small cottage and so far as Isobel could recall, there were plenty of brothers and sisters younger than her. She'd have been well used to working hard for her mother. A day off now again would do her good.

Clouds of steam could be seen rolling over the hedges right of the station towards Downpatrick. A movement to their left caught Isobel's attention. That man again. The one that stared. She stood up smartly and faced down the platform towards the engine that was now in view. Sarah Heaney also stood up and pressed in behind her. Perhaps she didn't like that man either. There was more movement now as the engine came whooshing and heaving into the station and that man blew a whistle and waved a flag and all around was bustle. As it came to a halt a guard got off and opened the door for them.

First Class was quiet. Just two other ladies and three officers. Isobel sat down and motioned Sarah to sit. The sun was shining, and the wind tugged and pulled on washing strung up on lines that they passed on their way into town, but it looked like it might stay dry all day.

The train hissed and puffed until it came into Queens Quay railway station and Sarah was immediately on her feet and lifting her shawl and grabbing the basket, then half-fell over as it lurched to a stop.

'Ladies never rush, Sarah,' Isobel said, smiling. 'And ladies' maids also never rush when they are out with them. Be organised, yes, but not in a flap.'

'Yes, miss.'

The carriage door was opened for them by one of the officers they'd observed on the train earlier. He held his hand out for Isobel to grasp, allowing her to step out carefully.

'Thank you so much. Very kind.' Her eyes glanced at his

uniform, his leather belt and holster and the badge on the peaked cap. 'Are you home on leave or just setting off?'

'Setting off, I'm afraid. They've requested replacements already.'

A stab of fear pierced her heart. 'That's not good news. Which regiments are you with?' She nodded in the direction of the other two men who were standing chatting with more soldiers.

'I'm joining the second battalion, Royal Irish. They took a bit of a bashing at Mons and a few other times this month. It'll be jolly good to take my turn against the hun!'

Isobel's heart had constricted, the sounds around her vanishing. All she could think of was Edward lying somewhere, injured. Or worse. The station seemed to swim around her instead of standing firm.

'Miss!' Sarah pulled on her sleeve. 'Do you need to sit down?'

'Miss! I say,' the officer exclaimed. 'I do beg your pardon.'

Between Sarah and the officer, Isobel felt herself being led across the platform and seated in the café. Sarah put a strong cup of tea in front of her and stirred it several times, adding plenty of sugar. The officer was all apologies.

When Isobel could speak again, she had to apologise for being foolish, but the officer wouldn't hear of it.

'No, please. I beg *your* pardon. You have someone who is fighting?'

'Yes, my fiancée is with the Royal Irish. Could you bring him a letter? I have it with me. It will be quicker going with you.'

'Of course, and I do beg your pardon. It was most unthinking of me to mention replacements. Is there anything else I can do to assist you?' The officer was younger than her, his chin still soft with barely a nick on it and his broad, confident smile expressed his pride at getting his chance to serve his king and country. His blond hair reminded her slightly of Edward, but his face was round with plump cheeks and it struck her most forcibly that he seemed fresh out of school.

'No, indeed. I have taken up your time already. It was most unthinking of me.'

'Please, consider that forgotten. I'm sure your chap is still safe.'

'Have you seen one of today's papers?'

'Yes, I have, and there were no casualties from the Royal Irish, so you may relax. Have you the letter you mentioned? Only I need to say goodbye to people.'

Isobel opened her damson velvet purse and removed her letter for Edward. She placed it carefully into the officer's hand. I'm Miss Harris, Miss Isobel Harris. I'm very grateful to you, sir.'

'It was a pleasure to make your acquaintance. I will deliver it personally. Good day.'

Once he'd gone, Isobel reclined wearily against the high-backed wooden bench in the café. 'Here, Sarah,' she said, pulling out a coin from her purse. 'Go and order a cup of tea for yourself and a bun for us both.'

'Really, miss? Thanks!'

'Yes,' she said, laughing. The officer's reassurances about no new casualties had lifted her mood again. It was the initial shock that must have made her feel faint, now she just felt hungry. 'Now off you go. One of those toasted teacakes for myself and you pick whatever you fancy.' The maid's eyes were popping out of her head. 'Well, I did promise you we'd treat ourselves, didn't I!'

Isobel watched Sarah wind her way through the busy café to the counter and place their orders. The buzz of so many people chatting helped to quell the nerves she would always feel, deep inside, but it was also positive too. She felt energised and alive instead of that awful enveloping nausea that had dogged her since Marseilles. She put it down to fear for Edward's safety. She'd had a letter from Cecily, and another one from the Finches, but the last letter from Edward to arrive had been posted from Marseilles. He'd arrived only days after she'd left. She carried it with her constantly, a little talisman of hope in the sea of despair that threatened to overwhelm her if she thought too hard about the war. He'd arrived in France; he and his friends were in great spirits, and he thought about her every minute of every hour and would do so until they met once again.

She was startled back to the present when the tea-tray arrived with a fresh pot of tea and two plates of teacakes. 'You all right, miss?'

'Yes, thank you, Sarah. I'm just thinking about my plans for the day.' She'd already sent her father a message to say she'd call on him, but she had plenty of time before then. They rested in the café for nearly a full half-hour before Isobel led Sarah out of the concourse and walked her into the city. She had paints to buy and a new uniform and supplies for Sarah. Keeping busy; that was the key to it all.

Chapter Seventeen

'Cigarette, sir?'

'Please, Blake. Cup of tea too if there's any going.'

'Might be, but no milk.' His batman bustled off after passing Edward the cigarette. Edward was more than pleased with Blake, who'd worked for his predecessor, a lieutenant from Cavan and who'd proved his mettle on the retreat from Mons. Blake was a quiet and serious fellow, which suited Edward immensely. The two of them had fallen into step within hours, Blake offering his services as soon as Edward had arrived that first night. Edward had no time for chatting about inconsequential things. Any spare moment he drafted out for himself were the last few seconds before his eyes shut and he sank into a fitful sleep, and he only ever thought about Isobel. Isobel and Cairo.

Edward was astounded how quickly he'd become accustomed to doing without things. Mainly sleep and being clean. So much for this being a decisive battle and we'll all be home for Christmas. It was nothing of the sort. A relentless slog of march, fight, march some more. If they were lucky, they might last more than a day in their billet and, if so, they got some decent sleep, a wash and a shave; but it rarely happened. Today they were in a decent-sized farm near the village of Courcelles. It gave him time to fill out their daily log, and more importantly, to catch up writing to the wives and parents of men they'd lost in the past week. All the men. All the time. He couldn't believe he could think this, but the actual deaths were the easiest to write. 'Your son fought bravely doing his duty and was killed instantly by a sniper when we were defending a village. You have every right to feel proud of a son who was a well-respected member of our company.'

The men who simply vanished – they were the hardest letters to write home about. 'Last seen defending his post in a village … there is always hope …'

What hope? Hope that he was captured, and the Germans were merciful, or hope that his death was swift and pain-less? Not much of a choice, but so many men were just unaccounted for. He'd only been here four weeks and it felt like four years, but a swift death, a bullet with your name on it, that was preferable to being half blown up, or a stomach injury that no one could treat and you died a long, lingering death lying in a ditch hoping beyond hope that your mates could find you and bring you back. Invariably it ended up with more soldiers being shot or worse, trying to retrieve an injured mate.

The dust that seemed to encompass the whole of this part of France lodged in his throat. He rubbed his face to try and clear it from his skin. A cup of tea would help right now. He lifted his pen; he had fifteen such letters needing his attention this week.

Blake returned, setting the tin mug and a battered plate next to him. 'Goat's milk, sir. Hope that's acceptable.'

Edward smiled. 'I lived in Egypt. Goat is fine. Thank you.'

'The farmer's wife is sharing her last pot of apricot jam, sir. Very nice it is too. Makes the hard biscuits more palatable.'

A huge roar ripped through the building, and they could

hear windows in the front of the farmhouse splintering and smashing. Edward coughed as a cloud of white dust showered down from the white-washed farmhouse ceiling. 'Close one.'

'Huns are busy tonight, sir. Anything else?'

'Thank you, no.' Taking slugs of his tea and ignoring the film of dust on it, he nodded in the direction of the front. 'Keep your head down and get some sleep. We'll be moving soon, I imagine.'

'Yes, sir.'

Summer Hill, Ireland, Monday 12 October 1914

Isobel finished the painting of Edward by the end of the first week in October and enquired locally about getting it framed. Every day she hovered close to the house hoping against hope that a letter would arrive from Edward.

She rushed back to the house, breathless with a pain in her chest when she saw the telegram boy cycling back down the drive.

'Mrs Cox! Where is it?' She burst into the scullery through the back door from the stable yard.

'Oh, Miss Harris. Don't take on so. I left it on the side table. Off you go, I'll bring tea.'

Isobel had already left at a run, down the corridor and into the breakfast room. The envelope had her name across the front. Her fingers shook, but she couldn't wait. She ripped it open. 'Oh!' She gasped in relief, sinking back into her favourite armchair which overlooked the sunny terrace. It was pleasant news. Nothing to be alarmed about.

'Everything all right, Miss Isobel?' Mrs Cox enquired,

peering around the door. 'I'm just brewing you a pot. I'll have it ready in a jiffy.'

'Yes, thankfully. All is well. Cecily is returning tomorrow. I shall meet her boat and stay a few days in town at Ballydarragh. If you see Sarah before I do, tell her to let her family know she'll be away a few days.'

'Yes, miss. That is good news for a change. I'll send her in with your tray. Have you finished with the newspaper?'

Isobel nodded. The list of casualties from the Irish Regiments grew longer each day. She should stop reading the paper, it made her feel sick with nerves every morning, and yet, if she didn't read it then she could do nothing else all day.

'Yes. Take it away.' She wanted to start another attempt at painting Summer Hill. The mellow autumn sun and the flower beds filled with copper-coloured dahlias and bronze-leaved foliage drew her outdoors each day. She'd already tried a watercolour but yearned to capture it instead with the luscious new paints she'd bought in town. The two new canvases she'd ordered and all of Sarah's new maid uniforms had arrived.

'Very good, Miss Isobel. I'll send Sarah in directly.'

Donegal Quay, Belfast, Tuesday 13 October

'Isobel, dearest! Let me look at you. You are too pale, don't you think so, Minnie?' Cecily hugged her tightly then released her again. They stood in the dreary damp afternoon on the quayside and shivered after the sunshine of the day before.

'I'm fine, Cecily, I am. It's all this worrying we are doing. Have you heard from Tom yet?'

'He's still in Egypt, and Wilfred is packing up and will be on the move soon. It's Edward I'm more worried about. And you.' Her forehead scrunched up, inspecting her sister. 'Really, Isobel, you don't seem yourself. I'm so pleased we're back to look after you and keep your spirits up. Any news at all?'

'One letter this morning. Come on though, I'll tell you everything once we get home. I got off the train at Bloomfield station, called at Ballydarragh and got Wilson to drive me down in the motor. Let's get back home first, shall we? And I'll tell you all about it.'

The sisters waited in the car whilst Minnie and their father's chauffeur organised the safe delivery of all Cecily's trunks. They drove out of the docks and onto the Newtownards Road. Red, white and blue flags were hung or draped outside a building. 'Whatever's that for?' Cecily enquired.

'That's the recruiting office, I expect. I've seen a few already. There's normally a crowd of men and young lads queuing up to volunteer.'

'Of course. It wasn't pleasant in Southampton, Izzy. The men were all disembarking from the ships, straight from the front. Covered in mud and filth and blood as we waited for our train. So many of them, Izzy! And hardly anyone to help them!'

'Don't! I can't bear it. He has to survive; he just has to!' Isobel covered her mouth to stop herself crying out in despair. 'Here, I cut this out of the paper before I left Summer Hill this morning.' She opened her velvet purse and pulled out a scrap of newspaper. Cecily took it from her and read it.

Casualties to British Officers. Following is the detailed list:-
Irish Regiments wounded and missing.

Barton; lieut H S, Royal Irish Regiment.

Isobel pointed at the piece of paper. 'He was a brother of my friend from school. That's the same regiment that Edward's in. One day that could be Edward's name I read there. Or Wilfred. Or Tom. How shall we bear it?'

'Well, we will, dearest. We will.' Cecily held her hand tightly all the way back through town and up the gentle slopes until they passed into the wide tree-lined avenues of east Belfast and pulled into Ballydarragh.

They took tea together before lying down for a while until the dressing bell rang for dinner. Isobel couldn't stop yawning all evening, even though it was a joy to have Cecily back with her. Both sisters begged their father to excuse them and went to bed early.

★

The next morning Isobel was up early and seated at her writing desk when she heard a gentle tap at her door and Minnie came in. 'I've come to help you dress, Miss Isobel, if you don't mind. I don't think young Sarah is looking after you well enough.'

'Oh, don't be too severe on her, Minnie. She does the best she can. Perhaps you could train her up, now that you are back. I like her company well enough, and I'm not too fussy on the rest of the details. I've kept myself very much to myself the last few weeks.'

'Indeed.'

Minnie helped her slip her robe off and then her night-gown. 'Now, where's your corset?'

'Oh, I haven't worn one these past few days. I'm finding them so restrictive. Nothing feels comfortable any longer.'

'That's why nothing fits well, Miss Isobel.' She moved to the chest of drawers and lifted out the half-waist corset that Isobel normally used. 'Come on now, step into it.'

'Must I? I feel breathless even looking at it.'

'Yes, you must.' Minnie struggled to pull the stretch satin half-corset up and around her waist. 'Are you sure this is yours? Perhaps I've mixed Miss Cecily's up with yours. I do beg your pardon.'

'It's too tight, Minnie. I can't breathe. I'm taking it off again.' Isobel struggled out of it again, whilst Minnie went to check on Cecily's underwear. She returned and measured the two garments against each other.

'This is yours, Miss Isobel. I don't understand it. It just seems too tight. I hope that wee minx hasn't shrunk it on you.'

'Oh, don't let's be cross. I just shan't wear one for now.'

Minnie wasn't listening to her but was intent on examining the two corsets. 'It's as though it just doesn't fit you any longer, Miss Isobel. How strange.'

The moment she said that, Isobel felt the colour drain from her cheeks. 'Don't say that!' she whispered, panic filling her body.

Minnie met her gaze, her mouth falling open. The only thing stirring in the room was the crackle of the fire and the clock ticking. 'Is ... is there any reason why that might be?' She couldn't even finish her sentence and swallowed nervously.

Isobel bit her lip. She thought she might swoon. She remembered Edward's words to her, that last afternoon. He said he'd been careful but ... there was always a chance. She nodded, her strawberry-blonde hair falling forward to shield her face. 'Minnie. Minnie, please tell me I'm not.' She could barely enunciate her thoughts out loud, her hands falling to cover her stomach.

'Oh, larks, miss.'

Isobel sank onto her seat at the dressing table. So many

times she went to say something, but couldn't; tears splashing down and leaving dark blotches on her camisole and drawers.

Minnie hovered in the middle of the room, neither coming nor going; neither setting the corsets down nor lifting anything else for her to put on. The fire hissed and spat in the grate, already lit an hour or so earlier this morning; lit before Isobel's world shifted beneath her feet. Another sharp tap on the door made them jump and Cecily bounded in, beaming from ear to ear.

'Ready for breakfast, Izzy?' She halted directly in front of the fire. 'What's wrong, why aren't you dressed? Minnie, why are you just standing there?' She grasped the atmosphere in the room as her voice shifted an octave higher. 'Tell me, Izzy! Have you had a letter? A wire?'

Isobel sat mute on the stool, unable to answer. Unable to do anything but let tears slide down her face. *She was having a baby.*

Chapter Eighteen

'A baby! You are having a baby?' Cecily's face turned a nasty shade of grey as she backed up to the wooden post at the end of Isobel's bed and slithered down it until she was sitting in a heap – skirts, petticoats, boots all in disarray. 'Isobel, tell me it can't be true!' she whispered.

Isobel couldn't answer. She couldn't lie either. She just nodded.

Both ladies turned to Minnie for guidance, who just kept opening and closing her mouth, the shock overwhelming her.

'Minnie. You're the practical one. You know about these things. Is she with child?' Cecily whispered again.

Minnie roused herself and placed the corsets on the bed. 'Let me think now, when did you last have your monthly?'

Isobel shook her head in despair. She couldn't think. Minnie prompted her. 'Remember when we were in Cairo. You had one then, because sometimes it takes you badly. I sent down for a nightcap, do you remember now?'

'Oh, I do.'

'Good, good. We're getting somewhere now,' Cecily added. 'Then you went off to France with the Finches. That was in early June and it was exceedingly hot. What about then?'

'Yes. I did have a bleed, but then Alice took ill and we raced back to Egypt.'

'Good. What about after that then?' Minnie asked.

Isobel wracked her brain for something; anything. There had been nothing since that, and she knew exactly why. Covering her face, she burst into noisy sobs. 'Oh, my goodness! What will I do? Edward said we'd be married by November if anything were to happen. What's the date now?'

'Wednesday October fourteenth. November is only two weeks away. It's not so bad, Izzy.' Cecily picked herself up from the floor and crept over to her sister who was still crying. 'Edward just needs to come home on leave and marry you, that's all. It'll be fine.'

Minnie was busy counting on her fingers. 'You're about three or four months gone, miss. We need Edward to get back to London sharpish and marry you in the next few weeks. It won't stop the gossip once the baby arrives early, but so long as you have a ring on your finger, you'll survive.'

'We can hide away in Summer Hill, Izzy, even delay announcing the birth. We'll manage, won't we, Minnie?'

'We just need a ring on your finger, Miss Isobel. That's the key.'

Isobel sprang up, clutching her head and pacing the small bedroom. 'I'll write to Edward immediately. His father is the commanding officer; once he explains that he *needs* to come home, I'm sure it will be fine.' This couldn't be happening. She couldn't be having a baby. She just couldn't be. 'Oh, Cecily! Everyone will know soon. What will Mother and Father say?'

'I don't know, really I don't, but why on earth did you …?' Cecily didn't seem capable of finishing her sentence. 'Isobel, women have been known to be, well, shunned because of this. No matter how much money Father has, it can't protect you from this. Why on earth didn't you think of that?'

'I'm sorry! I am.' Covering her face, she burst into deep

sobs and no amount of comforting by Minnie or kind words from Cecily eased her pain. 'It's all my fault, you know,' she explained, when she could speak. 'He suggested we marry in Cairo before I left and I put him off the idea.'

Cecily was aghast. 'Why didn't you?'

'For the first time in my entire life Mother was pleased with me. She was delighted to be planning a double wedding. I ... I wanted nothing more than to walk down the aisle with you, Cecily, and if I'd stayed there, who would have helped the Finches get home? So I said no.'

Cecily seemed to sag in front of her, mulling over the fateful words. 'Mother did you an awful wrong, dearest. All these years. She has wronged you more than anything if your main desire was to please her. You are worth so, so much more than just the accomplishment of marriage. As am I.' She held her sister close and buried her face in her hair. 'Have faith, Edward will return to marry you. As for me, whilst war still rages, and Tom is overseas, I am going to volunteer to be a nurse. We *are* more than just marriageable vessels. We have skills. All of us.' She looked at Isobel and Minnie. 'I am determined not to be judged by that measure from now on. You said that long ago, Isobel, and I foolishly dismissed it. Now you unfortunately need it and I do not. Write to Edward. The situation can still be saved.'

Isobel felt cheered a little bit by the decision. She'd had a momentary panic, but all would be well now. Edward had understood the risks and would return to marry her. 'Quickly, Minnie. Help me get dressed and I shall get a letter in the post immediately.'

'We need to return to London. Father will think that odd, but I shall merely tell him we have changed our plans and have decided to meet up with Mother and Rosalie for the next few weeks, before they sail for America and

Rosalie's wedding. You, Izzy, can tell him that you want to be in London for when Edward gets leave, and you will be married then.'

Everyone nodded and smiled at each other and tried to look confident, but underneath it all was the sense of panic. A wave of despair that hung on Edward staying alive and being given home leave.

Wednesday, 14 October

Dearest Edward,

Minnie has informed me that I am expecting a baby. Our baby.

I am overjoyed to think that we have created a child together and I'm eagerly awaiting its birth. I know you will be a wonderful father. But I need you to come home immediately.

Ask your father for help, whatever strings he needs to pull, let him pull them so that you can return, and we can be married. I am waiting for you in London.

All I can think of is that I am carrying your child. Our child. I am secretly overjoyed! No matter what happens I will love, cherish and protect our little one.

Wherever you are, my sweetheart, know that we are forever united together.

Hurry home.

Your heart, Isobel

Three days later they were standing on the platform of Euston station in the early morning. They'd sailed the afternoon before and taken the overnight train to London. Isobel rubbed her eyes – they felt gritty and her head pounded. A sharp wind whipped across the platform that chilled her to the bone, and try as she might, her winter coat from last spring, wouldn't button up. Was it only nine months since they'd arrived here all together; to meet up with Alice and the Finches and then set off on their trip to Egypt?! Nine months and so much had changed.

Across the station everything was different. Red, white and blue bunting swung in the stiff wind; the train just next to them was a hive of activity. Nurses in their blue and white uniforms were hovering over stretchers with soldiers fresh from the front. Soldiers were being helped into carriages to be transported to hospitals further north. Isobel averted her eyes, afraid she would break down inconsolably if she searched every face to see if it might be him. 'Their uniforms are caked in mud and blood, Minnie. The poor men. I hope to receive an answer soon.'

'Yes, miss.' They all held their breath walking past. The metallic smell of old blood and goodness knows what else clogged their nostrils, but the look of relief on the soldiers' faces at being back home was enough to bring even the sternest hearts to tears.

'Come, Izzy, don't look, dear. You're only annoying yourself. Head up.' Cecily marched her out of the station and into the family motor that was waiting.

Saturday 17 October

Dearest Edward,

We have arrived in London where we await your arrival. I can't sleep yet I'm so tired.

What a joy to be having this child. Yes, a joy! I will manage it and find a way. Cecily is so severe on me, yet also sad. But I am happier than I've ever been. I do not regret a thing between us.

I do not care for this term 'fallen woman.' I have not
fallen, I was flying. It was so wonderful. It was how life
should surely be meant to be lived. With love and passion.
Stay safe, Edward. Stay alive. Hurry home, my love.

Sunday 18 October

'I have written Edward lots of letters telling him of our
child, Cecily. A letter may go astray easily. I received one,
but it was from weeks ago. He hasn't heard so far. Oh what
if he doesn't get it in time? What will become of me?' She
paced the room so often Minnie had taken to complaining
that she was wearing down her shoe leather. She couldn't
be still, no matter how hard they tried to settle her. She
wanted to run, all by herself to Southampton and get on a
ship to France. At night her dreams were filled with faces and
groans and darkness. She feared she would go mad before
Edward replied. Her letters to him might have been warm
and positive, but inside she was desperate.

She was to be a mother. She could barely find time to
look after herself, let alone have a baby. Would she even be
able to look after it? To love it? Mother hadn't loved her.
How did she know she wouldn't be the same? She placed
her hand over her heart to steady her nerves. It didn't help.
Thinking about it all sent her heart racing and she thought
she'd be sick.

'He will come just as soon as he hears, Izzy, I'm sure of it.
Just be patient a little longer.' Cecily soothed her.

'I told him even if he could send a letter of permission, we could be married by proxy. Or I could travel to
Southampton, Calais even, and get a clergyman there to
marry us. It could be done.'

'Of course, dearest one. Let us not give up hope. As soon as he hears, he will come home. I know he will. Shush now. You need to save your energy. Mother is saying you look too pale, I'm fearful she will guess shortly unless we are very clever.' Cecily rang the bell and ordered tea up to their bedroom and asked Isobel to lie down.

Isobel reclined as she was bid, but rest she could not. The news from France was not good and every time Mother and Rosalie went out, they returned with more awful news from families they knew and sons and husbands who were no longer coming back. It was hard to be hopeful at a time like this.

Chapter Nineteen

North-eastern France, 19/20 October 1914

'D' Company had spent all evening digging in, after their advance across the flat field between Le Riez and Le Pilly. The heavy shellfire of earlier had ceased, and their machine gun had taken out two German snipers on the far side of the field. Now they rested as 'B' and 'C' companies covered the same field, bringing rations with them. An earlier bayonet charge right up the village street had routed the remaining Germans from Le Pilly, and the soldiers were determined to hold their new position.

Rain hammered down on the soldiers of the Royal Irish as they sheltered as best they could, in the shallow trenches near the back of the railway station and a nearby barn. The water rolled down their faces, soaking into shoulders, sleeves, down necks; anywhere that was exposed. Edward wiped his face for the millionth time, straining to see across the downward slope of the road and into the village of Herlie.

The moon had disappeared long before midnight and it had rained incessantly ever since. Fingers and toes were beginning to lose all feeling in the numbing cold of the wet night air. The Royal Irish fired at anything that moved, hoping to pin the enemy down until they received their next order to advance. The only thing that warmed Edward was a letter from Isobel in his breast pocket – newly arrived but, as yet, unopened. When their unit next got a reprieve from this madness, he would get Blake to brew him a cup of tea with a good slug of something stronger and he would savour every word of her news from home. Later, he promised himself, more than slightly jealous of his batman being at least dry if not warm back at HQ in Aubers. He was hoping with their good work he might be able to bag some leave and get back to England and see Isobel again. Three months they'd been apart; far too long for his heart to cope.

Edward crawled up and down his lines, checking on his men, assessing numbers of injured and keeping an eye on the enemy who as far as they could tell were still on the far side of the field. The frontline might only be eight hundred yards away, maybe more. With a fair wind they'd be able to push the enemy even further back in the morning.

With a French battalion on their left, and the 4th Middlesex on their right, the Royal Irish had fought their way forward, yard by yard, attacking the Huns. Edward was so proud of the company he belonged to. He knew they would always fight their very best.

Dawn was still too far away to be of use. Flashes of rifle fire on the far side of the field seemed to be spreading further and further to their right, and intense artillery fire was raining down on where he assumed the 4th Middlesex were entrenched. The Royal Irish were supposed to be pushing forward, making good their attack, but word soon came back. *Fall back, watch your flanks.*

Edward passed the order on, concerned now. The rain eased just as the first greys of the dawn stretched out on the horizon, slowly bringing into focus the outline of the village buildings. Small arms fire seemed to come from everywhere at the same time. The deafening rattle of numerous German machine guns on their flank and the front making it near on impossible to move anywhere.

'Fall back! Fall back!'

One unit was inside the railway building behind which Edward and his unit sheltered. The door faced east onto the road. High up on the west wall, one of their men forced open a hole between the roof rafters. 'Jesus, Mary and fucking Joseph, sir! Look behind you!'

The colourless countryside blurred with a mist that had enveloped it and slowly but surely a line of grey-blue figures crystallised out of the whiteness – they were approaching from every direction.

They were surrounded. How could they be? Where were the flanks protecting them?

'Sir! Lieutenant! What will we do?'

Edward swore. His only senior officer that he was still in contact with was seriously wounded with a stomach injury. There was no one else. A shout came through the grey morning light, the unmistakable clipped English vowels of their commanding officer. 'Put down your weapons. Stop firing. We surrender!'

Chapter Twenty

Isobel scrutinised herself in the tall bevelled mirror, turning this way and that. Her new walking gown had slightly more gathers in the skirt and a softer silhouette overall. She lifted her arms higher first to see what she looked like, then allowed Minnie to drape the loose kimono-style jacket in front. 'It's perfect!' It didn't solve her problems, but it disguised the problem for now.

'It is indeed, miss. That new American corset has done wonders for you. Will I order another each of the corset and the gown?'

'Please, Minnie. What other colours did they have?'

'Well, this one's known as dove grey, and it's grand like, but we need you looking more like yourself to keep your mother off your back.'

'How about a soft green?'

Minnie heaved herself up straighter, peering down her nose. 'Well, the girl in the ladies department offered me one called *seaweed* green but, honestly, I couldn't have you wearing a fabric known as seaweed! They have a nice blue, a military look to it, and one in a soft coppery-beech. That would be nice on you.'

'Thank you. Can you order those for me?'

'I will. I'll ask her to put an extra bit in the waistband,

and leave it unfinished, then I'll take it in a bit myself. That way we'll get plenty more months out of it. I was thinking we ought to get a pale cream one run up too. Ready for the wedding. Not too dressy though, something suitable for the times we are in, with a nice decorative coat to go over it with a fancy trim. You could always wear it in the evenings for a while, with a coloured voile. It could be very versatile.'

Isobel was pleased with the idea. She had refused to even consider getting anything made in the past week or two, her ever-present problem overwhelming her brain. But today she felt a renewed energy and so much more like herself. She was still admiring herself in the mirror when Cecily bounded in. 'Oh, dearest! You do look well. I don't suppose you fancy going out today?'

'I do actually. I'm feeling very positive and I think the distraction will be good for me.'

'Bravo! An excursion it is then. How about a museum and afternoon tea?'

'Why not?! Some fresh air will do me good, and it is a beautiful day.' The trees in the square out the front were glowing bronze in the morning sunshine. A slight breeze rippled through the leaves. After the slight frost overnight, it was just the day for a brisk walk through a park.

Rosalie was surprised to see her at breakfast but made no mention of joining them, much to their relief. Isobel and Cecily escaped twice that day, once for a refreshing walk, and then in the afternoon when they visited the Victoria and Albert Museum, at Isobel's request. She couldn't resist a visit to the Egyptian exhibits.

'What about going out one evening?' Cecily suggested over tea and cakes. 'I do love this café, don't you?'

'Yes, it is rather lovely. We should take more time to see things now that we are here. Once Edward sends me a telegram, I'll be infinitely busy organising things. Too busy for nice afternoons.'

'But once you're married, we'll be able to do more outings surely?'

'I suppose we can, but Mother will require you for endless dress fittings and other boring things. I already refused to go to America early with them. I will return to Ireland before Christmas and hide away at Summer Hill.'

'You make it sound quite jolly, Izzy.'

'Of course it will be jolly. And by then, the war should be over, and Edward can come home.'

'I'm not sure that will be the case, dearest.'

'It will if I think positively about it. Look at the papers.' She got up and borrowed the *Pall Mall Gazette* that had been discarded by a previous customer. 'Look at that, Cecily,' she said, pointing to the headlines. 'We seem to be doing awfully well.'

The headlines read: *Allies' Continued Progress: Enemy driven back 30 Miles.*

'That all seems very encouraging, doesn't it?'

Cecily was not convinced. Pulling the paper from her sister's hands, she turned the pages until she came to the list of casualties. Jabbing her finger at it, she looked her sister firmly but kindly in the eye. 'There are two columns of missing soldiers, Izzy. I cannot understand how, if we are doing so well, we can be so careless at misplacing our soldiers. I mean, where exactly are they lost?'

Perplexed, Isobel refused to acknowledge her and poured a fresh cup of tea which she proceeded to sip slowly, without catching her eye. So long as Edward's name wasn't on the list, then everything was going to be fine. She had to be positive from now on.

Cecily was still poring over the lists. 'How can they lose

so many soldiers from the same battalion, Izzy? They can't be dead, because they would say dead, but where are they, then?'

'I've no idea, Cecily, I'm sure it's just a mistake though, there being so many of them. Look, there's officers' names at the end. *Reported missing but now wounded.* There, see; just a mix-up.' Isobel sounded more convincing than she felt, but she felt invigorated today and refused to let negative thoughts overwhelm her. The two sisters sat a bit longer savouring their tea and the convivial atmosphere in the café, before walking home.

London, Thursday 22 October

'Isobel, I have received a letter to say Mrs Dunwoody and Wilfred will be calling on us soon,' Mrs Harris announced as she swept into the breakfast room where Isobel and her sisters were still seated at the polished oval table. 'I am delighted to see how much improved you are looking. You weren't blessed with many advantages to start with, but to lose what assets you did have would be simply careless.'

Isobel pulled a face. She was still in a buoyant mood this week and determined Mother wouldn't spoil it. She clutched a letter from Edward behind her back, her heart fluttering like a trapped bird; she was so eager to read his reply. Instead, she wiped her mouth and fixed a smile on her face. 'I was not aware that Wilfred was back, Mother. Does Mrs Dunwoody say when he arrived?'

'Indeed not. Nor,' she fixed her gaze firmly on Isobel, 'is it any of our business.'

It took Isobel all her reserves of strength not to retaliate in a way which would bring forth another rebuke. 'Well, how pleased Mrs Dunwoody must be to have one son safely home for the time being.' She tried to get Cecily's attention and pushed her foot closer to her sister, out of sight under the table.

'Are you slouching, Isobel? See that you don't. A woman must always look to her figure. Now, Rosalie and I are engaged for the day, but we shall expect to see you later.'

Isobel had to stop biting her lower lip before answering and inhaled deeply. 'Yes, Mother. We are looking forward to the performance of the Russian Ballet this evening at the Coliseum.'

'I am pleased to hear it. Don't stray too far for the next day or so. It would be most remiss of you to be out if the Dunwoody's called.'

'Yes, Mother.'

'Until Wilfred marries again, you will be the daughter-in-law to bring Mrs Dunwoody comfort. You should do more to cultivate that. None of this painting lark that takes up so much of your time. It's so selfish of you, when you could be socialising and making new friends.' Isobel had to sit on her hands until her mother and Rosalie departed, they infuriated her so much.

'Calm down, Izzy dear. Wilfred will be here. That's most fortuitous, don't you think?'

'Yes, I do. They must have arrived back in England from abroad for a quick spot of leave before embarking for the front, but he can get word to Edward for me, in person.'

Cecily clutched her sister's arm tight. 'You're not actually going to tell him, are you?'

'Oh no, not as such. But I will impress on him the importance of Edward getting home leave. I shall speak to him privately, though.' She was dizzy with her good fortune. This would be better than a letter. All her others might have gone astray, or perhaps the one she held in her hand right this second might hold good news. She pulled it out from where she had sat on it, hiding it from the prying eyes of her mother and Rosalie and held it against her breast, praying very hard that it contained good news.

'Go on then.' Cecily encouraged her.

She held her breath, wishing and wishing that this would be the letter that said he was coming home. *Make it this one, please*, she begged. She ripped open the envelope, scanning the contents for a quick clue that he'd heard. No. But at least he was safe and well. Wiping a quick tear that had formed she inhaled deeply. Not this one, but soon, soon he would hear the news and come home.

London, Friday 23 October

The Dunwoodys didn't arrive on the Thursday, but Isobel was hopeful they would arrive today. The ballet the evening before had been delightful, but the newsreel of war news that had been shown before it started had been excruciatingly hard not to cry over. The harsh images of the Belgian refugees trudging into Dunkirk was very emotional. Images of their own troops, bright and cheery, waving for the cameraman as they marched along the foreign roads did cheer her, but always the reminder of how many men were being killed. She had to be strong.

Friday morning, they stayed at home. Isobel got her sketch book out and attempted to draw Cecily, but she couldn't concentrate. The day was dull and dreary and neither of them wanted to venture out. Cecily rang for tea, but Isobel couldn't drink any. Her stomach was all in knots.

'Send someone out for *The Times*, won't you? Perhaps there's news,' Isobel asked.

Cecily raised an eyebrow. 'I will not. It does you no good and you only read the Roll of Honour anyway.'

'I do not. I read all of it.'

'Well, it does you no favours and you are grumpy and cross afterwards. Shall I play something? That would distract us.'

'Must you? Oh listen.' The doorbell chimed and they leant forward, trying to discern who had arrived. Wilfred's deep tones could be heard, but he sounded rushed. Not like himself at all. The door flung open, and he pushed his way through without waiting to be announced by the maid.

Isobel stood, her sketchbook clattering to the floor, her chest pounding.

'Isobel!' He came straight to her. His face was serious, dark eyebrows furrowed across his forehead.

She would swoon. She knew it. She looked wildly around for Cecily who rushed to her side.

'Isobel, it's Edward. I came as soon as we received the telegram.'

Isobel gasped, grabbing onto her sister for support, Wilfred on her other side. 'Tell me. Tell me now! Is he dead?'

'No, not dead. Please, sit down. Cecily, ring for tea. Or smelling salts or something.'

'What, Wilfred? Tell me exactly what you know,' she screeched. 'I just need the truth!'

'He's missing. But it's not just him. Most of his battalion is missing it seems. Father sent Mother a telegram yesterday. He's not going to rest until he finds out what has happened. I arrived late last night from Liverpool. I came as soon as I could.'

'Missing doesn't mean dead,' Cecily said aloud, for Isobel's benefit.

'No, indeed not. There is every hope that they will turn

up shortly. The frontline moves so rapidly that men get stuck behind the lines for several days and then just pop up again. Most of a battalion missing, means, at worst that they've been captured, and if that's the case then I'm sure they'll be treated very well.'

Images from last night came flooding back. The crying Belgium refugees trudging along roads having lost all their belongings. News reports in the papers that explained how the Germans had shot Belgium women and children for retaliating against the occupying force were replayed in her brain. Germans weren't decent sorts, or they would never have invaded. 'No, this can't be. How can this be true? Oh Edward!'

Tears came then; long, bitter tears for the danger Edward was facing and the hopeless situation she was in. They were both doomed. Their bright, happy future had been stolen from them.

Wilfred stepped closer, putting his arms out as though to comfort her, but then dropped them back to his sides, flexing his fingers. 'I am most terribly sorry for bringing the news. But please be reassured that we do believe he will be safe. As soon as we hear anything further, I will return. Perhaps I should leave you?'

Cecily nodded. 'I think until the shock has worn off, we might be better alone.' Minnie hovered in the doorway, ready to assist. 'My maid and I will take good care of her. Have no fear.'

'Right. Well, I'll go. I promise to return this evening.'

'Thank you, Wilfred. You must be feeling the uncertainty of your brother's loss as well. Isn't that right, Isobel?' She prodded her sister, but Isobel couldn't respond. She could barely think.

'I'll call at the War Office this morning. Any more news and I'll be over immediately.'

'Yes. Thank you.' Cecily barely said goodbye, she and Minnie were huddled around Isobel who was lost to everything but her anxiety over Edward. They didn't watch him leave.

Time seemed to lose its regular rhythms after that. One minute seemed like an hour, and hours would pass and Isobel barely noticed. She was undone. How could she go on? Every second of every day that he wasn't found, she was hurtling to a disaster of unmitigated proportions.

I am like Icarus the Greek God who flew too close to the sun. I was given more happiness than I deserved and now I must pay.

'I do not believe I can go on,' she said repeatedly that day, as Cecily and Minnie took charge of her. Bundling her up the stairs to her bedroom and restricting all other visitors.

Wilfred returned late in the evening with *The Times*. Four other officers from the battalion were listed as killed or wounded. But there were two whole columns of soldiers listed as missing. Wilfred had no other news, but assured them again that no stone would be left unturned in the search for his brother and the missing battalion.

Night came and Isobel tossed and turned, her eyes refusing to close. She lay awake, clutching her tummy protectively, not knowing how she would bear the future without Edward in it. When dawn eased itself into the gritty London streets, Isobel was wrapped in a blanket and seated in her armchair looking out at the square. The same trees that at the start of the week had seemed so cheery and bright, were now limp and broken. Dark brown leaves drifted down to the ground, only to be trodden on and squished onto the damp, sodden pavements.

She didn't speak that day. She couldn't. She gazed around

her with wide, staring eyes, but she was a different person. She was never going to be the old Isobel again. She was broken and she wouldn't be whole again until he was found and came home.

Chapter Twenty-One

Belgium: German occupied territory, 20 October 1914

It rained on and off all that long day.

'Throw down your weapons.'

Orders from the German unit that had captured them, translated efficiently by Walker, Edward's equivalent in B company. First, they had knelt in the mud of the dirt road; rainwater and blood combined from their own soldiers, running under their knees and soaking into their uniforms. Their injured had cried out for help and yet they'd been refused permission to touch them. Only those that had been able to move themselves into line had been helped. Bandages appearing out of pockets, spare socks being turned into pads to stop the bleeding. Then the order to march, and they'd been corralled through the village and out the other side before the church clock had struck the hour of seven. As they marched, arms high above their heads, Edward clenched his jaw every time he heard a shot ring out behind him. He counted them. Twenty-three. And they marched on, heads down, anger burning up inside.

Edward struggled to comprehend how this had happened. Who was left to let their families know where they were? A violent urge to vomit washed through him. Isobel! In a few days she'd be given news that he'd disappeared. That all of them had just vanished. His stomach heaved, and heaved, and he bent over just before the remains of his sparse meal from yesterday reappeared, splashing over his shoes and puttees.

'March! March!' the Germans continued shouting, hitting the men with the butts of their rifles to keep them moving. As Edward stumbled, so did the man behind him. 'Sorry,' he apologised. His brain desperately tried to calculate how many men they were leaving behind, killed during the night, or executed just now – a hundred, maybe more? How soon before the remainder of their battalion would come back and find them gone? Hours, or days? Or maybe never? He swallowed down more bile that threatened to undo him. His anxiety wasn't for himself, but for Isobel when she received the news. Oh Lord, give him strength. This could not be happening.

They walked all day without rations and with only the bare minimum of rest. They needed water badly. The adrenaline from the running battle over the last few days and the lack of sleep had burnt up all their reserves. They were parched and unable to quench their thirst. The men stumbled along, mouths tilted upward to the sky, trying to catch the rain. And they needed food. Men stumbled from hunger. The walking wounded were supported, but still they fell to the ground.

'Get up,' Edward urged one man. 'Come on now, Trenton. Come on. Up we go. It's the only way. Think of your home, your village, your mother. Think of anything you can, but get up again.' The wounded man was lifted under the arms and although his feet dragged, the men either side kept him moving. His back was soaked with blood from a head wound.

What chance did he have, Edward wondered? What chance did any of them have? He tried to calculate how many rations they might have, dispersed through the men.

Maybe a mouthful of chocolate each. Perhaps a hard biscuit, if they were lucky. Everyone had a mouthful or two at best. Tin cups were held out to fill up with water and were passed around. He thought of Isobel's letter in his jacket pocket. It was probably soaked through by now. Oh, Isobel. He would survive if he possibly could.

'Where're we going?' the men whispered as they stumbled along the road. Up and down the line their guards jabbed at them with their rifle butts, or stabbed the unfortunate ones with their bayonets, if they stopped too long.

The hairs on the back of Edward's neck bristled. They'd stopped late in the afternoon; there seemed to be some sort of disturbance happening. Leaving his place in the line, he went forward.

McCleland, a corporal from Waterford, was objecting to a couple of guards demanding he hand over his valuables.

'Zoovenirs!' they barked.

'Jesus Christ, man, my ring doesn't come off!' The Huns, in their grey-blue uniforms, stood over him. A sickening crump reached Edward's ears just as he got to him. A bayonet was plunged deep into the man's thigh bone, his screams piercing the whole line of weary, dejected men.

'Here. Please stop!' Edward twisted his own signet ring off his finger and held it out to them. 'Here, take it, and my watch. Souvenirs!' The young guards eyed them up as they lay on his palm, which quivered out of exhaustion and fear. Sneering, the nearest guard grabbed them and slipped them into his pocket, but it wasn't enough to help McCleland. His screams when the other soldier set his boot against his thigh and twisted the bayonet as it came out was too much to bear.

'Stop! Please stop!' Edward shouted but to no avail. A couple of McCleland's mates charged the guards to defend their buddy, but they were also bayoneted in the stomach, before a quick burst of bullets finished them off. Three more men now lay crumpled in a heap on the road, more blood draining away from Irish soldiers who'd never make it home. Edward and the rest of the officers still with the battalion shouted orders at the men to stay in their ranks. They couldn't risk losing more men.

'March. March.'

Hands gripped tight by his side, they marched past the bodies of their fallen mates. The injustice of it all burnt in Edward's throat. Having to abandon men who had fought fiercely all through the past few months hit him in the pit of his stomach. For them to be abandoned like that, with no burial, and the likelihood that they would be dumped in a mass grave with no grave marker, made him sick. He memorised the names of the three men and tried to fix in his brain the place where they were now, determined as soon as was possible that he would write home to their families to let them know. Thoughts of Isobel once more filled his head. He had to stay alive for her.

Darkness was falling as they marched into Lille. What civilians they passed had the dejected look of the conquered. Fearful of the occupying Germans, they scurried along the road, heads bent, shoulders hunched in the miserable weather. They whispered though, encouraging the troops as they stumbled on past, wearily dragging their feet. A loaf of bread was tossed into the midst of them, the bread owner scurrying away before the Germans could notice.

'This it, then?' voices asked, as they were unceremoniously shoved into a vast yard next to the train station. It was pitch black and they stumbled continuously from sheer exhaustion and since they couldn't see what was under their feet. Other allied troops were already penned in, their ashen faces lifting only to ask had they any food with them. They had not. They sank to the ground where they stopped and slept where they were, lying on the wet ground if there was room, or else their head leaning on their arms as they held their knees trying to consolidate body temperature.

Edward tapped his breast pocket where Isobel's letter was, then pulled it out. It would be his good luck talisman; something to look forward to reading. It was only partially damp; the contents should still be dry enough even though the ink with his name and address were smudged. He couldn't read it yet even if he wanted to, there wasn't enough light to even make out the faces of his fellow officers, let alone words on a page. He pressed it to his lips. *Good night, my love*, he whispered, *don't give up on me. I'll be home before you know it.*

London, 1 November 1914

Isobel had sent him a note and now Wilfred was here. Cecily and Minnie would have argued against it, but she was driven to do something. *Anything.*

There had been no more news; not from the War Office and neither from Edward's father. It had to be assumed that he was alive behind enemy lines somewhere, but so far there had been no definite confirmation. The only slight piece of explanation was that on the night the battalion went missing, the frontline had been fast moving and chaotic. Ground had been lost and regained several times over the matter of hours.

Today was Wilfred's last night before his battalion embarked for France. Isobel knew it was now or never. She was dressed and waiting for him at the bottom of the stairs. Minnie had carefully washed her hair yesterday – the first time that Isobel had allowed her since the dreadful news had arrived. She had eaten barely anything either, which although unwise in her condition, had been impossible to rectify. She had lost all urge to eat.

'I need to speak to you alone,' she said, as soon as he appeared in the hall.

'I see.' He too looked wretched. His previous confidence and poise gone.

'Shall we walk?' she asked.

'Are you well enough to walk?'

'I need some fresh air. Please, let's go into the square.'

'So,' Wilfred started, by her side, 'you said you must speak to me.'

Painful as it was, walking with Wilfred reminded her of Edward. His height and build were similar. Edward was blonder, of course, and his hair finer, so it flopped over his forehead, unlike Wilfred's which stayed where it was put. Isobel walked shoulder to shoulder with him just as she had Edward.

She had rehearsed this conversation so many times in her head, but now she could barely speak. She tried once but failed. 'Wilfred ...'

'I can't work miracles, Isobel. You just need to tell me.'

'I ... you see. Edward and I, we were supposed to be married in November.' He nodded. 'Only, during October it became *crucial* that I should be married as soon as possible, you see. And now Edward's not here.' Her words tumbled out and she felt her cheeks burning. She couldn't even meet his eyes when he stopped abruptly.

'I beg your pardon.'

She could hear the hesitation in his voice as he digested the full meaning of her words.

'Am I to assume, that you and Edward. That is to say ... the situation you find yourself in now, is very *delicate*?' He cleared his throat, obviously embarrassed at the situation she'd put him in.

'Yes,' she whispered.

'Ah.'

They stood side by side under a tree, neither moving nor talking. She had never noticed before how loud he breathed through his nose, but right this minute that was all she could focus on.

'I could marry you, but we don't have time. I leave tomorrow,' he said after a long sigh.

'No! No, I didn't mean that at all. Edward could be found next week lying in a casualty dressing station somewhere. He might have lost his memory or be so ill that he is unable to give his name,' she blurted out, wishing the ground would open up and swallow her whole.

'I see.' He twizzled the long end of his moustache, breathing heavily still. 'So, what exactly can I do for you?'

Isobel couldn't answer, her throat closed up in that dreadful way when you are trying not to cry. She shrugged her shoulders.

'This was after Alice died, wasn't it? In Cairo. I should string my brother up for leaving you in this position. Why on earth didn't you get married before you left? I shall personally strangle him when I find him.' He paced up and down the empty garden square. 'Well, this is a fine old mess now, isn't it? How long do we have exactly?'

'I should be able to keep it hidden until Christmas, but only just. I need him to come home,' she wailed. 'Please don't be angry. If war hadn't been declared, he would have come home, and we'd be married. None of us expected it to be this way.'

'It's hard not to be angry in this situation. And what if he doesn't come home?'

'Don't say that! Don't even think that.'

He returned and stood close by her, muttering under his breath, mulling everything over. 'I shall do my utmost to find him. I promise you that. If not,' he gesticulated with his hands, 'I shall send word to my solicitor that he is to advance money to you, whatever you need.'

He cleared his throat again. 'Please keep me informed of the situation. I asked you before, when we were still in Cairo, if you'd write to me, I mean it even more now.' His hand reached up to touch her shoulder before his eyes met hers. 'I will endeavor to cover your financial needs, but I can assume no one else knows of this situation?'

'Just Cecily. She's not going to tell anyone.'

'Right. Good. I just don't think it will be very helpful if other people were to know.' She nodded. 'I must go. Anything you want or need to tell me, write to me. If I rush now, I will catch my solicitor before he closes. I'm so very sorry for your trouble, Isobel, really I am, but we can't have this sort of thing known. You do understand. Our family has an impeccable reputation to uphold – this sort of thing is unthinkable.' He leant forward giving her a quick peck on the cheek. He spoke again, his tone softer this time. 'I need time to digest this news, Isobel. It is as much of a shock as Edward being missing, but I promise I'll do all that I can to protect you, should it come to it.'

'Thank you, Wilfred. Let's hope Edward will be found alive and well this week.' She stood taller, trying to be positive even though she felt ashamed even asking him for help. He was already moving away from her.

'I'll send a note with the details. Goodbye.' He walked briskly away, exiting the square and was out of sight within moments. Isobel sank onto the nearest bench with relief, her legs turning suddenly to jelly. She was doomed, wasn't she?

Edward, even if he was still alive somewhere, was unlikely to be able to marry her in the next week or two. The best thing she could do was to find someplace to hide away and be prepared to have the baby by herself. But no matter what anybody tried to make her do, she would never give up this precious child she carried. Never!

Seven days later a letter arrived from Wilfred.

'Cecily!' Isobel called, her strength having left her. The letter quivered in her hand. Isobel simply couldn't bear to open it. She screwed her eyes tight and forced Cecily to take it.

'Oh, my love,' Cecily repeated and repeated, her soft words doing nothing to soften the blow, as she read the news.

'He's dead, isn't he?'

'I'm so sorry, dearest. I'm so sorry.' Cecily held her so tight she thought her bones could shatter and then that would be the simplest thing and she could just vanish. How could this have happened? Her pregnant. Edward dead. The stars in Heaven must have decided thousands of years ago that her life was to be one of those ill-fated ones. Edward, the love of her life, was dead.

A Belgium refugee had passed on some personal letters belonging to Edward, which had been recovered from a field close to where Edward and his company had last been seen. The Belgian had reported that he'd hidden and watched German soldiers dig a mass grave and then unceremoniously thrown the bodies of the Allied dead into the grave. Once he'd been sure the Germans had gone, he'd searched through the trenches and gathered anything left behind. The Germans had removed anything of value from the bodies. Only worthless things like letters and photographs had been tossed aside.

In the letter, Wilfred apologised profusely to Isobel for being the bearer of bad news, but stated that with that testimony, they should assume Edward was dead, unless any other evidence contrary to that came to light. He reminded her of his offer of financial support and to keep him up to date with any news.

Edward was gone and she was alone.

Chapter Twenty-Two

Summer Hill, Ireland, Saturday 21 November 1914

Dank, dark clouds hung heavy over the meadow and the paddock that lined the drive up to Summer Hill. It had rained incessantly since they had returned home. Minnie had purchased a new coat for her to wear when they were in London, and Cecily had picked out two new cardigans, that draped and tied with a belt in the front. They helped to disguise the growing bump.

Sarah Heaney's little eyes missed nothing the first day she returned. 'Oh, Miss Isobel!' she whispered.

'Can you keep it a secret, Sarah? Please! I'm relying on you.'

'Of course I can, miss. Sure, there's plenty of bairns born too early or out of wedlock around here. You should ask my mam.'

'Your mother?' Isobel wasn't quite sure how to respond.

'Well now, I'm not so green as to not understand what my mother was at. She's managed to a degree.'

The girl had a point, except that Mrs Heaney was shunned by most of the village. Sarah had also seemed to have grown by another inch even whilst Isobel had been away, she was nearly the same height as her. It was hard to believe it had only been a month since she'd been in Summer Hill before.

Their day trip to Belfast to buy paint had seemed like a lifetime ago.

'Well so long as you know you can't breathe a word of this. Please, Sarah.'

'I won't, miss. But better than that, I'll tell you if I hear any gossip. Would that do?'

'Thank you. I'm very grateful.' The maid bobbed a quick curtsey and removed all the dishes that she'd been sent in to collect by Mrs Cox.

'And take no notice of Mrs Cox,' she added. 'They're just grumpy because they never normally have to keep the house open like this in the winter. And with you and your sister back, you see, and their oldest signed up and the second boy likely to go too. She'll come around, in time.' Isobel nodded her thanks as the maid bobbed around the room and loaded the tray before departing.

Isobel waited for her to leave, then retreated to the window and took up her favourite position, watching for the postman to cycle up the drive. Letters and newspapers were the only thing she looked forward to now.

'I received a letter today from Mrs Finch,' Isobel said to Cecily as they both sat in armchairs on the upstairs landing. The rain had stopped and where the morning sun had broken through the clouds, it managed to warm the small space upstairs where they sat and clumsily wielded knitting needles. Smoke grey wool was all they had, but both were determined to knit socks for the soldiers at the front that they knew. Tom was still in Cairo and didn't need woollen socks for the present.

'I had hoped she might offer some help, a cottage perhaps that I could live in. She says she has no cottage as they are all inhabited by her farm tenants and workers, but has offered to find a suitable couple near her who would adopt our baby once born. She is sympathetic, to a degree, but says I must get married or give the baby up.' Her voice quivered with emotion. 'I can't give our baby up. I can't. What if Edward should be found alive, and hears I gave our baby away. What would he think of me?'

'I'm so sorry, Isobel, but I can't see a different way through this. You can't have the baby and keep it. You just can't!' She set her knitting down and moved to kneel next to her sister. 'Edward's dead, my love, you can't keep hoping for miracles.'

'You don't understand, Cecily, I *must*!'

'Be realistic. Father will throw you out of here, you know he will, sooner or later.' Cecily tried to soothe her, holding her tight, but Isobel shrugged her arms away.

'Then I shall run away.'

Exasperated, Cecily stood up. 'And live on what, exactly?'

'Wilfred's money, perhaps, but I don't even care. I could sell things. Paintings?'

'Wilfred is in France, and he never said how much money he was prepared to give you. You are being unrealistic. Mrs Finch's offer is the best you have. You saw how Mr and Mrs Cox judged you when you returned. Another week or so and everyone around here will know and they will know you are unmarried.'

'Stop saying that ... that ... word! I can't bear it!'

'I'm sorry, dearest, but we must be practical. Write back to Mrs Finch and thank her for her kind offer. I shall send Minnie with you; you won't be alone. Mother and Father won't know a thing.'

Isobel broke into fresh sobs and this time allowed Cecily to hold her. 'You'll be so far away in America. Couldn't you refuse to go?'

'I think not. Minnie will stay and help you and be a

friendly face. It's the best solution we have. Who knows, Edward may *still* turn up. Mistakes are made all the time. Your baby isn't expected until April. A miracle might still happen.'

'I pray for it every night, Cecily! You must know that.'

'I do, my dearest.'

'I gaze at his portrait every day, remembering his smile, his touch, his voice. I pray that I won't ever forget how he made me feel so loved.'

'Don't ever forget that. Hold on, Isobel, and be strong. Every week, every month brings different news. Just be strong.'

'I'm trying. Dash these socks!' She threw her knitting down in frustration. 'I was never meant to have the patience to be a knitter.'

'I suspect not. Come on. Let's get some air whilst it's dry. Down to the train-line and back again.'

'Let's. Knitting is worse than a polite "at home" with mother.'

Isobel didn't want to accept Mrs Finch's offer. She knew deep down she'd never be able to give up her and Edward's baby, but perhaps she didn't need to say so right now. She just needed to keep out of the way until her father and Cecily sailed for America and Rosalie's wedding. And April was still a long way off.

5 *December, 1914*

Goodness, such a commotion Isobel thought, hearing the front doorbell of Summer Hill being rung continuously and then the door being pounded. Instantly alert, she put down her pencil and moved swiftly to the top of the stairs.

Footsteps from inside the house could be heard running down the tiled corridor. Isobel saw a brief whirl of grey skirts and white frilled apron belonging to Sarah, looking smart in her new uniform, as she ran to answer the door.

'Hurry up!' The unmistakable bellicose tones of her father interrupted her pleasant respite at Summer Hill. He barged in shouting all the while. 'Out of my way. Isobel! Isobel! Get down here this instant.'

Her insides plunged to her boots, and that unmistaken frisson of fear swept over her, leaving her brow and palms sweaty.

Cecily also heard the ruckus and came running. 'Father, dearest, how lovely to see you. What brings you here? Now, don't look so cross. Sarah, pour Mr Harris a whiskey please, we'll have it by the fire in the drawing room.'

'What is that, that *thing* doing here. I said she wasn't to be in my sight.'

Isobel had crept down the stairs and watched her father pointing at Sarah but refusing to look at her, the way he would treat a stray dog. It was awfully upsetting. She was very fond of Sarah and hated seeing her treated so. She'd picked up enough hints over the years that Sarah was her father's own illegitimate daughter – her half-sister, to be more precise. 'She's my maid, Father, and a great little worker. Don't take on so.'

Her father faced her straight on, fury burning in his eyes in a way she had never seen before. 'Don't speak to me like that, you whore!'

She gasped and staggered backwards as though he'd physically hit her.

'Father, please!' Cecily tried to intercede, edging herself between Isobel and her father. He pushed her out of the way.

'Isobel. In my study. Now.'

Sobbing, Isobel didn't even attempt to stop the flood of tears. He knew. That was the only explanation for his behaviour. He must know about the baby.

'Both of you. In here. Shut the door.' The two sisters crept into his study, supporting each other. Isobel clutched Cecily so tight as though she feared their father would rip them apart for ever. She couldn't even look him in the eye, she was so fearful of her future now. What only moments ago had seemed a manageable mishap, now, she felt dirty and ashamed.

'You have shamed me and our family. You have threatened the respectability that I have strived for over so many, many years. And by this, this...' he gesticulated to the increasing swelling around Isobel's waistline. 'By this act of gross lascivity, you threaten the happiness of your two other sisters. You always were the difficult one, Isobel. Always.'

'Please, Father. I'm sorry. I never meant it to happen. We were going to get married. We would be married if Edward hadn't been lost.'

'Edward Dunwoody? You threaten to besmirch the good name of a decent and upstanding local family with your lies!'

'They're not lies, Father! Edward loves me. We were due to be married. You know this. Cecily, tell him!' Isobel beseeched her sister for help. Her father was treating her like a common whore. To throw away the love she had for Edward was such an insult.

'It's true, Father. Isobel and Edward would have been married by now, the war just got in the way.'

He rammed his palm towards the two of them. 'Enough! I don't want to hear the sordid details, but I am positive if he came in that door now, his family wouldn't allow him to implicate himself in marriage with a soiled woman like you.'

'Father! How dare you? You don't even know him.'

'I know his parents, and they would not allow it. And don't you ever speak back to me again, my girl.'

Isobel sagged against Cecily's strong embrace. She sobbed with the injustice of it all, but deep down she knew worse was to come, and that fear hung over her like a black cloud.

'You are to be married this week. It's been agreed already and before you say anything,' his voice boomed above the protests from the two sisters, 'you have no choice. Mr Derby from the station has been very kind in offering himself to marry you, so that's that.'

'What? That can't be! No, Father! No!'

'Oh yes, Daughter. That will be.' His vehemence on the matter was obvious. 'You will marry him and be grateful. I've arranged a small sum of money to be paid monthly to help towards the upkeep of you and the child,' he spat the word out. 'You should be downright grateful I'm even arranging this for you. The other option is to be sent someplace, by yourself, and you would never come home again. You have heard of those places, haven't you?'

Isobel shivered. She'd heard whispered tales of girls who got into trouble and they just disappeared. Families never spoke of them again. She wasn't sure where these places were, but she understood the threat well enough.

He yanked the bell cord beside the fireplace. Minnie and Mrs Cox appeared almost instantaneously. The whole house must have heard what was going on. 'Mrs Cox, escort Isobel to her room. Lock her in, and under no circumstances is she to be allowed out. Is that clear?'

'Father, no!' Isobel begged. 'Please no.'

'Take her, Mrs Cox, if you still want your job.' The dumpy housekeeper was remarkably strong for the size of her. Isobel's arm was pulled hard and she toppled sideways. Cecily gripped all the tighter on to her.

'You!' Mr Harris shouted, pointing at Minnie. 'Pack Cecily's clothes. She'll be coming back to Belfast with me today and won't be returning. You can send her trunk on later.'

The two sisters still clung to each other, weeping and wailing and promising each other that everything would be alright. Mr Harris couldn't bear the noise. He swept out from behind his desk and pushed himself between the two of them.

'Take them,' he demanded. Mrs Cox yanked Isobel, and Minnie held onto Cecily, soothing her tears. Isobel cried and cried, kicking and struggling to get away, but it was futile. Her father had decided her fate and Mrs Cox, who needed to keep her job, was supporting him.

It was done. She was heaved up the stairs and pushed into her room. Her father lifted the key out of the inside of the door and slammed it shut before she even had a chance to regain her balance and rush back to the door. The sound of the key turning in the lock finished her. She sank against the bed and sobbed and sobbed.

Cecily wasn't allowed back up to say goodbye. Her coat was fetched, and she was bundled straight into the motor with Mr Harris. The last Isobel saw of her was her forlorn face as she waved out the side window as she and her father were driven away.

Isobel lost track of time. She no longer cared what happened. Her family had been snatched from her; her kind and loving sister yanked from her arms, her only solace in the storm.

Minnie slipped a short note under her door that evening before she too was despatched down to the station sitting up beside Mr Cox on the pony and trap. It was pouring down and her shawl was pulled up tightly around her head.

Much later, when all around was darkness bar the small sliver of light under her door from the hall lamp that had been lit, a slight tapping disturbed Isobel from her semi-conscious state of misery.

'Miss, miss!' The small voice called softly to her from low down. 'Miss Isobel. Can you hear me? It's Sarah.'

'Sarah?' Isobel rolled over, painfully, where she lay curled up in a heap on the bed; the early exertions having strained her body. 'Sarah! It's good to hear your voice. Can you open the door?'

'No, miss. I would never dare. But I've smuggled you some food up. Mrs Cox was ordered not to bring you anything until tomorrow, but I knew you'd be starving. Open your window, miss. I have a wee basket. I'm sure we can manage it that way.'

'Oh, bless you, Sarah. You're my only help now. Bless you.'

Sarah had a small bundle of bread and cheese begged from her own family, all tied up in a small linen tray cloth, nestled in a small basket. She opened the window on the landing, and, leaning out as far as she could, swung it along to Isobel by way of a walking stick. Isobel leant out of her window and missed the first swing but grabbed it the second time. No one would see them do it, for at night there was no one around.

Isobel hauled the basket in and closed the window against the bleak night. Sinking once more to her knees, crawling to the door, she sat hunched, holding her knees and leaning against its solid, unyielding presence.

'Miss,' Sarah whispered again. 'Miss.' Her fingers slid under the door, reaching around for Isobel's.

Moved by such a small act of faith, Isobel placed her own hand over the tips of Sarah's fingers that just poked through.

'Miss, don't be scared. Me and me mam haven't abandoned you. Mam said to tell you she's ever so grateful that you took me on and treated me so well. I know you have to marry Mr Derby, but you'll not be on your own. I'll come down and help. Mam already does his heavy cleaning. I know it ain't going to be no picnic like, but we'll look out for you.'

'Thank you, Sarah. I appreciate that.' Her tears slid once more down her cheeks, silently this time.

'I'll slip up and talk to you tomorrow, miss. And bring you stuff. Do you need anything now?'

'No.' Isobel sighed, her chest heaving trying to keep her voice calm and under control. 'Will you post a letter for me though?'

'Aye. I'll post thirty letters if you need. Don't be scared though, all right.'

'Thank you.'

'I better go.'

'Yes, before Mrs Cox hears you.'

They kept their fingers touching for another while until Sarah slipped hers away and Isobel heard the rustlings of her skirt and her feet tiptoeing down the stairs. She was alone once more.

Chapter Twenty-Three

Summer Hill, Ireland, 7 December 1914

'Miss, miss, it's me, Sarah.' Isobel woke from her afternoon nap to find the young maid hovering next to her armchair, shaking her arm. The oil lamp beside the bed had been lit, but the girl spoke in hushed tones. 'You need to get up.'

'What time is it?' Isobel asked, rubbing her eyes. She hadn't realised before how exhausting being pregnant would be.

'After six, miss. Now you gotta listen to me. You need to get up and get packed. You have to leave on the seven-thirty train this evening for Belfast, and then the steamer for Heysham. You have to get away.'

Isobel sat up, alert now, trying to take the information in. 'Has Cecily come for me?'

'No. You're leaving by yourself. Get up now and get ready whilst I pack for you. I went down to Cyprus Avenue yesterday with your letter and to speak to your sister. She and Minnie helped me with a plan. A letter came this afternoon for you, but they sent it to me mam's cottage. Cecily can't get away from the house, but Minnie will meet you at the train station and see that you get away. But you need to go now.'

Isobel staggered to her feet, her head reeling at the news, but she did as she was bid. Sarah had brought a small bag with her and was now pulling drawers open and placing underclothes and skirts and a spare cardigan into it. Isobel undertook a brief toilette, and pinned up her hair again, setting down her silver brush and mirror back on the dresser.

'Give me them, miss. I'll pack them.'

'They'll be too heavy, Sarah. I'll hardly be able to carry my bag as it is.'

'We have to be practical. You can sell them if things get desperate. Miss Cecily has sent money and Minnie will pass on some pieces of Miss Cecily's jewellery for you to sell too.'

Tears stung Isobel eyes and she sank back onto the bed. 'Why are you helping me?' she asked Sarah.

Sarah stopped right in front of her, clutching a small hand towel to her chest. 'Me mam and I had a bit of a chat yesterday. Mr Derby at the station, well … he's not right, miss. No one could marry him. Especially not you. He's always trying to get under my skirts as it is, dirty bastard. I couldn't let you marry him. Honest I couldn't. You have to get away tonight, before Mrs Cox knows you're up to something and your father returns.'

Overcome with emotion, Isobel stood and hugged Sarah tight. 'You are an angel. I'm going to miss you. If I managed to set myself up somehow, with an income, would you come and join me?'

The maid beamed. 'Course I would. I can't wait to get away from this place. I'd follow you anywhere, miss.'

'I don't deserve you, Sarah.' She cupped the girl's cheeks in her hands and gazed at the familiar face looking back at her. 'Thank you.'

They pulled away, both wiping a few tears that had crept into their eyes. 'What about my oil paints? I can't be without them.'

'Your leather satchel will have to do. I can send things on to you if you write back with your address. It will have to be to my house though, miss. Just in case your father comes after you. Best to keep it secret.'

'Of course. I'd like the large painting of Edward too if we could manage it, but that seems hardly possible.'

'Well, let's see about that in the future. Now, be ready to go, but keep your coat and walking shoes hidden until Mrs Cox sends up your dinner. I'll hide your bags in the outside porch. She'll never look there. As soon as your dinner is here, be ready to go. She never looks in on you again.'

The maid did one last check for Isobel's clothes, then closed the bag and slipped quietly down the stairs with it. She returned briefly for the satchel and this time turned the key in the door again. Isobel listened carefully to her tiptoeing down the stairs. She pressed her ear against the door, but could hear nothing more. She waited, her stomach in knots – hardly sitting for long before pacing the room again. Just when she thought all was lost, she heard the heavy footsteps of Mrs Cox on the stairs. Isobel sat nervously in her chair, and pretended she was reading the bible.

The key turned loudly in the lock, the handle turned, and a pause whilst she steadied herself before the door was shoved open. Mrs Cox backed in, wooden tray in her hands. 'Soup and bread for you.'

'Thank you,' Isobel replied, trying to sound grateful.

'I've added a glass of milk too, seeing as … well … you need to keep your strength up.'

'Thank you. It can't be easy for you all this … disturbance.'

'Aye, well. T'will be better for everyone once you're married.'

Marriage. She'd fought against it all her years – hated that she would always be measured against it, but she couldn't escape the necessity of it, after all. She coughed slightly to hide the gulp as she swallowed down her fear and Mrs Cox waited a minute longer, hovering for what Isobel didn't know.

'You'll just have to get used to Frank and his ways. People will forget about all this in a year or so. You'll just have to manage.'

Isobel was taken aback by the words but didn't want to keep the lady talking. She lifted the spoon, even though every mouthful left her feeling as though she would be ill. She set her spoon down and buttered the roll. She wouldn't eat it though. She'd slip it into her pocket to eat tonight. Mrs Cox mumbled goodnight and left. The bedroom door clicked shut and the key scraped in the lock again. Isobel held her breath until she was sure the housekeeper had gone downstairs.

Isobel was ready when Sarah crept back up the stairs. The key scraped open for a third time and without a word the two of them slipped downstairs and out through the front door. Sarah held Isobel's bag, and Isobel pulled the strap of her satchel over her head. 'Hurry,' Sarah whispered when they were out of sight of the house.

There was no one to see them go though, as the rest of the house was in darkness. The two women stumbled down the drive in the dark, the cold night air whipping their skirts and stray hairs that escaped from hats and tugged at Isobel's scarf. Sarah was wrapped up tight with a black shawl over her head and arms. The wind in the beech trees whistled and snapped and the two of them had a few moments when they both jumped. Dark corners behind bushes seemed scary when they couldn't see far in front of them.

The orange glow from the first house at Railway Street came into view and Sarah pulled on Isobel's arm. 'Wait here, miss, until I check the station is quiet. We don't want Mr Derby getting wind of you escaping.'

Isobel put her mouth near Sarah's ear. 'What about my ticket?'

'Me ma bought you a third-class one. We couldn't do anything else. It'll have to do.'

Isobel nodded and waited as Sarah scouted the platform. The minutes ticked by before she returned. 'Listen now, if Frank turns up, I'll distract him. I'll not be able to say good-bye to you on the platform. Here's your ticket.' She pulled it out and pressed it into Isobel's gloved hand. 'Don't let it blow away now and don't forget about me, sure you won't?'

'Oh, Sarah. Never! As soon as I can, I'll send for you. You've been so kind to me.' She pulled the maid into her arms, forever grateful for her help.

'Come on. We need to get across before the gates are closed. We'll hang back out of sight though and only go up on the platform at the last minute.'

The two of them crossed the tracks just as a railway worker ambled out to start pulling the white gates across. The two gas lights on the platform cast a pool of orange, but left acres of shadow where they hid out of sight. The tracks began to vibrate and the next they knew the train from Newcastle was screeching and shuddering up the line, steam and smoke filling the platform. One last squeeze of Sarah's hand and she felt the maid push her forward, out into the open, head bent and heading for the third-class carriage. No one saw her climb in. She held her breath, hoping Mr Derby wouldn't appear at the window demanding to know where she was going.

The whistle blew and no one turned up demanding she get out. The carriage jerked and she steadied herself. She'd escaped for now. Every time they stopped at a station on the way up to Belfast her hands trembled, petrified a railway official would be waiting to drag her out; or her father. But none came.

The train pulled into Queen's Street and Minnie was waiting in the corner. A nod of her head was all she did to indicate she'd seen her. They scurried out of the station and caught a cab across the river to Donegal Quay. The night had turned wintry and sleet blew in front of them as they were driven across the bridge. Minnie paid the driver and helped lift Isobel's bags into the waiting room. The steamer didn't leave for an hour, but the tiny café was open, knowing it would still get a few customers. The smell of greasy pies, diesel and fish caught in the back of Isobel's throat.

'Sip that. It might help you,' Minnie said, pushing a cup of tea across the table to her. The white china had a band of blue around the rim which had worn away in places. The saucer left a puddle on the table. 'Open it.' Minnie placed an envelope on the table next to the tea, keeping her voice low. A thin gold ring was nestled in the corner as well as Cecily's pearl earrings, an engraved silver bangle and a pair of silver hair combs studded with small jewels. 'Slip the ring on and put the other things away carefully. Keep your bag tight against you at all times, you hear, I've no doubt someone will try to rob you if you don't mind yourself.'

Isobel couldn't speak. Words formed in her mouth, but no sound came out. She didn't trust herself not to cry. Instead, she reached inside the envelope and slipped the wedding ring on. She had no idea where Minnie had acquired it.

The maid leant across the table, keeping her voice hushed. 'You're married now and don't forget it. Pick a name, pick Edward's, it doesn't matter. Try not to get engaged too deeply in conversation with anyone. You're going to stay with friends in London as your husband has been injured. Use the Royal Irish if you must, but keep details vague.

Cecily is distraught she couldn't see you off, but Mr Harris expected her down for dinner. We'll meet you in London just as soon as we get back from this wedding in America. Cecily has written to a few London hospitals to see if they will take her as a volunteer.' Gulping down her tears, Isobel could only hang on to Minnie and nod. She couldn't break down now.

The windows had steamed up inside the café, but the commotion outside was enough to let them know the steamer had docked and it was time for her to go. 'Cecily insisted first-class all the way through to Euston. You'll be in by lunchtime tomorrow. Book a few nights into a nice hotel and send Mrs Finch a letter. She said she might be able to help you. If not, start looking for a small place to rent. You can do this, you're stronger than you realise. We'll be back by February. Smile; off you go now.'

Isobel's legs were like wood and she hardly felt them move. Everything felt wrong as she bit back her tears. Head up, shoulders back, she smiled at the man waiting to check her ticket and allowed the porter to carry her bag up the ramp. She couldn't look back. Her old life was behind her. From now on, she'd be Mrs Dunwoody whether she was entitled to it or not.

Chapter Twenty-Four

Bloomsbury, London, December 1914

London was damp and grey instead of biting cold. Large, dirty drops of rainwater hung suspended from every available iron railing and road sign. Isobel walked from the station to Russell Square. She thought about the hotel there but decided against it as it was thronged, and it seemed careless of her to lose so much money on just a few nights in a hotel. She wandered up and down a few streets near to Regent's Park, looking for a smaller hotel. Before she went in, she slipped on her set of pearls and tidied her hair.

It was easy. She remembered Cecily's words that first night in Shepheard's after she'd overheard Mrs Dunwoody – *pretend you are confident, and everyone will believe it*. She paid for three nights, smiled, and tipped the bell-boy. Everyone had to believe she was a married woman in town visiting her sick husband. As soon as she was shown up to her room, she wrote a letter to Mrs Finch and one to Wilfred's solicitor. The hardest part was over – she had escaped from a potential marriage with Mr Derby and now, for the first time, she was in charge of her own life. If her heart didn't feel like breaking whenever she thought of Edward, she should have been happy.

Sitting in the train on the long journey down to London, she had plenty of time to come up with a plan. Being away from her mother and being alone in London used to be a dream for her. Now it was a reality. If she could accomplish it, she would set herself up as an artist and make her living by painting; but how was she going to do that? She had a vague idea, inspired by listening to her father when her mother would have preferred she didn't. He was very successful in Belfast with a large store and she had learnt something from him. Offer people something for free and they are likely to buy something that costs more.

She was talented; she could draw exceptionally well and fast. Trying to sneak in visits to garages and shipyards when she shouldn't have had made her an expert in quick sketches. Starting tomorrow she would find a hotel lounge, or fashionable tearoom, one where people with money would frequent. She would find a young soldier in his shiny new uniform and she'd draw him for free. If she was fortunate, she could drum up some business. And soon. Perhaps she should get some business cards made out too. She'd have to be Mrs Isobel Dunwoody, portrait artist. Favourable rates. It would be easier if she had a permanent address though.

A flat – that was the other part of her plan. She would walk the streets every morning enquiring for rooms to rent suitable for an artist and keep an eye out for small galleries who might be favourable to hanging a piece of her artwork. That would be in the future though. She was certain the hotel manager would not be pleased if she stank out his hotel room with turpentine and linseed oil.

She let out a deep sigh. In her head it seemed like a reasonable plan that a confident young woman could accomplish – the reality was that she wasn't confident, and she was also pregnant. She instinctively placed a hand over her increasing bump, fearful of both their futures, but also thinking fondly of Edward.

Her stomach grumbled. She'd barely eaten for days. Daylight was beginning to fade outside, and the small bedroom appeared cheerless and slightly worse for wear. She was pleased it had electric lighting though, that would help in the coming evenings – she could work for longer in her room.

She put most of her jewellery on and hid the rest in a dirty paint rag in the satchel and got ready to go out. She would find a small café close by and have tea. So long as she didn't order expensive evening meals, she had faith that her small stash of money would last until Christmas. She smiled ruefully; she would be completely alone this year. Not completely, she reminded herself. Not whilst she was pregnant. Knitting! That was something else she'd need to make a start with. She sighed, hoping baby garments would be easier than socks.

She lifted her hat, scarf and gloves and left her hotel room. Her first day in London she could afford to treat herself to whatever bun she fancied.

She'd been in London for three days and had no luck finding a flat that was suitable. They were all so expensive, or they were in areas that made her feel unsafe or the owner took one look at her increasing bump and shut the door in her face. But she wouldn't give up yet. She hadn't heard back from Wilfred; perhaps he might have a solution. The Finches hadn't replied either. Every day she sat and cried at some point before wiping the tears away and trying to find some small thing to be grateful for.

This afternoon she had been determined to get a commission. She spent ages in front of the small mirror in her bedroom which she'd named the Draughty Dormitory (the wind seemed to whistle down the chimney no matter what way it was blowing from), she'd put on her brightest outfit and tried to imagine how she'd look to a potential client. She needed to look artistic, yet elegant. On her walks in the neighbourhood, she'd kept an eye out for young ladies who seemed rich and in style. She'd also bought a pot of rouge in Selfridges beauty department and a brightly coloured chiffon scarf which floated as she walked and helped her feel stylish, even if she wasn't.

With a salmon pink lip colour and a forced smile on her face, she sallied forth into the large lounge in the Russell Hotel on the edge of Russell Square. Mr and Mrs Finch had a house nearby, but she didn't recall ever knowing the address. She allowed the porter to take her coat and ordered a pot of tea. She hovered for a few moments, taking it all in, deciding where best to sit. There was a large family group dominating a bay window, to the left of her there were couples holding hands. Then she spotted a potential client. A pink-cheeked, smooth-faced young man, in a brand-new officer's uniform sat by himself near a large chimney place looking uncomfortable and out of place.

Be brave, Izzy, she scolded herself.

Taking a deep breath, she walked over and warmed her hands in front of the fire, smiling at the young man. 'Such a miserable day, don't you think? Might I join you? I've ordered some tea. Would you care for a cup?' She introduced herself.

He blushed beetroot and Isobel felt sorry for him, he looked as though he'd just left school. He stood up immediately and reassured her that of course she should sit down. He declined tea at first, but once Isobel beckoned the maid over, he thought perhaps he might take a cup. Isobel smiled as warmly as she could and asked him questions to keep the conversation flowing. As she did, she lifted out her sketch pad and started to draw.

Her bold hand skimmed across the paper, dashing hither and thither, confident in her skill. 'There now,' she said, as the young soldier drained his second cup (she was hoping he'd suggest he'd pay for it), she moved the sketchpad around so he could see it.

'Gosh. That's extraordinary. You are clever.'

'Thank you. It's just something I do to keep myself amused.'

'There's my mother.' He stood and beckoned to an immaculately well-dressed lady, a bell-boy trailing behind, laden with her parcels. 'Mother.' He kissed her on the cheek. 'Do sit down, this is Mrs Dunwoody, she's an artist. Shall I order more tea?'

His mother smiled and sank into the velvet sofa opposite Isobel. 'Shopping is such a bore, isn't it? Tea would be lovely. I'm Mrs Trafford and this is my son Toby, although it looks like you've already met.' Toby immediately ordered a fresh pot and sandwiches for his mother and Isobel and then effused about her drawing.

Isobel signed the sketch, and carefully pulled it out of her drawing pad and gave it to him. 'Please take it, it's been such a joy to have company this afternoon. Your son has been so kind keeping me amused, Mrs Trafford. Have it as a memento of our little afternoon together. He looks so smart in his uniform, you must be so proud.'

Mrs Trafford peered at the sketch, then took it to examine it further. 'Such extraordinary skill, Mrs Dunwoody. Do you take commissions, only I have a daughter who'll be eighteen shortly? She'll be back for the Christmas holidays. A watercolour of each of them would be something to treasure.'

'Of course I could. I'm in London waiting on news of my husband. Painting would be a good distraction right now.'

'I'm so sorry. So thoughtless of me not to think you might have someone away ...' Her eyes fell on Isobel's bump. 'Are you sure it's not too much trouble?'

'Not at all. I'd rather have something to concentrate on right now, and home is so far away; but I said I wouldn't return until I had better news, so here I am.' Isobel was trying not to look too hopeful, or desperate. She couldn't believe she'd been so fortunate to secure not just one, but two paintings already. They spent another little while making small talk until Isobel decided it would be fortuitous to make her departure. She carefully wrote Mrs Trafford's home address down but agreed to make a start on Toby's painting the next day. He only had a few days before he was due to leave. Isobel reassured both the mother and son that she could make some preliminary sketches to capture his essence, before working on the watercolour once he'd departed for France. (She didn't want to suggest an oil painting just yet.)

She nearly skipped out of the front door of the hotel so delighted was she with her good fortune. She wasn't looking where she was going and bumped into another lady coming in.

'I do beg your pardon,' she apologised profusely, blushing like mad.

'Isobel, my dear child. What are you doing here?'

'Mrs Finch!' For a second, she was fine, and then her emotions overtook her. All the drama of the past few weeks became too much and seeing a friendly face made her cry.

'Now, dear,' Mrs Finch said, slipping her arm through hers. 'We're just across the square. Come home with me now and you can tell me all about it. I sent another letter to Summer

Hill the day before yesterday, but I received no reply. I have done nothing but worry over you, and here you are.'

Clutching her friend's arm tightly, Isobel accompanied her home.

Mrs Finch led Isobel through the large square garden and out the other side. The trees were bare now, all their leaves having been spirited away by wind and rain leaving only stark grey branches. Neatly trimmed box hedges lined the paths and empty mud-brown soil sat exposed to the elements.

'It's very tranquil in the summer,' Mrs Finch said, as they traversed the garden and missed a small white dog which insisted on standing its ground and barking like mad. 'Afternoon, Mrs Bishop,' she said as they nodded at the lady and stepped neatly past the white ball of fluff which strained against its leash. 'She has a husband and two sons fighting already.'

They crossed the street and walked up the steps of a fine three-storey town house with neatly painted railings and a shiny letter box. She opened the door with her own key. 'Mr Finch is still out, I presume, and my housekeeper just left. We'll have to fend for ourselves if you don't mind. We've been eating at The Russell most nights.' She set her gloves down on the side table in the hall and switched on the electric lights. 'That's better, isn't it? Not so dreary. I can't abide coming back when its empty and dark.' Her voice cracked just a little.

Isobel understood. It hadn't even been six months since Alice died. Six months was nothing when you were grieving the one person that your whole world revolved around.

'You'll have to come into the kitchen, I'm afraid. I need to hire someone new, but I can't face the interviews.'

Isobel helped to boil the kettle and make tea, but she

didn't need to eat anything just yet. She was still full after meeting the Traffords. Isobel returned to the front sitting room and lit the fire which was already set in the grate. By the time Mrs Finch walked in, pushing a tea trolley, the room was feeling much warmer.

'Now, tell me all about it, Isobel. Mr Finch and I haven't been home to Bexley Hall in a week. We've handed it over to become a hospital, so whilst they are getting it set up, the whole place was at sixes and sevens, so we just brought ourselves up here, out of the way. When did you arrive?'

'Tuesday. I ran away, I'm afraid.' Her heart pounded, thinking of it again. She wondered what her father had said once it had been discovered she'd gone. She looked imploringly at her friend. 'I couldn't stay. Father wanted me to marry this awful man. He locked me in my room at Summer Hill. I'm not sorry, I'm just not. I've called myself Mrs Dunwoody, and I've already got two commissions this afternoon for portraits. I shall be independent and when Edward is found he will marry me, I know it!' She burst into tears at the end of her emotional speech. The grief of not knowing what had happened to Edward, and the shock of how her father had treated her and having to flee in the night – it had all caught up with her. It was so reassuring sitting with dear Mrs Finch again.

'There, there, Isobel. You're safe now. Mr Finch and I were so upset when we heard your news. We blame ourselves you know, but I understood Wilfred had news to say he was dead. Has there been other information?'

Isobel shrank a little. She knew she should accept the finality of Edward's death, but she just couldn't. 'I know everyone says he's gone, but I don't feel that inside here.' She tapped her heart. 'I think I'd feel it here if he was truly gone and I don't.'

Mrs Finch squeezed her hand but shook her head, looking at her with big sorrowful eyes. 'He's gone, Isobel, and you'll feel better when you stop hoping that isn't the case. It will hurt, I understand that, but we need to think about your situation now. I'm just so sorry, I feel this was our fault.'

'Oh please, it wasn't your fault. How could it have been?'

'But if Alice hadn't died this wouldn't have happened, would it?'

'Well no.' Isobel stared into the cup of tea Mrs Finch had poured and placed into her hands.

'As I thought. And we were all caught up with the hospital idea when you wrote, and I couldn't think. But we've talked of nothing since. We want to help, my dear, so why don't you stay here for now? There's plenty of room. We need a new maid of sorts though, to live in.'

'What about Sarah Heaney, the maid from Summer Hill. I promised I'd bring her over as soon as I could. This man I was to marry, Mr Derby, he seems to … well, he's very inappropriate with Sarah. In a bold way. I promised I'd get Sarah away. She's a hard worker around the house, but not very accomplished with the finer things like cooking.'

Mrs Finch's hands shot up then fell back into her lap. 'There it is then. The perfect solution. We'll not worry about food for now. You send for Sarah, and we'll keep her out of harm's way too. Come, let me show you the rooms.'

They wandered up the stairs and Mrs Finch showed her around. On the first floor there was another cosy sitting room at the front, and then two bedrooms which belonged to the Finches. On the top floor there was one larger bedroom at the front and two small rooms at the back nestled under the eaves. One was full of unneeded belongings, but the other still had a bed and chest of drawers and a small wardrobe. 'Up here will do very nicely for Sarah and myself. We won't be any trouble. The front room has plenty of natural light, it will be perfect for my painting.'

'I'll leave it up to you. I'm only sorry I didn't think of it earlier. Is there anything else I can help with?'

'Could Cecily write to me here, but address it to you? I'm afraid of Father finding me and dragging me home. I couldn't bear that.'

'Of course. Come up with a way that won't get us muddled. You're very creative, I'm sure you can arrange that. Now, when do you want to bring your cases over?'

'Tomorrow?'

'Tomorrow it is. Mr Finch will be relieved. We both feel responsible, and, truthfully, we shall like the company.' She squeezed Isobel's hand tightly. 'Christmas is a dreadful time of the year, isn't it?'

Of course it was. The Finches were missing Alice and had nothing to look forward to. Their future of grandchildren ripped away just as painfully as when Alice had died.

Isobel slept soundly that night, a huge weight lifted from her shoulders. The Finches were dear, dear friends and with them for company she didn't miss Cecily and Edward quite as much. Once she'd got settled in that first morning and she'd written to Sarah, she established a new routine. Once they'd breakfasted together, Isobel started her own work and Mrs Finch got her messages accomplished, and then mid-afternoon the two of them went out. Sometimes it was shopping, other days a nice refreshing walk into Regent's Park, and if it was wet and cold, they visited a museum or just took afternoon tea in The Russell.

Sarah arrived the week before Christmas and stared open-mouthed at all the finery that London had on show. The war didn't seem quite so real when the shop windows were decorated with toys and trees and fairy lights. Sarah had managed to sneak out four of Isobel's smaller landscapes of Egypt and the Riviera, but the painting of Edward reclining at Mena House was far too big for her to take without Mrs Cox catching on. Isobel would just have to manage without it for now.

Chapter Twenty-Five

Bad Helberg Prison camp, Germany, November 1914

The sharp tones of the German guards woke them from their stupor. 'Up! Up! Move!' Shouts around him in the steely-light of dawn woke Edward up. Not that he was ever fully asleep – he, and most of the men around him, slipped in and out of a light, uncomfortable doze all through the extra days they waited for a train. Food had been little but watery soup and a horrible unappetising hard black bread. Latrines were nowhere except a drain in the corner. Officers and men squatting over a filthy hole. The stench was horrendous.

Other groups of captured soldiers had arrived whilst they waited, and they too were starving. The French and the Belgians were treated better than the British for some reason, but thankfully shared what little they had been allocated.

'Move. Move.' The guards barked orders now at the soldiers, who helped each other up and into line. If they weren't quick enough, they got a rifle butt in the head. Edward and Walker peered through the feeble light checking to see if all their men had made it into the lines. The gate opened and they were pushed forward up onto the railway station. A cattle train was waiting for them, doors open; the cavernous hole swallowing each of them up as they were forced to clamber in. Grunts and exclamations echoed up and down the train as the injured amongst them weren't given time to ease themselves into the truck. If they couldn't walk, they were carried by their mates and set down onto the dirty floor of the truck.

'Walker?'

'Here. Behind you.' It was hard to see him, but Edward was relieved all the same. The two of them had bonded well these past few weeks together. Ominous clanging noises rang out as the sliding doors of the trucks were shoved back in place before being locked.

'Water. Water! Give us some water at least!' men shouted through the small open bars at the top of the trucks.

'Where are we going?'

'The bastards are going to starve us to death! You filthy hun!'

The engine let out a huge whoosh of steam and slowly at first it jerked forward, causing all inside to fall, then steady themselves, before it did the same again. Edward tried to peer out, calculating where they could be going, searching for landmarks amongst the town of Lille.

Someone further up the train, in a strong Dublin accent, sang the first line of a song they all knew.

It's a long way to Tipperary.

Up and down the train, despite their injuries, their starving bellies, their fury at being captured and their shame of how they were treated, the soldiers joined in. Opening their mouths and singing with gusto, so that as they chugged through the town of Lille, all would know that the British army wasn't beaten yet.

The journey deep into the heart of Germany took nearly a week. The train they were on got shunted into sidings more times than Edward could remember, where they waited hours, or even a day, until it moved off again. Sometimes they got some of that watery soup, sometimes nothing.

Just survive. *Stay alive for Isobel,* Edward told himself every night, as he tried to sleep again. His stomach was eating itself from hunger. He tried to calculate how much weight he must have lost, and how much food they needed to consume before they could actually die of starvation. Water, that was critical. *Clean* water, though.

The day before, the train had stopped, and all their non-commissioned men were marched off. It was a stab in the chest for Edward. He tried to remember who was left from 'D' company. He still felt keenly that they were his responsibility.

Now, the cattle train that stank to high heaven with men's excrements from the past week finally came to a halt in a small village. From what he could see, they had travelled east, and mountains rose up all around them. When the doors were finally thrown open for the last time, he gulped down lungfuls of the clean, fresh air. It was so cold that it felt as though it would burn his lungs, but the scent of pine needles was sweeter than any gift. It reminded him in a way of the Mourne mountains, back home in Ireland, but there were more trees here.

Night had fallen when they were ordered off the train, their limbs stiff and aching. No matter, the officers were ordered into line and if they weren't quick enough the familiar rifle butt was smacked against any part of their body available.

'Not very good aim though, are they?' Walker commented, after ducking from a heavy-built guard.

'We stink. They can't aim when they won't stand closer than three feet. Be thankful for small mercies.'

'Silence!' someone shouted. 'March.' Off they trekked, out of the village, ducking every now and then as housewives who should have been in their beds threw potatoes or rocks at them. Their march was far shorter than they feared, only a mile or so from the village. Fancy metal gates, that had not been painted for a while, had a name spelled out in wrought iron.

Bad Helberg.

'Good grief. That's the worse sign I've ever seen. We're headed for hell, that's for sure.'

'It's a spa. Don't panic. It might not be too bad,' Walker said.

Scanning their surroundings, Edward thought the hope misplaced. Once in the gates, which were covered with barbed wire and a small hut where guards were stationed, the road surface was poor and badly maintained. Grass grew up the middle of it. They marched a further half mile amongst dark, looming pine trees, before they reached a second fence. Higher this time and again, secured with more guards and barbed wire. The buildings in front of them, even in the shadow of nightfall, looked dishevelled and unkempt. The nearest building must be a manor house or similar, with stables and outbuildings behind. Grass grew everywhere, the paths weren't tidy, and window frames needed painting. It might have been a spa at one time, but the visitors must have been ghosts by now. A restrictive band formed around Edward's chest as he fought to suppress the panic. The gates were closed behind them, and in the pale light of lanterns, they could see guards and menacing dogs which strained at their leashes, lined up to greet them.

'Velcome to Bad Helberg.' One of the Germans had stepped forward. 'I am your kommandant. Ve vant no trouble here. No trouble. All good.' He nodded at them, inbetween puffing on an oversized cigar, the tip of which glowed in the darkness. 'I am sure you are all tired and hungry.' He gestured with his arm and two orderlies struggled forward with a large tureen of something which steamed in the cold night air. Using his gloved hand, he lifted the lid, wafting the steam towards them. They sniffed the air in anticipation. Edward's mouth salivated at what might be in the pan.

'You vant this, yes?' The kommandant, marched up and down in front of their ranks, eyeing them all up, holding the lid in one hand, his cigar in the other.

Hope. He was offering them hope. Edward's gut twisted – this didn't feel right. Good food after they'd been treated so abominably badly all this time. Hardly.

'You vant it?' he said again, encouraging them to come forward. 'Come. Come.' His gloved hand directed them towards the steaming pan.

Most of them hadn't even a cup to hold water, let alone steaming hot soup. Edward's nerves were on fire. Further up the line, guards pushed the first men towards the pan, jabbing them in their backs. There was a group intake of breath. Everyone was on edge. As the first men came to within touching distance, the kommandant laughed at them. 'Not today though.' He kicked the pan, spilling the steaming-hot contents onto the ground where it gushed towards the men who were down slope from it. Hot fish heads swam towards them and the guards burst out laughing as some of the British made a dive for them. The Germans immediately started kicking at the soldiers as they were on the ground.

Bastards! Edward swore under his breath. He had a feeling Bad Helberg was going to be an accurate name for the camp.

They were then marched off into the building which was to house them. House was a loose term, Edward thought. The ceiling dripped and sagged in the middle and mold grew in several spots, beneath which puddles of water had gathered. Bunks had been erected in lines. I should be grateful at least for a blanket, he thought, climbing up into the bed allocated to him. His coat was damp. His feet were like blocks of ice. The blanket was at least dry. He lay on his back and closed his eyes. Instantly he opened them again. A surge of panic rolled right through him. The vastness of defeat hit him. They were hundreds of miles from the French or Belgium border. No one knew they were here. Beads of sweat gathered on his forehead and scalp, and he breathed deeper and deeper to get a grip on himself.

'Easy, man, easy,' Walker said from below him, tapping the side of his bunk. 'One day at a time, mate. Don't think too far ahead. Think of better things.'

He tried, but every time he closed his eyes he was overcome by a black hole of panic. He couldn't explain it. Fear, sheer fear of never getting out of this place ate away at him. Walker must have felt the shudders as his body fought off the terror.

'Open her letter.'

Isobel's letter. Maybe he would. That would give him something to look forward to. Maybe he'd eke it out. Just a line tonight. Another line tomorrow. He would open it. His fingers searched through his jacket to the pocket where it lay. It still crackled as he touched it. That was good. It was dry. He felt in the dark for the edge of the envelope so he could open it, before it hit him.

'Bloody bollocks, Walker. There's no bloody light to read it by!'

A throaty laugh erupted from the bunk below. 'I know, but at least it stopped you panicking. Now go to sleep.'

'Bastard!' Edward retorted, but he knew he was beat. Walker was right. He replaced the letter for now. He *would* read it in the morning though, it was something to look forward to.

Somehow, he drifted off. When daylight dawned late the next morning, he was ready. He ripped it open, anticipating reading her words.

Wednesday 14th October

Dearest Edward,

Minnie has informed me that I am expecting a baby. Our baby.

I am overjoyed to think that we have created a child together and I'm eagerly awaiting its birth. I know you will be a wonderful father. But I need you to come home immediately.

He stormed out of their bunk room and smacked the first boche that he saw. He also lost his letter and the next ten days of his relative freedom. He was lucky not to have been put in front of a firing squad, Walker reminded him when he was finally allowed out of solitary, another five pounds lighter.

'You're fortunate that the boche you punched was one of the friendly ones, now go and apologise.'

'Must I?'

'Yes. Think of it as part of your escape plan, your training. Do it in German.' Edward scowled at him. 'You are to speak German every day and be courteous and nice whilst you are at it. We will get out, you and I, and make it home. After all, you're going to be a father now so you have to.' He pulled out Isobel's letter, that he'd saved from the guards and gave it back to Edward. 'Now, for God's sake find a nice quiet place to read this and don't hit anyone again.'

Chapter Twenty-Six

Christmas passed quietly and bleakly. The weather was freezing, and snow blew in from the continent. It was like nature was saying you all deserve to be miserable. News from the war was just as harsh and a continuous line of trains decamped injured men at train stations across England. The hope of the nation that the war would be over by Christmas had been proven horribly untrue.

During January, Isobel spent a couple of weeks in Surrey painting the Traffords' daughter Harriet, and she completed the portrait of Toby only two days before his mother sent her a wire saying he'd been killed fixing barbed wire out in no-man's land. She cried. She understood all too well the pain of losing someone.

Mr and Mrs Finch had moved back to Bexley Hall after the New Year and nobody had talked about what was going to happen when her baby arrived. Isobel knew she'd fight tooth and nail before she allowed anyone to force her to give it up for adoption.

The front door rattled one afternoon in early February and Sarah shot upstairs to where she was painting. 'There's a man downstairs, miss. Says he knows you. Captain Dunwoody, miss.'

Isobel's heart sank. Wilfred. She hadn't got over that awful meeting with him in November. Perhaps he had news though? She unbuttoned her painters' frock and patted her hair into shape. She didn't take any longer with her toilette though, because she knew all he'd focus on was the size of her expanding bump. Now that she'd come back from Surrey and Mrs Finch had returned to Norfolk, she'd barely left the house.

'Ah, Isobel,' he said when she walked slowly into the sitting room. 'Ah.'

'Wilfred. How nice.' Hadn't he ever seen a heavily pregnant woman before? Probably not. 'Oh, your hand! Is it bad?' Her eyes had seen his bandaged right arm and the sling.

'Minor injury, but it's put me out of action for a few weeks. I've been sent home for a rest. It was a bullet thankfully. Nice and clean. I'll be as right as rain in days.'

She nodded and sat down heavily into the armchair opposite to where he stood. 'Any news?'

'Sorry. None. I will keep my ear to the ground though. I promise.' He cleared his throat. 'I got your letters. I just wanted to see how you were fixed for ... things.'

'I'm fine as you can see. The Finches are looking after me and I'm expecting Cecily soon when she returns from America.'

Sarah reversed into the room pushing the tea trolley with silver teapot, cups and saucers and a plate of her lemon thins of which Isobel knew she had spent ages perfecting the recipe.

'Can I sketch you?'

'Must you?' he said, plucking at a thread on his trousers.

'Well, if you want to sit and chat, I might as well draw at the same time. I'm always looking for a new subject.' He didn't object after that, so she sent Sarah up for her pad and pencil and she proceeded to draw him as he sat. As she was concentrating, he seemed to feel more able to talk.

'Are you keeping well?'

'I am. How's your cousin, Roger? In uniform yet?' Her hand kept up the fluid strokes across the page, filling in the details that she saw.

'Soon. He wants you to write to him, if you wouldn't mind.'

'Why would I mind? We've known each other for years.'

'Well... you know...' He waved his hand towards her.

'I'm having your brother's baby. Not an elephant. Women have babies all the time.'

His face fell. 'I know.'

'I'm so sorry, Wilfred. You and Alice were looking forward to your own. I do apologise.'

He looked down at his hands then crossed and uncrossed his feet. 'The thing is, I didn't have time to think about that. We didn't know before she left. Also,' he cleared his throat, 'I've had plenty of time to think, laid up in hospital recently, so I thought it best if I did marry you.'

'No, really!' She was alarmed at where the subject was now going.

'Please!' He held his hand up to stop her, then squinted at her. 'You have paint on your cheek. Did you know?'

'I'm an artist, Wilfred. I'm always painting.'

'Yes... well, I didn't realise I would miss Alice and our... well. I do. I'd like to be a father to your baby. It's only right. Give him a proper name.'

Isobel's pencil dropped from her hand, breaking the silence that had enveloped the room. She swallowed. Twice.

She'd only seen him blush the once before and that was when she'd told him she was pregnant. He was now flushed around the neck and up to his ears. She let her breath out slowly.

'The thing is, Wilfred, that's very, very, kind of you. I'm awfully touched. You'll be a wonderful uncle and can see him or her whenever you want, but I can't marry you.'

'You could,' he said, turning his head away and looking at the embroidered cushion next to him. 'You must.'

'I can't,' Isobel replied firmly. 'What if Edward is found in a camp and comes home and we are married – how awful would that be? He'd be so hurt. His own child recognised as yours! No, it's very kind of you, but I just can't accept.'

Wilfred breathed heavily. He even seemed somewhat wistful. But pity wasn't enough reason to marry him, Isobel knew. 'One day you'll fall in love again, I promise.'

He nodded without looking at her. 'You need to re-consider and if you do, the offer will still be there. You've changed, I think. You have always been on the wild side but I recognise a strong woman when I see one. Like Alice was. I like that. You and Edward both understood that you wanted to follow your own ideas. I wish I had been strong enough not to follow Father into the army.' He paused, gazing out across the desolate garden in front of the townhouse. 'I understand you're calling yourself Mrs Dunwoody; just don't get caught out. Mother will be furious.'

'As though Edward and I had married.'

'He's dead, Isobel. Dead. You need to face facts. I have permission from my commanding officer and now that I am here for a few more days, I think it imperative that we do this. Mother will not support you as an unmarried woman. Not in the slightest. I'm not asking for … things,' he blushed a deep beetroot colour, 'not yet anyhow. It's just as likely that I'll be killed soon too. But Alice would have wanted me to do this.'

'You don't even like me, Wilfred. I displease you!' He had completely astounded her. How could he suggest marrying her when he didn't like her? 'Don't use Alice to convince me.' She could see his face contort as he fought his own emotions; God knows he'd tried to hide them so many times from her in the past. Tried to keep the upper hand, the composed I'm-better-than-you stance. He fought against it yet she swore she saw his lip tremble.

'I don't dislike you, Isobel. I'm sorry if it always seemed that way. I admire you, I do. And now you need a husband and your child needs a name. The Dunwoody name, if I'm frank. Who knows how long this war will last? But your child will need my name if they are to have any decent future at all. You know this. Deep down you do, Isobel. I want to marry you. If I survive this war we can even be happy together. I'm prepared to make a sacrifice and you need to do the same.'

She felt sick. The feeling deep inside that told her he was right. Oh God, she didn't want to. Really, she didn't. She'd always fought her mother against getting married for the sake of it. This marriage would be everything she didn't want it to be – it wasn't for love. It just stood for propriety and security. Her whole soul bucked against it, but, deep down, deep, deep down she knew he was right. That independence that she'd always craved, to be in charge of her own destiny – choosing who to fall in love with – she was giving it all up. She'd even fought her father against being married off to Mr Derby at the station. 'Can you give me a few hours to think it through?' The words came out so slowly it was as though she'd never said them.

He breathed heavily. Exasperated at her, she assumed.

He stood and nodded stiffly. 'I'm awfully tired, actually.

And my head is pounding. Would you mind if I lay down for a few hours?'

'No. Not at all. I should have realised. You can sleep upstairs. I'll bring you up some water and something for your headache.' He followed her up the two flights of stairs and barely said a word as she pulled the coverlet off her bed and gestured for him to lie down. His features were pinched, barely seeming to focus on her. She hurried downstairs and returned with a bromide tablet for him, but he was already asleep, fully dressed, his boots still on. She tiptoed away, heart heavy and not wanting to think about what he'd suggested earlier.

The afternoon light slipped away, and the lamps were on when she heard a strange sound. She couldn't place it to start with, like a cat or wild animal caught somehow. Even Sarah heard it and tiptoed to the bottom of the stairs with her, face white as a ghost.

'What is that?' Isobel whispered. The noise seemed to come from upstairs.

'That's like the banshee that comes on wild winter nights, so it is!' Sarah declared.

They both strained to listen as the eerie high-pitched keening sound trickled down the stairs.

'Oh.' Isobel knew. 'It's Wilfred. I must go to him.' She went upstairs, not knowing whether he wanted her, or was he awake, or what even the noise was. But it was definitely him, that was for certain. She waited for a moment outside her bedroom door, as his breaths gasped and spluttered the other side of it. She peered in, afraid he was choking. By the light from the landing, she saw his limbs contorted, but rigid, his eyes glassy, staring at some such demon miles out of reach, and his body sobbing and gasping for breath. She was by his side immediately.

'Wilfred,' she soothed him. 'Shush now. Shush. It's Isobel. It's going to be all right.' She sensed, more than saw, that he relaxed a tiny bit at the sound of her voice. She knelt on the floor and kept talking to him, trying to reach him through his nightmare. What horrors he must have seen already, she wondered. 'Shush, Wilfred,' she kept repeating, and little by little she kissed his ice-cold hands, and then pressed her lips to his forehead as though it was Edward before her, injured.

His nightmare eased, and his body gradually relaxed. 'Alice?'

'It's me. Isobel. You're safe now.'

'Sorry. The nights are so hard. So sorry if I was behaving badly.'

'Not at all.' Now she was embarrassed. It was awkward. Too personal. She should have brought Sarah upstairs with her.

He moved and helped her up. She sat down beside him, her knees sore and aching. They sat next to each other, not speaking, just leaning shoulder to shoulder in the dark. After a while, Wilfred spoke.

'I miss Alice. You miss Edward. Perhaps we can make it work, for this one.' His large hand slipped gently over Isobel's bump, stroking it reverently.

She should be grateful, shouldn't she? But inside she wanted to cry. She desperately wanted to say, no. Never. But she already understood she couldn't hurt his feelings. 'Can I give you an answer tomorrow?' For the first time she saw the man Alice fell in love with. A sensitive and shy man.

'I have three days left before I embark again for France. May I call tomorrow? Same time? You can draw some more if you want. I've already spoken to the rector of All Souls. We need a special licence. He can organise that.'

She barely nodded. He was lonely and missing Alice and

the baby he'd never hold. Being in France must have been dreadful. He seemed changed, that was for sure. He'd always been the oldest whenever the two family groups had met up in Belfast socially. He'd been sterner, or perhaps just more confident. He'd bossed her about so many times, yet she had so many memories of her and Edward playing tricks on him or setting him up in a race that she knew she could beat him at. Perhaps she didn't know him well at all. Dear man. If it was company he needed then she would do her best to provide it. 'Thank you. Yes. It would be nice.'

She showed him out herself, watching his back as he walked down the steps and paused, fixing his cap on his head. Her heart fluttered inside at the familiarity of the two brothers – this is what Edward must have looked like in his uniform. Same height, same shoulders. Same walk.

But getting married now was accepting Edward was dead and it hurt far more than she expected. She closed the door behind him and sank to the ground holding her body tight, fighting the deep, ragged breaths that threatened to undo her. She was considering marriage after all and she hated herself.

Chapter Twenty-Seven

She penned a letter to Mrs Finch immediately, then screwed it up and tossed it into the fire. 'I wish Cecily was here,' she murmured into the flames. She'd tell me what to do. Furious with herself, she wrote another letter, again to Mrs Finch.

Mrs Finch,
   Wilfred has proposed. What should I do?

It was obvious though, wasn't it? She didn't need anyone to advise her – she was jolly lucky a nice, reserved, respectable man like Wilfred had offered to marry her. Even though it went against everything she'd fought, every principle she'd clung to, she knew she had to go through with it.

It didn't make her a nice person though. And if she dared cast her eyes too far down the road... oh goodness! She groaned out loud.

'Miss! Miss! Are you unwell?' Sarah came running into the parlour.

'I am a horrible, despicable person, Sarah. Make no mistake about it.' Tears streamed down her face, dripping onto her collar. She looked up beseechingly at the young maid, begging her to help find solace in her decision.

'Why? What have you done?'

'I'm going to say yes to Wilfred Dunwoody.' She cried out when she spoke his name, it was such a betrayal of Edward.

She was going to marry his brother in order to save herself and her child. She was hateful.

'Oh my,' Sarah said, wide-eyed. 'Maybe I should pour you a drink.'

'Just a cup of tea please. And get one yourself, Sarah, because I cannot be alone,' she said, sobbing. 'I always vowed never to marry but if I did it would only be for love. And now look at me. His brother!'

'Stop, miss. If Cecily and Minnie were here, they would tell you it was the right thing to do. If that nice Mrs Finch was here, she'd say the same. Fairy tales and happy endings only exist in books, and this ain't no fairy story we're living. Marry him. Get a ring on that finger and no regrets.'

'But what if Edward's alive? What then?' she shouted, holding her large bump. 'If he is alive, in a camp some place, and he hears I've got married to his brother, I would surely have killed him as if I'd shot him with a bullet.'

'Stop that silly talk. Where is he then, if he's alive? Why hasn't he written? It's been three months since he vanished. Three! If he was still alive, then he would have written to you in Belfast, or here in London. Or even Summer Hill.'

'But I'm not in any of those places. What if he has?' she wailed, becoming hysterical.

'Or to his mother then.'

'She wouldn't tell me.' Isobel knew that Mrs Dunwoody wouldn't want her hearing in the slightest.

'Maybe not personally, but she wouldn't be able to stop the news leaking out. She would rejoice if her son had been found. It would be in the papers, and someone would have heard.' She stared down at Isobel, who was curled up in the chair, rocking herself. 'Face facts, miss. He's not coming back. Wilfred is very kind to do this. You have to marry him. You just have to. Write that note for Mrs Finch and I'll pop out now to post it. With luck she can come and stand in for you. Moral support and all that.'

Nodding, Isobel barely heard her. She didn't want to feel sensible and grown-up. She wanted to wallow in deep misery like she deserved. *Forgive me, Edward, I'm such a coward.*

The wedding was set for the day after next. Mrs Finch sent a reply immediately and said she'd be honoured to attend and offered Mr Finch to stand up for Wilfred. No one else would be present. Cecily wouldn't be home for another few weeks.

'Don't be scared, Isobel, you are doing the right thing.' Mrs Finch said, when she arrived.

'How can I be?' Isobel cried out. Her chest was so tight it was as though her heart could break in two. 'I feel I'm abandoning him.'

'It's another level of grief. That's all,' Mrs Finch replied, wiping away her own tears. 'If Alice was alive, she would have helped you. She and Wilfred would have taken in your baby – Alice loved you that much. She wouldn't have seen you suffer. Even though the two of you had very little time together, she always said you had an immediate connection. Like the sister she never had.'

'We did.' Isobel clutched Mrs Finch. 'We got on so well. I just wish we'd met years ago.'

'But you also need to face facts. You've refused to talk about what will happen when the baby comes. I've tried countless times, but you've avoided it. But you have to realise that you just couldn't keep the baby.' Isobel went to interrupt, but Mrs Finch stopped her, holding a hand in front of her. 'It's harsh, I know, but facts are facts. You say you want to be an artist, a professional artist, which you undoubtedly have the talent for and I know you've a desire to exhibit at the Royal Institute of Oil Painters – but do you think they'd spend one second thinking it over if you had a child out of wedlock? No. They wouldn't. You'd be shunned. Utterly and painfully. And this child, your baby, would also suffer in the same way. Good schools would be closed to him, men – if it's a boy – would close ranks against him. Society doesn't like its rules broken, and that's the truth.'

Isobel's whole body shook. Mrs Finch had never been so forceful before.

Mrs Finch stood back, her usually kind eyes stern. 'You and Edward broke the rules and now you have to fix it. Marry Wilfred,' she added, softer this time. 'You won't get a better offer.'

'But how can I ever be the right wife for Wilfred? He's not Edward. He dislikes my painting. I must paint, you know.'

'Wilfred knows that too. Just give him a chance. The soldiers we see down at Bexley Hall are broken men, dear. This war has turned into a war like no other. Wilfred has reached out to you, as a way of dealing with his grief of losing Alice and their baby, but also of losing Edward. Trust his intentions. Give him a chance, won't you?'

'I– I … I just don't want to lose myself, you see.'

'Marriage, real marriage takes work and commitment on both sides.' Mrs Finch opened up her arms to hug her.

'But that's what I'm afraid of. This isn't just a little fix for the sake of the baby. This is a commitment to Wilfred for life. I don't know him!' She wailed, burying her face into Mrs Finch's shoulder. 'He's practically a stranger.'

'Alice loved him and respected him. I'm sure you just need to get to know him better. Right now, he's hurting badly, as are you. Surely you can find some common ground there?'

'But is that enough?' She was sure it wasn't. It was never going to come close to the love she felt for Edward.

'For the sake of your baby, then yes. It has to be. You are doing the right thing. Mr Finch and I know Wilfred better than you. Please trust us. This is the best solution.'

Although Isobel agreed verbally, she spent the rest of the day in a blur. She was lost in a fog and couldn't escape. Everyone around her kept saying it was the best thing, but deep down a little voice was screaming no! And no matter what she did, she couldn't stop the fear circulating within her that she was making a huge mistake.

Wilfred arrived and she spoke when she needed to and enquired after his health and organised tea for him, but inside she was a mess.

'Come outside for a walk, Isobel?' he suggested before he left. Mrs Finch was staying the night and Mr Finch would arrive the next morning. Nothing was going to be like she had imagined her wedding to Edward would be. That was a good thing, she thought.

The wintry afternoon sun filtered through the bare branches of the trees in Russell Square. She was barely outside these days, trying to keep herself out of sight.

'Some fresh air might help us both,' he said.

Sarah brought her hat and coat, although it didn't fasten over her expanding bump now. Instead, the maid draped the scarf in front, covering the buttons that wouldn't fasten. At the last minute she spurned her gloves but snatched up her drawing pad and pencil instead.

Wilfred held the door open and then held out his arm for her to hold. Swallowing first, she accepted. This was just the first time of a multitude that she would now act as a wife. Not an acquaintance.

Slowly they circumnavigated the park. Past trees dead to the winter – their branches stark and bare. Past clumps of decaying foliage standing in the flower beds, waiting for the grip of winter to pass. That's what it feels like to grieve, Isobel thought. To be defeated and decaying inside of yourself.

She tried to make conversation, to break the awkward silence between them, but the harder she tried the more she homed in instead on his heavy breathing. That's what it will be like at night, lying next to him in bed. She fought down the impulse to flee. 'Let's sit, shall we? The sun falls nicely just so, across the grass.' She withdrew her arm from his and awkwardly lowered herself onto the bench, setting her drawing pad on her knee and selecting a blank page.

'I hadn't realised quite how cumbersome …' he gestured with his good arm. 'It looks uncomfortable is what I meant.' His breath formed a little cloud as he spoke, the daytime temperature not far above freezing. 'Are you warm enough? I could run back and get you a blanket.'

She was touched by his thoughtfulness. 'Thank you, but I'm fine.'

The flower bed nearest their feet had drifts of snowdrops lifting their heads out of the half-frozen soil, and beside them green spikes where crocuses were just peeking through. Across the park, another officer appeared, bundled up in his greatcoat, hat pulled well down over his features. He sank onto a bench and virtually disappeared into his collar.

'Is he all right?' Isobel leant forward in her seat. 'He seems …' She couldn't finish.

'Are any of us all right?' Wilfred answered, his voice thick with emotion. He coughed to clear his throat.

Isobel's instinctively started to sketch – the park, the sky, the desolate trees, but mostly the defeated slouch of the officer, all but invisible in his coat. She lost herself for a while, hand skimming the crisp white page, filling it with grey lines, but gradually, where there was nothing before, the figure emerged.

'Can you paint him too?' Wilfred asked, his tone serious.

'Why yes, of course.'

'You have a rare skill, Isobel. I do admire it. But promise me one thing?'

She was surprised by his praise. 'Yes?'

'Tell the truth. Tell the world the truth about what we are going through. The blood and death, exhaustion, the never-ending fear and anguish that we face day in, day out. We give ourselves freely, but it is not the picnic they paint in the papers. Paint that officer, notice the mud still caked to his puttees, the shake in his hand before he buried it deep out of sight. The complete exhaustion within his features. Get it all down.'

Turning her head, Isobel looked closer at Wilfred, but he couldn't acknowledge her. Instead, she slipped her hand back through his and squeezed it. Gently, little by little, she edged closer to him, shoulders touching. He needed her, perhaps just as badly as she needed his name.

'I just want a wife and child to come home to, Isobel,' he said quietly. 'Something to make all this worth fighting for. It has to be worth something.' He dipped his head a fraction, his hat awkwardly knocking into hers. It wasn't much, but it was a connection. A tiny fracture into his soul. Isobel prayed she would be equal to it.

They sat a while longer before the cold got the better of them and they retreated back indoors. He kissed her cheek when he left that night, standing on the doorstep, ignoring the blackout rather carelessly. 'I haven't told Mother. I fear I shan't just yet. Is that all right with you?'

'Yes. I'm not in a hurry to tell my family either. Just Cecily when she returns.'

'Time enough when the baby has arrived safely. I'll tell her in my own time. Until tomorrow then.' He tipped his hat and left, walking swiftly into the looming darkness and fog that had descended once the sunlight had gone, and he was swallowed up by the dense whirling mist before he'd even reached the end of the street.

That will be me tomorrow, she thought, swallowed up by marriage. Isobel Harris no longer, forever known as a wife. An appendage to a man. Invisible to the world.

Chapter Twenty-Eight

The ceremony was set for 11 o'clock. Mrs Finch and Sarah fussed over her outfit and, as an afterthought, Sarah nipped out, returning with a small posy of snowdrops set off nicely against a couple of dark cyclamen leaves. The thoughtful act brought Isobel to tears. 'Thank you,' she whispered, kissing the maid on the forehead.

'There's a good girl now,' Mrs Finch intervened. 'Get our coats ready. It's time we were leaving. Mr Finch has sent the car back for us.' She waved Sarah off out of the way before turning to Isobel.

'Now. Chin up. Be strong, no tears on your wedding day. Wilfred is doing you a great kindness, so pay him back with the same smile you'd give if it was Edward. You're a very lucky girl. It might not feel like it, and God only knows what will happen to poor Wilfred when he returns to the front, but that man is being very gracious towards you and his brother, so don't ever repay him with a cold heart. Alice loved him, and I'm trusting you to do the same.'

Isobel's legs wobbled. If she could turn and run, she would. It was wrong. So very, very wrong. But coward as she was, she was going through with it. The reckless, impulsive, rebellious young girl had vanished and a cold-hearted expectant mother stood in her place. She walked woodenly down the stairs, and let Sarah help her on with her coat. Her wedding dress was no more than Mrs Finch had been able to rustle up from Selfridges the day before. Smart, but plain. Her coat was trimmed with a chestnut brown fur collar and a matching hat, and she noticed Sarah had tucked a couple of snowdrops into the band. She was suitably dressed for the day.

She did as she was bid by Mrs Finch – walked when she was told to, sat when she had to and smiled when expected. She had slipped off the pretend wedding ring last night. She was ready.

Wilfred and Mr Finch waited discreetly inside the church. Her heart lurched when she saw him at the altar rail. From behind, if she didn't know any better, it could be Edward. It wasn't though. He turned around as she and Mrs Finch walked up the aisle and the slight squeeze on her arm reminded her to smile at him.

Wilfred's eyes followed her up the aisle. His expression, if she had read him correctly, was one of bashfulness as his eyes finally dropped to her feet when she was beside him. A quick flick of her head towards him and the tiny lift of his lips suggested he was pleased to see her. She let out a deep breath.

It was plain to see the censure on the face of the minister, but there was no avoiding the fact that her bump was large. The service was short and to the point. No hymns, no sermon, just the vows and then the register to be signed and witnessed. It was complete. They were Captain and Mrs Dunwoody now. No going back. He squeezed her hand gently, before carefully tucking her arm in his as he led her back down the aisle.

There was no heading to a nice hotel for a celebratory wedding meal, instead Mrs Finch had ordered food to be delivered to the house. It all tasted like sawdust to Isobel. She sat next to Wilfred at the table and winced when Mr

Finch insisted on opening a bottle of champagne to toast their good health.

From her place at the table, she could see the other officer had returned to the square again and slouched on the bench. Wilfred would need more than a toast of champagne to keep him safe. His knife rattled occasionally on the dinner plate, like a drum roll or a tattoo. He was as jumpy as she was, but she couldn't tell was it marriage to her or because he was due back to the front.

He wiped his mouth and set down his cutlery, leaving half the dinner untouched. 'I'm sorry,' he apologised to Mrs Finch. 'Counting down the hours is harder than I realised.'

'Of course, of course it is. I just didn't want to let the day go past without marking it in some way.'

'It was very kind of you,' Isobel said, reaching across and gently touching her dear friend on the hand. 'It's all very different this time ...' She couldn't finish. Of course, it was hard on the Finches and Wilfred. The last time he'd exchanged marriage vows it had been with their daughter not much over a year ago. What dreadful misfortune they all had suffered. The world had turned upside down since they'd been in Belfast last year.

'Such a waste of food.'

'Never mind. It can't be helped.'

'Might I speak to you alone, Isobel, before I leave?'

'Yes. Inside or outside?' She looked across the table to the square. The sun was out. 'I wonder would he care for some food?' she wondered, looking at the soldier outside.

'A drink I should think.'

'Won't he be freezing cold, out there all afternoon?'

'It's dry, Mrs Finch. Dry feet. Dry clothes. So many men have been affected by awful problems with their feet. Standing in freezing-cold water day in, day out, never getting dry socks to change into and, even then, the dry socks only lasting a few hours.'

'Still, it seems a bit churlish of us not to check on him, when we have food to spare,' Mr Finch said, getting up to head outside.

'We'll ask him, Mr Finch. Don't get cold. Isobel?' Wilfred looked across at her, his expression pained.

She noticed his demeanour. It was like a mask slowly slipping across his face. He was saying words, but beneath them he was losing himself. His tone, his smile, his eyes. All were vanishing into a pea soup of blandness, as though he was withdrawing. She wondered for a moment was it her – having to be married to her instead of Alice. Was it such a burden? 'I'll call for Sarah.'

'Are you all right, Wilfred?' she asked, as the front door closed behind them.

He sighed heavily, but didn't answer her immediately. 'Let's walk the long way around. I've a few things I need to say first.' He offered her his arm and they crossed the street, Wilfred directing them to walk around the outside of the square for now. Taxi cabs ploughed up and down the road next to them, and a Harrods delivery van was pulling into the next street. Wilfred waited for a quieter moment before speaking.

'I've written a new will. You and the baby will be looked after should ...'

'Oh, please don't say that!'

'I *must,* Isobel. We have to face facts. Edward is dead. I could be next. None of us are invincible like we thought we were. I've spoken to Mr Finch this morning. They are good people and I shall rest easy now, leaving you in their care. I'm sorry I wasn't more help in November. Things ... took me by surprise. But now I can return to the front knowing I have done my best for you.'

'I'm sorry.' She was a burden to him. An uncomfortable, awkward burden. His duty. Well, that was correct for sure.

'At least it was Edward. I'm not such a saint that I would have taken on someone else's child, you understand.'

She bit her lip. There was nothing much she could say to that.

He turned away from her so she couldn't see his face, his breath deep and heavy. Neither spoke for a few minutes. 'You'll be put down as my next of kin when I return and will be due my pension if necessary.'

'Thank you.' She was supposed to be grateful, but why did it feel so humiliating?

'Have you thought of any names?'

'I ... no.' She hadn't.

'Alice would be nice if it's a girl.'

'Oh, absolutely. Alice would be perfect.' Alice *would* be perfect, but she had wanted the freedom to choose for herself.

He continued. 'I'd rather not Edward though, for a boy – just too ... obvious, if you get my drift.'

'Perhaps George. Quite ... regal for the times.'

'George.' Wilfred repeated it a few times, as though trying it out to see if he would like it. 'George Dunwoody. Mmm, yes. You'll have to add family middle names though. That would be expected. George Edward Wilfred Dunwoody. That has a nice ring to it, doesn't it?'

'Yes.' That was it then, she patted her bump. Named already. She tried to smile at him as though she meant it. 'Well, that was nicely arranged, wasn't it?'

'Yes. It gives me something to look forward to ... out there. One finds it hard, you see ... going back.'

She could see that, poor man, but this was just awkward. 'Shall we walk some more? The snowdrops were pleasant yesterday.'

'Send me a wire, won't you? I do want to know. A photograph too. Only when it can be arranged, but soon. I should like to see the child, perhaps of you, too. If that's not too forward of me.'

She was dying inside. This was all getting drawn out and awkward, but she ought to be grateful he didn't ask to share her bed tonight. Oh lord, what had she done? The next time he came home he'd expect that, wouldn't he! She tried to hide how she felt by speaking more brightly instead. She pulled him along the pavement and in through the wrought-iron gate and followed the path in its circuitous route. She'd forgotten all about the officer on the bench until Wilfred shouted.

The uniformed figure was no longer slouching, withdrawn within his overcoat. His body had tipped sideways onto the bench, his hat knocked off and his eyes a wide-open stare. Two scarlet puddles lay beneath the bench where his blood had seeped away whilst they had been choosing baby names.

'Oh God! Avert your eyes, Isobel,' exclaimed Wilfred. 'Poor man's topped himself.'

The officer on the bench who killed himself came to be what Isobel thought of every time she thought back to her wedding day.

Pain. And a desire by men not to return to the awful horror of the trenches overtook any fragment of love and hope that might have existed between her and Wilfred. Not that Isobel ever thought she was 'in love' with Wilfred, or him of her. She knew he was driven by duty, but also his love of Alice and her wishes, had she been alive.

Isobel stood at the first-floor window of the house in Russell Square that afternoon and wondered if the young officer had killed himself from fear of going forward, of returning? Or was there something else? Wilfred made huffing noises about 'duty' of course. And doing your bit. But she considered a whole multitude of other reasons why he'd done it. Perhaps he'd come home on leave only to discover his fiancée had married another whilst he was away? Or a husband whose wife had died in childbirth? She shuddered, thinking about that possibility. Or a man who had come face to face with killing someone for the first time and discovered it was something he simply couldn't do again?

Even as the motor ambulance trickled out of the square with the body concealed within and Wilfred said goodbye for the second time, she considered how she might honour the young man's life. She would paint him, of course.

Wilfred had said to tell the truth. Well, she would. On canvas. She had weeks yet until the baby was expected, so starting a new painting would fill her time.

Chapter Twenty-Nine

A murky grey February moved into a March with bitter winds, and the news in the newspapers was grim. Column after column of names were published in *The Times'* Roll of Honour, as it slowly dawned on the public that the conflict hadn't ended by Christmas and there was no sign it would end anytime soon.

Now that she had a genuine ring on her finger, Mrs Finch encouraged Isobel to come out shopping with her some more.

'You need a few more clothes for yourself, and we should think about provisions for a nursery.'

'I don't feel like it today. I received a letter this morning. Do you remember my first commission, Toby Trafford?' Mrs Finch nodded. 'His mother asked me to do the same painting again in oils.'

Mrs Finch looked doubtful. 'You need to rest, dearest. Not keep yourself too busy.'

'Toby was killed a few weeks ago. She wants an oil painting of him done as soon as I can before I forget him. She means herself naturally, but I don't want to disappoint a grieving mother.'

'Oh, the poor woman. So sad. Of course you must, but don't neglect your own health either.'

'I won't.' Her hand automatically smoothed over her bump. Sleep had been difficult the last few weeks as she was so uncomfortable, and the baby moved so much, but also her mind wouldn't switch off. All the unimagined horrors of what Wilfred was going through and of what Edward might have suffered in his last moments was enough to keep her awake most of the night.

'You'll be glad to have Cecily with you finally.'

The thought of Cecily's return had been Isobel's only solace. She had written to say she had been accepted for voluntary nursing training at the Royal Free Hospital on Gray's Inn Road, and now that Isobel was staying in Russell Square, she and Minnie would join her there.

'Oh dear. What if Mother insists on coming too?' She hadn't meant to say it out loud, but it slipped out, nonetheless. Mrs Finch understood her meaning though.

'It's going to come out soon enough though, darling. Your mother might already know about the baby.'

'Unlikely. She would have written me a dreadful letter by now.'

'She didn't have an address though, did she? Even Cecily hasn't had this address too long. And,' she continued, 'neither of them know that you're married yet.'

'True.' Her thoughts went from her mother to Edward's mother. What would she say once she found out? She couldn't cut off Wilfred too. He was her only surviving son. What parent would do that? But her stomach roiled with nervous anticipation anyway. She'd heard Mrs Dunwoody's opinion of her far too often and just because she had a ring on her finger did not mean she was suddenly going to welcome her into the family with open arms.

Some mornings, when Isobel couldn't sleep, she got up early and walked to the Tube, taking her sketchpad with her. When her pencil was in her hand all her other panicky, chaotic thoughts vanished – if not for ever, then at least for a short time. She sat down on a bench and watched the trains arriving and departing from Waterloo. She captured couples saying their last goodbyes before the man, dressed in khaki, boarded a train and disappeared, and she watched orderlies and nurses waiting on the platform and attending to scores of injured soldiers as they were disgorged onto a freezing platform.

Her hand captured the exhausted men, sinking down onto mud-caked kit bags, grateful for a cup of tea and a bun, handed out by multitudes of lady volunteers and other men who lay, some in their own filth and stained bandages, fresh from the battlefields. More than once she stopped drawing because she could no longer see the page in front of her and fat tears smeared the graphite marks.

'You shouldn't be here, miss.' One gentleman stopped beside her one morning.

'Yet I can't not be, for if I don't capture it, then these precious partings and returns have been for nothing, haven't they?' She spoke more harshly than she meant, but she was biting back her own emotions.

The speckled-haired gentleman didn't answer immediately. 'May I?' he asked, gesturing towards her pad.

She shrugged. What was the point of her sketching them, if not to share them with an audience? She watched his well-manicured moustache twitch as he poured over her sketches.

'Don't I know you?' he said, peering closer at her. 'Egypt perhaps?'

She looked closer. 'Mr Hodgkiss? You and your daughters were at Mena House.'

'That's right, and I admired your work back then. Let's see what you're painting now; not the pyramids, that's for sure.'

'Well, Mr Hodgkiss, I want to capture this.' She pointed towards the maelstrom of activity before them. The queues of motor ambulances, never ceasing, just waiting for their patients before departing. The constant trickle of orderlies bearing the patients toward the ambulances and the nurses bent over the men, attending to their needs, all at temperatures hovering close to freezing.

'Do you see someone in particular when you draw?'

Her heart lurched painfully, causing her to examine him more closely. No one had ever asked that before. 'Do you?'

'My son. Since you ask.'

'Is he missing?'

'He is. A line in a newspaper, an explanation on a letter – but it doesn't seem to explain anything. You?'

She wanted to say her fiancé, but choked it down. She was married to Wilfred and showing every sign of a new baby. She said, 'a friend', and part of her heart died inside. This is how it will be, she told herself.

Lying.

Always. Every time I have to explain something in the future it will be one lie after another. Trying to do the right thing within society has turned me into a grotesque person and yet nice people will approve. I did the right thing in the end, they will think. As did Wilfred. What a nice, dear man he was to save me.

'Do you hope to see him here sometime, even though you've been told it is an impossibility?' Mr Hodgkiss looked across the platform, scanning the stretchers as he spoke.

'I do.' Her voice choked. 'Every day I hope that. I try to keep myself busy and not come down, but then I think, what if he was here, lying injured and I missed him. What would I do? I'd have let him down.' She stifled a sob.

'Me too.' He scrabbled in his pocket for something; Isobel

thought he was looking for a handkerchief, but it wasn't. 'My friend has a gallery, near Regent's Park. That's the address. Gabriel Wellbeck. Bring something over for me to see when it suits you. I won't forget you again, Mrs ...'

She hesitated using the name. 'Mrs Dunwoody.'

'Well, send something over, Mrs Dunwoody. I'd like to see if you can paint this as well as you painted the pyramids.' He tipped his hat at her and was gone.

She sat a while longer lost in her own thoughts, tears seeping from her eyes. Oh, Edward. What would you make of me now? You wouldn't even recognise me.

Chapter Thirty

Straining to get out of bed, Isobel rolled gently onto her side before sitting up. Her swollen belly weighed her down so much she felt like a lumbering camel from the markets in Cairo. It couldn't be too many more weeks to go, surely. The baby seemed to sit so low in her body she felt she needed to hang on to it in case it slipped out. Sighing heavily, she forced herself to tackle the day. Thank heavens Cecily would be arriving tomorrow, it had been too long since they'd been together. She had left Belfast last week and was spending a few days in Oxford with one of the friends she'd met in Cairo.

Isobel could hear Sarah busy in the kitchen, the clink of pots and pans, the gushing of water as she was pouring something. She was so grateful to that young girl. She'd become more than a general maid over these last few months. She was company, a friend, a soul mate for the dark moments in her day when she thought she couldn't go on any longer. Sarah's cheery face and the little songs she would sing or hum as she went about her day were a marvellous tonic to her weary soul.

'Come on, miss,' Sarah said, entering her room with a breakfast tray. 'Mrs Finch wants to take you out, in case you'd forgotten.' Isobel hadn't, she just wasn't ready to move yet.

'One more day before your sister gets here. That'll be nice for you.'

The motor was waiting for them outside and the cheery spring sunshine did lift her spirits a little. Snowdrops had been replaced with crocuses and now daffodils bobbed their cheery heads in the square. There was the hint of lime green as the first new leaves were emerging from trees which lined the streets they drove through.

'Nearly there.' Mrs Finch patted her hand as they drove past the British Museum and onto Oxford Street. 'Last outing for you now until baby arrives. Any new books or art paper or pencils you require, now is the time to get them.'

Mrs Finch had stepped into the shoes her mother might have taken, had she been here. Which was unlikely because Mother wasn't inclined to be maternal, except of course, now that Isobel was married to Wilfred, she wondered whether she might have made an effort. Or even Edward, had things been normal. But she didn't want Mother anywhere near her, so she was glad for all that.

'We'll just do a few messages, then I've booked us in for an early lunch in the Palm Court, and then home. How does that sound?'

'Lovely.' Isobel was already imagining how soft her mattress would be when she lay down again.

'That's my girl,' she replied, squeezing her hand some more. They both looked away then, pretending they had grit from London's smoke-filled skies in their eyes.

Mrs Finch's driver dropped them off outside the door and Isobel was helped out. She felt like a ship in full sail and wondered again how she could manage even another day with the baby lying as low as he was. 'Smile,' Mrs Finch reminded her gently, as they sashayed their way through the ground floor, through Perfume and the beauty hall. Mrs

Finch reminded her countless times since Wilfred returned to France that she had to pretend, even if she didn't feel it, that she had every right to hold her head high now. 'Look confident and everyone will treat you with respect – shop girls, waiters, bell-boys, bus conductors. You are a well-dressed woman of society, so behave like one.'

She tried. She just didn't quite believe it. She smiled at the shop girls they passed. She spoke in soft, modulated tones for the lift operator. She smiled and looked engaged when Mrs Finch placed an order to be delivered to Russell Square for three new linen nightgowns trimmed with Irish lace, two new bed-jackets in a warm wool and four new hand-knitted shawls, plus other smaller, more personal items.

'There now, that wasn't too hard, was it? Lunch?'

'Yes, please.' Her whole body ached and she desperately needed to sit down.

They retraced their steps to the ornate black and gold lift and waited patiently until it arrived. Isobel slumped into the dining chair when she got there, grateful to rest herself and did not look about her surroundings as others might whilst the waiter arranged their napkins on their laps.

'Oh dear.'

'Oh dear, Mrs Finch? Are you troubled?'

'Mrs Dunwoody is at a table in the corner. She is sitting with her back to us, but she moved as we came in. I don't believe she's seen us though.'

'Good. I don't think I can face her just yet.'

'Me neither. She is with a party of other ladies, and they seem to have just sat down as we have, so perhaps we will be finished sooner than they and that way we can avoid any unpleasantness.'

'I don't think I could be pleasant let alone deal with unpleasantness today.' A twitch at the corner of Mrs Finch's mouth indicated that she felt similar. She motioned to the waiter and they placed their order immediately. Isobel only wanted something light and refreshing so they both ordered the soup and the Dover sole. It made it worse, though. Isobel's stomach churned.

'Is it very warm in here?'

'Are you warm, dear? I find it just pleasant.' The potted palms were spread out to give the diners a modicum of privacy, but they would be seen for sure if Mrs Dunwoody got up from her table. 'Perhaps it is. The temperatures are so unpredictable right now.'

Isobel managed to consume the soup and a glass of water but nothing more. 'Please excuse me, Mrs Finch. I don't seem fit for anything today. I shall just take a short walk into the corridor, perhaps it will be cooler.'

'Of course. Don't go far. We shall go home directly we have finished eating. Now I am beginning to get anxious.'

'I fear it's just the worry of...' she inclined her head where the erect back of Mrs Dunwoody was still sitting at the table. 'Perhaps if I splash some water on my face it will refresh me.'

'Of course, dear, do.'

Isobel already had the conversation in her head three times over just in case she came face to face with the lady, and she was so engrossed in the activity as she walked slowly up and down the corridor that she was taken completely by surprise.

'It is you. I said it wasn't. I said it couldn't possibly be, but I'm shocked to find it is.'

Isobel opened and closed her mouth. Her ability to say anything at all evaded her at the precise time she needed it.

'My acquaintances said, doesn't that look like the girl Edward was engaged to. And we looked, and we looked again.' Her eyes were like daggers towards Isobel's tummy and Mrs Dunwoody practically hissed the next two words. '*With child.* You are out in society, *with child.*'

Isobel held herself protectively, but remained firm. She thrust her chin that little bit higher, remembering all the unkind words the lady had said of her in the past.

'And yet here you are, out, bringing shame on me and my family.'

Isobel felt a burning, a frisson of anger shoot through her – she should hold her tongue, but she didn't. With a half-smile on her lips, she tilted her head to the side and looked Mrs Dunwoody confidently in the eyes. 'I hope I have a girl,' she said, smoothing her dress further over her bump. 'A girl I can send to the best, most progressive schools that money can buy and I'm going to educate her to think, to dream, to create, to study Mathematics and Science, and to explore. And I hope she upends your world – yes, I do. You see I am not prepared to live my life quietly on the sidelines, being meek and polite and missing out on the enjoyments and experience that life has to offer. I won't be prepared to let my daughter suffer. Mark my words, Mrs Dunwoody, the world has changed under your very nose. Your sons, your friends' sons, when they return – *if* they return – they will have changed. Nothing… *nothing*, will remain as it was.' She stopped for a moment, as a stabbing pain caught her deep and low. 'Good day, Mrs Dunwoody. Wilfred and I are married by the way, so I guess that makes you Mrs Dunwoody *Senior* now.'

Mrs Dunwoody didn't respond immediately. Only her chest heaving and her lips held so tight together indicated that she had reacted to the words. Isobel heard her sharp intake of breath through her nose and realised from whom Wilfred had inherited it.

'Well, he's a fool then,' Mrs Dunwoody hissed. 'He should have understood that your kind were just a bit of skirt. To have fun with occasionally. You were never the marrying kind. His father knew that and so did yours. It's not as hidden as either of them would like.'

Her words were enunciated so meticulously, and her emotions held in grip so firmly, Isobel wondered if she had a heart at all.

'You always were flippant in your attitude to life, now you've proved just as insincere in love, exactly as I expected. I just hope the news that you married his brother won't kill Edward when he hears.'

Isobel swooned, clutching her side. Mrs Finch appeared by her side and held her tight, interrupting the conversation that threatened to get even further out of hand. 'We're leaving, Isobel. I've said to the waiter. Come away, dear.'

'Why do you say that?' she gasped, gulping down air to try and ease the pain in her chest. 'Edward's dead. Wilfred has said so constantly.'

'Well, Wilfred was mistaken. We've had news this week that Edward is in a prisoner-of-war camp. So, like I said, I hope the news that you and his own brother betrayed his love doesn't take him to his grave.'

Isobel didn't know how she made it to the lift and out through the beauty hall without Mrs Finch by her side. One minute she was standing her ground with Mrs Dunwoody, the next, the words had become like splinters inside her head.

'Deep breaths, keep walking,' Mrs Finch kept whispering to her as they pushed through the lunchtime crowds. Never once did she let go of Isobel's arm.

Another pain caught Isobel off guard as they waited for their driver to bring the car around. She clenched her jaws together not saying a word, just biting down hard on the pain that, deep down, she understood she deserved. She'd betrayed him. She had.

The minutes until they reached home seemed like hours, and as another pain came and went, all she could do was breathe hard through it and think of him.

Of Edward.

Her love. The father of her child. And she'd let him down.

'Sarah!' Mrs Finch called the second they arrived home. 'Send a telegram immediately.'

'To who, Mrs Finch?'

'Whom. It's, to whom, oh never mind. To Cecily. Just say, come tonight. Urgent.'

'Right you be. Why?'

Another wave of pain swept through Isobel as she stood like a marble statue in the hall. Grabbing onto the newel post she gripped it firmly, the whites of her knuckles telling their own tale. Her breath came deep and ragged and sweat pooled on her brow.

'Oh! Oh, Miss Isobel. Never fear. I'll go now.'

'Yes, you will. Run, child, run, and when you get back, we'll get a nice hot bath run and we'll call for the doctor that we engaged.'

'Yes, miss. Right away, miss.' Sarah ran back to the scullery to grab her coat from behind the door and Mrs Finch thrust her purse at her when she ran past.

'Just take it, dear. As quick as you can now.' The door slammed behind the maid as Isobel's waters cascaded down her legs and created a puddle on the floor and her heart broke into huge, gasping, shuddering cries.

'He's alive, Mrs Finch! I heard that correctly, didn't I? He's actually alive!'

★

235

Pain after pain gripped Isobel until she no longer knew where one stopped and the next began. Her nightdress stuck to her from the perspiration that covered her body. Each contraction was a wave that had to be endured and every single one threatened to engulf her, but yet she survived. When she opened her eyes, Cecily's face was next to her, smiling and reassuring. Cecily had arrived late last night and had been up with her all night. The darkness had come and gone and dawn was now breaking.

The lamps had been lit hours and hours by the time the doctor arrived, but he took a quick look and told her she was ready to push whenever she felt like it. He told Mrs Finch he'd wait downstairs in case there was a problem, but a good tall girl like her, young and healthy, should manage well by herself.

'Lazy man!' Mrs Finch exclaimed when he'd gone.

'Aye. Putting the feet up no doubt and happy to be paid over it too.' Minnie clucked and clucked about the room. 'We should have saved the money. We can manage without him. Come on now, miss. Push when you want.'

Isobel was lying in the bed now and it was far harder than before the doctor had turned up. She was so tired and the pains so strong she didn't think she could do it.

'Come on, love, come on!'

Screwing up her eyes she bore down hard every time and pushed for all she was worth. Finally, as the clock downstairs chimed the hour of eight, Isobel delivered a fine healthy boy. She lay back on the pillows and Mrs Finch handed her the baby wrapped in a shawl.

'Oh, Edward. Edward,' Isobel cried. 'Mrs Finch, he looks just like his father. Oh, my boy!' Her emotions surged. She was filled with so much love for this tiny newborn in her arms. Oh, how she wished Edward could have been here too.

236

For him to have been pacing the floors downstairs, waiting for the good news would have made all her pain worth it. But this wee bundle in her arms was perfect. She kissed his tiny fingers and rubbed her cheek against the downy fuzz of blond hair, just like his father. He was perfect.

Chapter Thirty-One

The whole household tiptoed around in a daze for the next few days. A new baby in the place seemed to lift everyone's spirits and they all beamed at each other and stood over his cot, and time passed and no one noticed.

Mr Finch came and went, bringing presents for the baby and flowers for Isobel. They were all cocooned in a little burrow and outside and bad news didn't seem to exist.

Mrs Finch had sent a telegram to Wilfred almost immediately.

George Edward Wilfred arrived safe March 16th STOP
All well STOP.

Outside the weather flitted from days of dull sheets of never-ending rain and biting winds to pea soupers that drowned them for days and then, finally, the sun came out again.

'Isn't he a darling?!' Cecily exclaimed for the third time that afternoon. 'I could watch him sleep all day.' George was sleeping in the bassinet in Isobel's room, which Cecily also shared. It was a bit of a squeeze for now, but as Cecily reminded her, she'd be starting her training shortly and Mrs Finch wanted to move the new family back to Bexley Hall and use the nursery there. Sarah, for all the age of her, had declared she'd be the nanny seeing as she had more experience than the rest of them and, so far, was doing an excellent job.

'So could I. I can't imagine how any mother could give their baby away, could you?' Isobel replied.

'You are very fortunate Wilfred married you, and don't you forget it. *And* that the Finches have been so generous spirited through it all.'

Isobel looked away, a pang of guilt within her chest. She was lucky in some ways, she knew that, yet, one day Wilfred would come home and then where would she be? She shuddered, a ripple of pinpricks down her spine thinking about what he would expect.

The doorbell rang far below them in the house. 'You need to send Mother and Father a letter soon, Izzy. Before they hear from anyone else.'

'Can't you do it? I've been putting it off because nothing I say sounds right. If you do it, you could keep it more formal – Dear Mother and Father, we wanted to let you know that Isobel is now married to Captain Wilfred Dunwoody and has just delivered a fine boy called George Edward Wilfred. I'm sure you'd like to join me in wishing them well on their good fortune … blah blah blah. How's that?'

'Perhaps we should have added one of Father's names in there too, to help soothe relations?' Cecily worried.

'His brother was George, had you forgotten? And their father was also George. I didn't pick it on purpose, but it is convenient. They're all so particular about these things.' The sound of footsteps on the stairs interrupted them, and a quick tapping sound before Minnie stuck her head round it.

'Begging your pardon, ladies, I thought you'd want to know that Mrs Dunwoody is downstairs. She's heard about the baby.'

The two of them froze. They'd discussed this many times

over the past week or two but not made any decisions. Now it was thrust upon them. 'I'll go down,' Cecily bravely volunteered.

'I'm not even dressed yet,' Isobel wailed. Her heart beat faster than it should and she stared wild-eyed at Minnie. 'What sort of mood is she in?'

'Well, that one always looks as though she's sat on a poker, but I do think this is as hard for her as it is for us. Remember she might want to see the baby.'

Isobel and Cecily exchanged glances. This they had talked about. She had every right to see her grandson, but was not going to be given the opportunity to interfere. Isobel had been very determined that way. Neither would her mother, if she arrived.

'Right. I'll go. Do I look suitably dressed, Minnie?' Cecily asked. Minnie checked her over, passed her as acceptable and Cecily left.

Isobel couldn't rest. She flung the covers back and got up, pacing the room. She felt sick. What did the woman want? If she had ideas about taking George, she'd soon have to think again, for Isobel knew she'd fight tooth and nail before that happened.

Minnie returned, slipping into the room quickly. 'Don't panic. She's fine. She's spoken to Cecily about putting a proper birth announcement in *The Times*, that's all. Cecily will fill you in afterwards. She does want to see the wee nipper though.' A pain shot through Isobel's chest and a whimper escaped her lips before she could stop herself.

'Come now, it'll be fine. He'll be waking for his next feed soon and as soon as he opens his mouth to cry, she won't want him around. Cecily won't let anything happen to him,' she said, doing her best to reassure Isobel.

The heartache as Minnie disappeared down the stairs even

for a short time with her baby in her arms hurt so badly, it reminded Isobel again of why she'd married Wilfred. She could never, ever, have given this baby away. Never.

She didn't go back to bed but hovered on the upstairs landing, trying to hear anything at all that was happening downstairs. True to form, it was only a short time before the piercing wails of a hungry newborn baby filtered up the stairwell. Two minutes later and she heard the door opening and Minnie returned up the stairs, with the lusty cries of George demanding to be fed echoing through the house. She opened the front of her nightgown to be ready for him and by the time Cecily returned, baby George was contentedly feeding at Isobel's breast.

'So? What did she want?'

'Be calm, Izzy. Everything is fine. She heard the news from Wilfred, and they have decided that the birth needs to be announced properly in the paper.'

'Must we?'

'You must. Stop people gossiping, she said. She will decide on the proper wording and use the occasion to mention the marriage too. Whether you like it or not, some things have to be done properly.'

Isobel pulled a face, but the tight, pinched feeling in her brow faded a little. 'Anything else? I was dreading it in case she demanded to take charge.'

'Luckily, no. It was difficult on her, but she did seem to admire George. She said he looked a fine fellow and Wilfred will be pleased.'

Isobel winced. Edward should have been the one to be pleased, not Wilfred. 'The only other thing you should know is that their cousin has died. The older one, Maxim Dunwoody. He was killed at Neuve Chappelle a few weeks ago.'

'Oh, the poor man. That is bad news.'

'It is, because don't forget he was the heir apparent. Now his younger brother Roger will be.'

'It never stops, does it? Isn't he at the front though, too?'

'Not yet, but soon. But what she was at pains to point out, was that the line of succession has just got closer. If anything happens to Roger, then Wilfred would inherit; after his father, of course.'

'Oh heavens, that's hardly likely though and so far in the future it doesn't affect us.'

'Izzy, she was at great pains to point out that George here is registered as Wilfred's first born, his male heir. So it does matter. Who knows how long this war will continue for? But, whether you like it or not, you are now part of the Dunwoody family and all that entails.'

Isobel groaned and buried her head against George's soft, downy one. How could anyone think that far ahead, when the baby was barely a few weeks old. She wouldn't think further than the summer. And she still hadn't forgotten that Edward was alive in a prison camp somewhere. She'd heard about The Red Cross setting up registers to help women like her, and, as soon as she was up and about, she would start writing letters again. She could hardly ask Wilfred or his mother for that information.

Bexley Hall, Norfolk, May, 1915

Isobel remembered the drive from the small village of Bexley. She had been just once before, in the spring of 1914, when she and Alice had just been beginning their friendship, and crocuses had covered the lawn with a vast lake of purple and gold petals, glinting in the early spring sunshine. Today was overcast and grim, one of those days in early summer that feels more like winter as angry indigo clouds roll continuously in from the west bringing gales and cause the fruit trees to drop half their precious load of blossom and the tulip garden turns into a sodden mess. The gardeners, quartered now in their number and consisting of just the very young and the very old, hid deep inside the potting sheds, praying for it all to pass.

Mrs Finch was waiting for them on the steps. 'Welcome, my dears, welcome.'

Kissing her on the cheek, she turned and led Isobel up the steps. 'I hope you will be very happy with us, Mrs Dunwoody.'

Isobel nearly faltered. She was still struggling to become used to her married name. She felt like an impostor using it, especially so when letters from Wilfred arrived addressed to Mrs Dunwoody. Words from his latest letter rippled through her head.

My dear Isobel, do tell me all your news. That is what I live for here at the front. If I ever get leave I'd like to spend some time by the coast listening to the sea. Would you like that too? It could be our honeymoon. Tell me about George, is he healthy? I know nothing about babies, but he's my future now. Write again soon.

She must remember to add little sketches of George and his new nursery in her next letter to Wilfred now that they had arrived safely.

Mrs Finch introduced her to the housekeeper and the butler before directing her inside. 'We've given you rooms next to the nursery, Isobel. I hope you find that satisfactory. Life is a little different right now, as I'm sure you understand, but we're so excited you're here. Having a baby in the house will brighten us all up. Now, I hope you don't mind, I've a couple of things I must do, but Mrs MacDonald will show you to your rooms. I'll see you downstairs for tea soon.' She hugged her tight, and it was easy to see how delighted she was to have them here. Isobel hadn't seen her looking so alive since before Alice had died.

'Mr Finch said you like to paint, so although we don't have a spare room as such, the landing up there has a lovely window with a west-facing aspect and it's very spacious. I've had an armchair brought up and another table. I'll show you both the way.' The housekeeper Mrs MacDonald, or Mrs Mac as she was known, smiled at Isobel and nodded towards Sarah, who was holding George in her arms.

'The drawing room and dining room are for our soldiers now, as you see. Family rooms are restricted to the breakfast room and Mr Finch's study. But we've made it as cosy for you as we can. Mrs Finch manages everything so well for the soldiers.'

'I'm sure it will be pleasant, Mrs Mac. Mrs Finch explained as best she could.' Isobel's eyes flitted all around her as they walked through the large hall, and up the wide staircase. Mid-afternoon, she could see several soldiers resting in armchairs in the drawing room; some upright and alert, others slumped, looking at nothing in particular. 'How many are here at present?'

'Twenty. None of them will be returning to the war, Mrs Dunwoody. This hospital is for recuperation. No doubt you'll get to know them whilst you are here. We have plenty of ladies who visit from the village to read to them or play board games; anything to lift their mood.'

As they climbed the stairs, they passed a soldier, a bandage obliterating his eyes, shuffling along the landing, arm in arm with a nurse. Isobel recognised the same uniform that Cecily had just bought and experienced that sharp twinge deep in her tummy whenever she thought of her sister. Cecily was brave and selfless volunteering for nursing.

'Good afternoon, Mrs Mac.'

'Good afternoon, Captain Harte.'

'You have guests with you, Mrs Mac?'

'Well done, Captain. You are getting so much better. Allow me to introduce Mrs Dunwoody and her son Master George.'

'Good afternoon, Mrs Dunwoody, although it seems a little dreary today does it not?'

Isobel stretched out and shook his hand. 'Pleased to meet you, Captain Harte. The weather is very inclement today. It might take another day before it passes through.'

'Indeed. Where's your little chap then? I can hear him awfully well.'

George was snuggled in Sarah's arms, sucking his fists and making the occasional noise. His eyes were darting about taking in his new surroundings. Isobel nodded to Sarah, encouraging her to step forward to the captain and guide his hand towards George. George made a grab for the hand that was offered, immediately drawing it to his mouth to chew on. 'I do apologise, sir, he is teething at the moment.'

'Not at all, Mrs Dunwoody. I have a son myself, similar age, I think. It's nice to hear his baby noises.'

'Well, I do hope you won't be disturbed by his young voice too often, Captain Harte. Especially not at night.'

'Come now, Captain, let's not detain Mrs Dunwoody any longer. I'm sure she needs to get freshened up after her long journey,' Mrs Mac said firmly.

'Yes, of course. Good day.'

They moved to the side and let the captain be guided

past before his hand alighted on the wooden handrail and he and his nurse continued down the stairs. 'Up here, Mrs Dunwoody,' Mrs Mac called, bustling ahead of her. 'You're on the next landing. There's an excellent view of the park from the window.' They kept climbing up and, as promised, the staircase opened onto an upper floor with a large picture window where a comfy chair had been placed. 'The nurses are sleeping down that corridor, and you and George are at this end.' She opened a door into a spacious suite of nursery rooms and then a smaller bedroom just off the landing. 'Your room isn't very large, I'm afraid, but Mrs Finch assured me you'd be just as content up here next to the nursery.'

'Oh, it's lovely!' Isobel said, walking into the nursery. She could visualise her dear friend Alice playing up here as a small child. There was a fireplace and two chairs, a rocking horse and bookcase and two windows that also faced west. Sarah's box room faced east. 'We shall be very content up here, Mrs Mac. Thank you.'

'Well, I shall leave you to get settled then, Mrs Dunwoody. Sarah, anything you need, please ask.'

Isobel sank into one of the armchairs in front of the cosy fire and fed George whilst Sarah bustled about finding new linen for him. Noise in the corridor and the sound of maids indicated that Isobel's luggage had arrived. There was a gentle tap on the door and a maid popped her head round it. She bobbed a curtsey at Isobel before telling her she would unpack for her. Tea had been laid out downstairs, and Mr and Mrs Finch were waiting for her if she wished to join them.

'Thank you. I'll be down soon.' She smiled. It wasn't going to be perfect living in someone else's home, and she still had no news about Edward despite her letters to the Red Cross, but the Finches were such kind souls that she felt she could be happy here. She would never, *ever* get over her guilt at marrying Wilfred, but for now she and George were going to enjoy their little sojourn in Norfolk.

The month of May at Bexley Hall came and went, and Isobel and George settled in well to the routine of the hospital. Mrs Finch insisted that the soldiers weren't patients, but guests. Both Isobel and Mrs Finch kept themselves busy keeping a pleasant home from home atmosphere. They played board games or wrote letters for the men, read books to those that were blind, made decorations, sang after dinner around the piano, and organised entertainments. Once or twice a week they had dancing in the evenings which not only helped to lift the mood of their 'guests', it was all part of helping the men to rehabilitate and to return home. Some were blind, others had lost one or more limbs, but none would ever return to the battlefields of France and Belgium. And every night Isobel knelt in her small bedroom and prayed that Edward was still alive and well someplace and would one day come home to her.

A telegram arrived shortly after breakfast one Saturday morning in early June, informing them that more patients would be arriving that evening. They were already full to bursting.

'Isobel, dear, here is a pickle! Two more men due tonight. Where on earth can we put them? I understand that they are going to need nursing, rather than just our normal convalescing care. What can we do?'

'Ring for Mrs Mac, she's very pragmatic. You'll come up with an answer for beds, I'm sure of it.'

'Perhaps two of our staff might stay in the village, just

for a few days and we will have to move some of our more capable men up to the top floor. What do you think?'

'I'm sure everyone will pull together. Minnie and I can move into the nursery if you need us to.' Minnie was now also down at Bexley Hall. She had stayed on in Russell Square for a few more weeks until Cecily had started her training and to get a new maid started, Agnes, Sarah Heaney's younger sister.

A little while later and all arrangements for the new wounded had been made and Mrs Finch and Isobel had gone for a walk around the garden. Minnie was hovering in the hall when the two ladies returned to the house. She bobbed a curtsey at Mrs Finch and did a mix of a wink and a jerk of her head at Isobel. 'Let me take your coat, Mrs Finch. Your two new arrivals are already upstairs. Dr Matthews is with them and Matron. Shall I ring for tea?'

'Thank you, Minnie. No, don't disturb the kitchen for tea. They'll be run off their feet today as it is. I shall wait for dinner.'

'Certainly, miss.' She bobbed another curtsey, her arms full of Mrs Finch's coat and hat.

'You go on ahead, Isobel dearest. I shall see you later at dinner. It was a good day today, wasn't it?'

'It was. It's always better to be busy and useful. I pray these men aren't too ill with their injuries.'

'Indeed. I'll pop up now and see if they need anything.'

Minnie kept Isobel in the hall, making a fuss of taking her coat, until Mrs Finch was well out of earshot.

'What is the matter, Minnie? Has something happened?' Isobel whispered.

Minnie was practically hopping from one foot to the other in her impatience. 'I can't say for sure who it is, but I was here when the two soldiers arrived. Both officers.' She eyed Isobel keenly. 'The Red Cross nurse in the ambulance said the second soldier was Lieutenant Dunwoody. I couldn't see for sure; his face was bandaged up so, but I'm sure it's one of our Dunwoody soldiers.'

'Oh, Minnie!'

'Now stop getting your hopes up. It's not Edward,' she whispered. 'He couldn't be anywhere near the trenches, so don't be thinking that. It could be Roger though, unlikely Wilfred because she said Lieutenant, not Captain.'

'Oh.' Her insides flipped upside down. The guilt she carried about marrying Wilfred had mangled up inside her so that she felt she had indirectly cursed him and every day she thought something bad would happen. She couldn't shake off the feeling that his time was limited on earth because of her wrongdoing. She tried to sound stronger than she was. 'Mrs Finch will know for certain. Come, let's keep busy. She will come and find me as soon as she knows. Oh, I don't know whether to pray it is one of them and they're now safely here, or that it's not one of them because they are injured!' They climbed the staircase side by side, hovering on the first-floor landing, eager to hear any news, but there was no movement from either of the rooms of the new arrivals, and Mrs Finch wasn't to be seen at all. They could only be patient for now.

Shortly before dinner, Isobel heard a sharp tap on her door, and she rushed to open it. Mrs Finch was there, her face a whole mixture of emotions. Isobel tried not to second guess at what this meant, but she could feel her hands tremble as they hung on tight to hers.

'Roger Dunwoody has been brought in downstairs – the cousin. He's terribly ill, dearest. I needed to wire his family in London, you understand. I must ask them to come immediately, in case …' She didn't say the words, but they both understood. Tears filled her eyes as she gazed at Isobel.

'That's perfectly understood. His mother needs to visit her son. I'll just stay upstairs out of the way when the family are here. I'd rather not bump into any of them.'

'But that's not all, dearest. I have news!' Her voice broke then, as she tried to articulate what she wanted to say. 'Matron handed me his personal items, so I might contact his family. She didn't know I already knew him. He had some letters on him. A very recent one from Wilfred. I recognised his handwriting. I'm afraid I opened the letter, completely wrong of me, I know, but I'm glad I did.' Her cheeks flushed the deepest pink.

'What? What are you not telling me?'

'Edward's definitely alive, Isobel. He's a prisoner in a German camp, and Wilfred has heard back from him. Oh, my darling, isn't that the best news!'

Isobel sank to the ground, her knees not able to support her. Minnie came running when she heard the thump as Isobel slithered to the ground. 'He's still alive! That's all I need to know right now. He's alive and safe!'

Chapter Thirty-Two

Bexley Hall,
Norfolk,
15 June, 1915

Dearest Wilfred,

May I offer you my deepest condolences on the death of your cousin, Roger. All of us at Bexley were devastated at his death, Mr and Mrs Finch included, but please be reassured that the staff here did their utmost to keep him comfortable in his last few days. My dear, it brings a timely reminder for you to keep yourself as safe as you possibly can, so that one day you will be able to return home to George and myself.

I apologise for speaking out of turn, but circumstances arose whilst Roger was with us that entailed Mrs Finch having to look through his personal letters to find an address for his parents.

Wilfred, I'm surprised and delighted to know that you've had news from Edward and that he is a prisoner of war. Please, if it's not too much trouble, could you write back with an address for him, or at least with a little more information. I understand the worry you might have over this situation, but I fully remember my wedding vows before God, and just want to be reassured of Edward's health and wellbeing.

I've enclosed a new photograph of George. He is three months old now and so bright and full of joy. The soldiers here like to see him as he's such a happy baby. They all say he reminds them of their own children. I've added some more sketches of our daily life as you said you liked them.

Please take care yourself. George and I need you to come home to us safe and sound. I pray for you every night and think of you as I go about my day.

With all our love,

Isobel and George.

June moved into July, and Isobel had one letter from Wilfred.

I'm dreaming of Devon, or perhaps Cornwall. A small hotel. Seaside walks and fresh seafood for dinner. Would you like that? You could draw and I'll just sit in a deckchair and watch you. When does a baby start to sit up or walk? I've no idea. I have all these plans for after the war. Edward is alive, but I'm sure things are difficult in the camps. Please leave all the correspondence to me, it's for the best.

The anxiety of it all stopped her sleeping and she took to painting every hour of the day when the light was good. Some days she feared she'd go mad with the not knowing. How many was too many letters to write to her husband and demand an address for the man she really loved? Mrs Finch urged caution. 'Loyalty, Isobel. You need him to feel you are still committed to the marriage.'

'Couldn't you ask his mother, Mrs Finch? It wouldn't look as bad coming from you.'

'I could ask, but it's unlikely to meet with a favoured ear. If Wilfred hasn't given you an address, then you must respect that.'

Isobel didn't respect that – she burnt with the knowledge that he was alive someplace and there was nothing she could do about it. She became obsessed with scouring the papers for news again and asking the soldiers if they knew of other camps. If she couldn't write to the correct address, then she would write to all of them until she had an answer.

Isobel's artwork also took on a fevered determination to be finished and to be as authentic as she possibly could. She poured her broken heart into her biggest painting so far, a combination of the many sketches she'd made at Waterloo station when she'd still been pregnant.

'Isobel! Isobel!' Mrs Finch's voice could be heard coming up the stairs, breathless. 'Isobel!'

She set down her paintbrush, wiping her hands on her smock as she went. 'Coming.' She got to the top of the stairs and bent over, Mrs Finch leaning over the banister below her.

'Do come down, dearest. We have news.'

Whooping with unladylike delight, Isobel took off down the stairs, running down lightly and jumping a few every now and then for expediency. Her hair was still tied up with a scarf over it, keeping her locks out of the way. One day she would chop it off, just like that film star. She pulled the scarf away, smoothing her hair as best she could, and trying to undo buttons as she went. She got to the bottom of the stairs, busy with a couple of soldiers walking through and two orderlies wheeling a bed. 'In here, Isobel!' Mrs Finch's voice carried from the morning room.

Her eyes were bright and sparkled with hope. 'Sit, dearest, for you won't believe the news. This is Mrs Babstone. Mrs Isobel Dunwoody.'

'Hello.' They both smiled and shook hands.

'You tell her,' Mrs Babstone said.

'No, you. It's your letter.'

The young woman beamed at Isobel. 'Very well. My husband is a prisoner of war, Mrs Dunwoody. Mrs Finch here explained your brother-in-law was missing also.'

'Yes.' Isobel's eyes darted to and from each of the ladies.

'I received a letter this morning and I came straight over. I always want to share my news – it helps to keep them alive somehow. Others don't seem to be interested the same way.'

Isobel held her breath, clutching at Mrs Finch's hand for support.

'I'll read it, shall I?' The others encouraged her by their expressions. '*Dearest Effie,* (that's me) *I am happy and well. Things are not bad at all. Please send more food and books if you could. It can be awfully dull around here. Some novels would be very welcome and also my workbook for Japanese that I was learning. Some fellows have got up a university of sorts here, it helps to keep us all occupied. I plan to teach them Japanese.*

Your knitted items were gratefully received. Do send more socks and comforts in time for the winter. A few shirts would also be helpful.

I met a fellow in here. He asks to be remembered to our mutual friends, the Finches, at Bexley Hall. He said, 'tell them he's looking forward to climbing the pyramids again with IH'.

'He goes on then to close with personal messages you wouldn't be interested in.'

Isobel didn't hear the ending anyway. Edward! He was alive and thinking of her.

Mrs Finch rang for tea. Isobel excused herself, mumbling about checking on the baby. She returned fifteen minutes later, her eyes bright with a mixture of exhilaration and grief. Nothing could undo her marriage to Wilfred, but with all her heart she had to dream that one day Edward would come home.

'Thank you so much, Mrs Babstone. Might I trouble you for your own address, and the one for your husband's camp? We have been desperate for news, and now you have brought us such relief,' Isobel asked.

'Of course, dear. I'd be delighted. If I'd realised you'd heard nothing, I'd have brought his other letters too. He describes the camp quite well. Shall I include a message when I write again?'

'What a good idea.' She paused, wracking her brain to think of something suitable. 'Tell him that Mrs Finch was reassured with the news and delighted that you were able to pass it on in person. Encourage him to write to Mrs Finch, here at Bexley, won't you?'

'I will, of course. They are only allowed to write two letters per month though, and there are times one hasn't arrived. The Germans don't seem very organised, is what I've gathered.' She offered Isobel the letter. 'Copy down the address before I go.'

Isobel took the letter and with hands that could barely grip the fountain pen, she wrote down the precious address. She had it now. Everything would be fine; she could feel it.

She posted a letter to Edward immediately and included a photo of George and one of herself. He was so close now, she could almost feel him. The large painting of Waterloo, a composite of the different soldiers she'd sketched over the last few months, was also finished and sat upstairs drying out. This autumn would be different, she convinced herself. She wrote every week to Edward, but couldn't bring herself to mention she was married. When he returned she'd have time to explain it all. But by letter it just felt too impersonal, and for now she could only dream of him coming home – as

255

guilty as she felt though, Wilfred didn't exist in the dreams. She completely obliterated him from her thoughts, as though she lived in a parallel universe. And she hated herself for doing it.

Chapter Thirty-Three

Bad Helberg Prison Camp, Germany, August 1915

The sun baked his skin to a crisp.

Rivulets of sweat dripped down every inch of Edward's torso.

Flies danced on the congealed blood of the crusty cut at the corner of his eye and made merry on his exposed skin that he couldn't reach. The skin around his wrists burnt and every muscle in his body shouted its abhorrence at being tied up like this. His sweat stung his eyes as the midday sun crept slowly across the sky. How many more hours of this torture could he endure?

Werner came out of his office on the shady side of the courtyard, appearing cool and calm with his white open-necked shirt and his immaculate breeches and boots so shiny one almost imagined you could see your reflection.

Werner flicked the short whip right across the exposed flesh across Edward's back. 'So, are you sorry yet, Dun-Voodie?' he asked him, striking him once more across damp, sticky flesh. The sound of it hit him hardest, assaulting his ears like wet leather – the burn registered a split-second later and he recoiled in pain.

'No,' he gasped, gritting his teeth. 'Never.' He would never apologise for standing up to Werner and the rest of the guards for the abuse they constantly dished out. Punching one of them in the guts now and again was always worth it; even if Walker disagreed. Casting his eyes around, Edward could see he wasn't alone. The other officers always kept up a continued vigilance when someone was being punished. It would all be witnessed, remembered and written down for the future. Walker nodded at him in a sign of support from where he perched on the low stone wall, trying to look nonchalant.

'Shame. You won't want to receive this wonderful love letter then from a woman called Iz-obel.' He smirked, holding out the white envelope in front of Edward's face. 'Such a shame, she writes you lovely words and sentiments, but you'll never know them, will you.'

Edward let a guttural roar from deep within his belly. Werner's fake smile was instantly replaced with a snarl as he kicked Edward hard in the side of the knee, whereupon he winced in agony and slipped to the ground. Crumpled on the old cobbled courtyard, Edward could only watch in despair as Werner pulled the letter from the already ripped envelope, eyes half-shut against the fierce sunlight, the German officer didn't notice the two small squares floating out. Instead, he pulled out a lighter and with a sadistic curl of his lips, lit the letter directly under Edward's face, the flame burning his nostril hairs. Edward's whole world existed in that letter! He would die, right here, if only he could hear the words. Isobel! Isobel, his only hope in this sorry, squalid existence and she'd written to him but Werner was burning it in front of him. There were not enough words to describe how he felt towards that man.

Walker, on watch duty, instantly took up a jolly good song from the shows and sang it with gusto, and within seconds several British Officers had appeared and proceeded to march up and down and generally make a nuisance of themselves and cause a distraction. A dripping wet, cold sponge was doused over Edward's head and a second offered to him to suck the liquid out of, whilst the rest of the men linked arms and engineered an impromptu Parisian can-can, keeping Edward out of harm's way.

Werner tried to shove the men, and kick through their legs, but gave up. The afternoon sun was just too hot to be outside for too long. Stepping back, he tossed the letter onto the cobbles and waited only long enough for it to burn up before disappearing inside into the cool once more.

'All right, old chap.'

'Hang in there.'

Men patted him gently on the shoulder and brought more water for him to drink and a soaking wet shirt to drape over his head. He hardly noticed; the pain was unbearable, but the pain inside his soul was unimaginable.

Walker dropped his head closer to his ear. 'Hang on, Woody. You can stick this. I rescued two photos for you. I'll keep them safe.'

'Photos?' he mumbled.

'Yes. Do you want to see?'

'Can't. Eyes.'

'Righto. Tonight it is, then.'

Edward slumped, head lolling towards his chest for a while, oblivious to everything but the pain in his knee and the one in his heart. Every hour the British officer on watch would walk past and check he was still alive and squeeze cold water over his head and into his mouth. The afternoon wore on and pain became one massive howitzer hole that he fell headlong into and nothing could alleviate it.

Finally, when the sun dipped low in the sky, and the bats that lived in the eaves of the stable block began diving and swooping through the sticky night air, Edward was cut free from his bonds. His compatriots came out in force, marching and singing again, drowning out his agonised yells as the blood crept into his arms. A lukewarm bowl of water was sitting ready to sponge his chest before he was lain down into his bunk. The only medicine was a good dose of homebrew, spooned into his mouth every half-hour by Walker who sat up with him, and some disgusting soup.

The moon rose high in the night sky before Edward remembered. 'Photos,' he mumbled.

'Yes, of course. Here.' Walker pulled them out of his shirt pocket and handed them over, propping them up against a small bible.

Edward had only one eye that he could see through right then, one was swollen up with one of the first fists that Werner had meted out this morning. Two photos, six inches from his face; his most favourite people in the whole of the world. Isobel and such a sweet, sweet baby boy. 'He looks like me,' he mumbled again.

'He does. A fine strapping baby boy if ever I saw one.'

Tears seeped out of both eyes. Even crying was too painful. Edward closed his second eye against the dim light and their images were imprinted on his brain.

For them he would survive.

For them he would endure anything Werner and his lot threw at him.

He would get back to them one way or another.

Chapter Thirty-Four

Sarah's younger sister Agnes had joined the household in Russell Square during the summer and lived in Sarah's old room. Isobel did wonder how long she'd last since the amount of late-night singing and tapping going on the lino in the kitchen would suggest she saw herself only as a temporary maid – future stage star! But she was a very convivial girl and so long as she did her duties around the house, Isobel couldn't stop her dreaming of a better future treading the boards. The fact that the position had been in London must have been a highly attractive bonus.

Isobel went to London every now and again during the day. Zeppelin raids had started to occur and gave her nightmares about George being killed when she wasn't with him. And still no letter from Edward. Nothing. She'd written more than was a decent amount, but Mrs Finch cautioned her about writing too many. Isobel had even gone into Bexley Village to call on Mrs Babstone and enquire whether she had any news. She'd heard nothing at all during September and was becoming anxious herself.

The doorbell chimed as she entered the Wellbeck Gallery. Autumn in London held ominous memories from last year. Waiting for news from Edward. Being pregnant and unmarried. Yet she was still here.

'Good morning, Mrs Dunwoody, good morning!' Mr Hodgkiss greeted her, his leathery hands reaching out to clasp her soft ones. 'We're so thrilled, my dear. Gabriel and I have already admired your painting. Come and look.' He led her towards the back wall where she stopped. Her heart was overcome, tears threatening to fall. There it was, her painting. Well, hers and Edward's, and Wilfred and all the lost souls who struggled to return home. The broad canvas stretched three feet wide by just one foot tall. Waterloo station staged the scene where a soldier lay on his stretcher, gazing upwards at a nurse, supported by another comrade and then more figures behind him and even more descending from the train newly arrived on the platform. The figure on the stretcher represented them all and epitomised the hope that every parent had that their son might be the lucky one to return home.

Isobel was proud, rightly so – when she admired it now, every brush stroke, every layer of paint that she'd applied, hadn't been in vain. It was a love song to the lost. A heart song to a generation. She'd also used as a palate her favourite mix of moss greens and heathers that belonged at home in Ireland – especially the Mourne Mountains.

'Do you like it?' Mr Hodgkiss asked. 'Gabriel chose this wall to set it off especially well. The shapes, the colour, textures, everything. You put your heart into it, my dear.'

She couldn't answer straight away. A wave of emotion was building inside her, a wave that she'd been scared to let go of. Mr Hodgkiss too, by the look of his watery eyes. He opened his arms and she fell into them, his elderly arms hugging her tight. 'They'll never be forgotten. Never!' she said between sobs.

Later, Isobel was celebrating having her painting hung by taking Agnes out to see a show at the Lyceum on the Strand.

It was supposed to be with Cecily, but a fellow VAD had fallen ill and they were short staffed at the hospital. 'Just me and you then, Agnes.'

'Yes, miss,' the girl said, beaming. 'We're going to have the best time. Have you seen the lead actress? Mavis Spark? She's got the best legs and the best singing voice in the whole of London.'

'Is that so?' Isobel answered, smiling at the young girl. Her adoration of the star of the show was helping lighten Isobel's mood. 'We're having tea at The Savoy too. Wait until you tell your sister. She'll be green.'

'Oooh, miss! Really? Am I dressed right enough? I don't want to let you down now.'

Isobel eyed the slim girl in front of her. 'Well, you're turned out very nicely, but since it's a special occasion, I will allow you to dress up a little more. Run upstairs and put that lipstick on, I know you own one.' Agnes blushed beetroot. 'And borrow my green hat. It will set your curls off nicely.'

'Thanks, miss. Of course, miss.' Agnes sprinted off up the stairs and appeared back down before Isobel had caught her breath. She had rouged her lips, changed hats and also carried a satin purse, stitched all over with glass bugle beads.

'That's beautiful,' Isobel eyed it up. Far too expensive for young Agnes to have bought it. 'Where did you buy it?'

'I didn't, miss. I made it, in me spare time.' She had the grace to blush a little more. 'I used the sewing machine in the attic. I should have asked, begging your pardon. But the satin and beads I bought myself. It looks fancy, but it's an old cushion cover all stained at one corner, which I found at the market. Do you like it?'

'It's exquisite,' she said, fingering the purse and admiring the stitching. 'If you weren't so set on the stage yourself, I would suggest you went into costume-making instead.'

With Agnes still beaming from the praise, they left Russell Square and walked to the tube station and took two stops onto the Strand. It amused Isobel, watching her companion. She didn't behave like a maid; she kept her head up and admired everything around her. Neither was she overcome with anxieties at being out with Isobel, among people way above her station. Agnes adjusted her enunciation and copied everything that Isobel did. She had plenty of pluck, that was for sure, and it highlighted how much things were changing. Agnes wasn't going to stay a maid for ever. Not that Isobel minded, she could get along reasonably well by herself if she had to, but society was changing. The woman who was hanging on the back of the bus that was driving up the Strand, taking fares from the customers, was testament to that.

Isobel had matinee tickets for the two of them, and the show was enjoyable. Their afternoon was going awfully well, even when they arrived at The Savoy and the maitre'd didn't bat an eyelid at Agnes. Amused by the young girl's acting skills, Isobel let her choose her own tea from the menu and her lively chatter ensured the afternoon passed quickly.

'Let's walk down to the river, shall we? Seems a shame to go home too early,' Isobel suggested. 'We can just as easily get a train back from down there.'

Their only problem was after they'd left and, owing to the pleasant evening, Agnes talked Isobel into walking up and down the Strand a little more, just admiring passers-by, and drinking in all the atmosphere. Isobel didn't even notice her purse was missing until they stopped at the underground.

Agnes looked at her, open-mouthed. 'Miss! You've been pick-pocketed, so you have!'

Irritated, Isobel tried to remember the last time she'd held it. The tickets for the matinee. Then she'd definitely been holding it because she'd paid at The Savoy. Afterwards, though?

'You bought a newspaper, at the corner, remember?'

Agnes was right. She had. 'I tucked the purse under my arm when I was reading the headlines.'

'That's it then, miss. You either dropped it, or someone nicked it.'

'Oh dear. Well, we've no money for the tube, I'm afraid. We'll have to walk home.'

'Oh, miss! It's a heck of a walk. Thank lord it ain't raining.'

It was gloomy though. Night had fallen and they had a longish trudge home. It was one of those autumn evenings though that smelt of smoke and kippers and onions, and the effluent that had drifted in off the Thames stung their eyes a little. The tree-lined avenues which they walked past stood sentry as they marched on, the night air, still and mellow with the sound of crispy leaves as they detached themselves from the branches and drifted straight down to the pavement, tickling the other leaves as they passed, encouraging them to follow in pursuit. A slight hazy fog was drifting in from the river and the buildings and people around them were slowly fading from sharp outlines, to a fuzzy blur. Neither of them noticed the enormous bulbous balloon of the Zeppelin above the rooftops of London.

They had retraced their steps, back from the riverside and back up to the Lyceum, in the hope of spotting Isobel's purse. 'My feet hurt, Agnes. Let's call back into the hotel. Perhaps I can find someone who would drive us home.'

'Of course …'

Agnes never finished what she was saying. A huge blast surrounded them both – the heat first, sucking the breath from their lungs, followed by a rush of hot burning air and the tinkling sound as thousands of fragments of glass were blown every which way around them and the other Londoners beside them. Isobel coughed and choked and spluttered, gasping for air, calling out for Agnes. Before the air had stopped moving or the ground ceased shaking, a second blast erupted again. There was a man's voice, shouting, screaming at passers-by to run. Then nothing. Just blackness and an overwhelming sense of weightlessness before everything around Isobel went dark.

Chapter Thirty-Five

Bad Helberg Camp, October 1915

'Nice to see you back again, Woody old chap,' Walker greeted him as he arrived into the bunk room after yet another punishment in solitary. 'Any other year I might jest and suggest that a holiday usually improves your spirits, but I shan't risk it with you. You look a trifle glum today.'

'Funny.' Edward eased himself gingerly into the only remaining wooden chair at the wobbly table in their dorm. His head still pounded much of the time and his skin was a mass of crusty, weeping sores. He seemed to spend more time in solitary these days than with Walker. Werner had developed a particularly nasty streak when it came to Edward. 'Any news?'

'Well yes, if you're up to it.' Neither of them had to clarify what they meant specifically; the only news Walker and Edward were interested in was the ongoing intricate planning for their escape. 'Cigarette?'

'God, no. A drink and something decent to eat would be an improvement.'

'Yes, of course. Sorry.' The bunk room was never quiet that morning, men constantly coming and going, keeping themselves busy doing nothing. *Appel* had been another charade when someone had been carted off to solitary because they had dawdled in late on purpose.

Edward and the rest of the officers had discovered that it infuriated the Boche no end if they refused to be correctly and smartly attired for roll call. The Boche felt that as fellow officers, they should uphold standards, instead, they took it in turns to be late, and 'forget' things like ties, and socks, and even on occasion, trousers. Anything they could do to irritate their captors and show them that the British army was still fighting their corner. Down, but not out.

Walker returned with a bowl of salty water and another one of clean water and a towel. 'Here, have a wash, then soak your burns. Some of them are pretty rancid-looking, if you don't mind me saying so. That Werner is a bastard with his cigarette.'

Edward made grumbling noises but did as he suggested whilst Walker made him a cup of tea and found a tin of tapioca pudding to eat. 'The bread would knock your teeth out and we have to keep your handsome looks for this girl of yours.'

Edward washed himself as carefully as he could, but ten days of filth on top of open crusty cigarette burns was not easy. 'Goddam,' he swore through gritted teeth. If there was even the slimmest chance of getting out of this hell-hole and back to Isobel, then he'd take it. Within minutes of washing off the dirt and grime, he was sweating again, the stinging pain of the saltwater burning his skin just as surely as the first time Werner had tortured him. Walker set down a small chipped tumbler of homebrew and pretended not to notice Edward's pain.

'So,' Walker said. 'Seems Werner is going to be celebrating his birthday in a couple of weeks.'

'Happy Birthday, Werner,' Edward muttered, stabbing a blunt knife into the squishy bar of soap.

'Nein!' Walker replied, raising his eyebrows. 'Alles Gute zum Geburtstag.'

'Ja?'

'Ja! And may he have a blessed and happy one, with plenty of drink!'

Ah … now Edward understood it. They had a date, a night when the guards would be otherwise compromised. 'Have we entertainment lined up for the occasion?'

'We do. And costumes to keep it authentic. I've been training up a choir to sing some Gilbert and Sullivan songs. That ought to put a smile on their faces. And I've been asking around for a few props, and accessories that we might use. It's cost me a heck of a lot in tobacco and treats for a few of the more friendly guards, but we'll be ready for the night of the twenty-ninth.'

The officers rehearsed like mad the song they would sing in honour of Werner's birthday and saved up treats from any parcels from home and promised the more junior German guards that they wouldn't miss out on the celebrations but that they could join the allied prisoners that night and sing songs and enjoy themselves. There was a lot of back slapping and being congenial to their more favoured guards, so that everything would be in order when the day arrived.

Werner's Birthday

The evening was crisp and dry, a late autumn day that held warmth in the sunshine, but the lack of cloud cover brought a chilly evening. Edward, Walker and their entire bunkhouse had rehearsed a special version of the Major-General's song from *The Pirates of Penzance*, just for Werner, and then they would carry on entertaining the remaining guards with other songs from the shows and a cabaret act. Their own Major Corky from the Scottish Highlanders had just enough of a rotund belly and fine singing voice to carry off the major-general, and then half the choir were dressed in workman-like labourer costumes, and the other half had drawn the short straw and had shaved their legs and chins, rolled up their trousers and contrived to look like gorgeous young dames as best they could.

'Ready?' Edward asked Walker.

'As ever as I shall be. What did you pack?'

'Some food, a map and my photographs. That's all I'll ever need to guide me home. You?' Edward replied.

'Same, and a good book. Who knows how long we'll be lying low in different places? You can gaze over your loved ones and I'll keep myself occupied.'

'Fine. Best of luck anyhow.' They'd been told every man for themselves. Split up and don't draw attention to themselves.

'See you on the other side.'

'Without a doubt. Come on, I promised Babstone I'd help him with a bit of rouge. Bet his missus was surprised when he asked her for her best lipstick from Selfridges.'

They weren't performing until after ten. Werner and his cohorts would have drunk enough of the best German beer and drunk the finer stuff too, no doubt. The tension amongst the prisoners was like a spark in an ammunitions dump. One wrong move, one bad comment and someone would blow their top. The French had arranged a gift of a large bottle of champagne and were to do a variety show also. There were some new prisoners just arrived from Russia; they had explained, in one officer's halting English, that they would perform a variety of dances from their native country. Each group of prisoners were checking out the others and not quite trusting their equivalents to also be attempting a mass breakout.

The choir from block D danced onto the makeshift stage, adrenaline high, flushed cheeks and eyes constantly scanning the audience. The sight of Werner sitting right in the front row made Edward's chest constrict. He had never before come across such a powerful feeling of pure hatred that he had for this man. Every time their paths had crossed since he'd been tied up, Edward seriously believed he could squeeze the last breath from the blond bastard and it still wouldn't be enough. Next to him, Walker dug him gently in the ribs. 'Easy,' he said through partially closed lips. Edward tried to breathe naturally, but just the sight of that man flicked a switch deep inside him which dulled regular sensations and scared him how easily he could have murdered him.

The Germans wolf whistled and clapped at the chorus, who only encouraged interactions by flashing their toned lower calves and pretending to act all coy. The music began and Major Corky strode around the stage belting out the popular tune. Walker had helped him change several lines into German and they'd taken the opportunity to poke fun at various well-known military figures. Around the room, the British POWs handed out small bottles of whiskey and slices of cake to Werner and his cronies and smiled and pretended they were having fun.

Edward twice went out to the latrines and chucked up – he had so much resting on this. If he didn't get out of this place soon, he would die. He knew it. He'd either murder Werner or Werner would go too far in his beatings and torture and kill him. He had to escape. Walker kept checking on him.

'Come on, Woody. Nearly there, old chap.'

Edward couldn't think straight, his mind was one huge

mass of sodden wool. He'd not even remembered the words of the song, never mind the details of how they were to escape. God! What on earth was wrong with him? Isobel, that was what. He had to get home to her.

Wilfred had refused to answer direct questions about anything to do with Isobel and just kept saying she was well. Now that Edward had those two precious photographs of George and Isobel, a small knot of fear had settled deep inside his chest that he couldn't shift. What if Wilfred had married her as a way of keeping her for himself when he didn't return? Oh, he knew that he had asked him to do it, that time he'd written a letter only a few weeks into the war, already understanding that he had no guarantee he'd make it home alive, but the idea that his brother might have gone through with it tore his heart to shreds. He had to get home before that happened. What if he waited in this hellhole another year, and Wilfred refused to give her up? What if Isobel forgot about him, or fell in love with Wilfred?

What then?

He had to get out. The jealousy and the not knowing was unbearable.

Edward and Walker were due to slip out at midnight, when the shift changed. Edward managed to keep his tension simmering just beneath his Bavarian woodsman costume. They went laden down with chocolates and wine and hung around with the guards acting all jolly and gaining their trust before a mock fight over one of the dames broke out. Nonchalantly lounging next to the guards on duty, the pair of them called out a well-rehearsed banter to their fellow prisoners. Which, like a well-regulated German Von Schliffen plan, went exactly to order and suddenly escalated and the pair in question rolled around on the ground, taking and landing punches amongst the bored set of guards. It was a moment of unremarkable quiet as Edward and Walker slipped into the dark space just out of sight under the watch tower and stayed hidden. There were no shouts, no shots fired, no immediate reaction of any kind. A second burst of faked argumentative wrestling kept the guards' attention and Edward and Walker rolled out of sight and crawled away from the perimeter fence. A hundred yards and they were still undetected.

No rushing, no sudden movement to draw anyone's attention, they simply walked free under cover of the trees. The plan had been rehearsed just as much as the major-general's song; out the main gate, down the drive under the tree line and end up a quarter of a mile past the sentry at the final exit to the camp. The fence had been loosened next to a post and was accessible by pulling it back and creeping through.

They paused for a second, listening hard – no approaching vehicles or unexpected patrols and then cross the main road and head due south-west, skirt the village and pick up the riverbank. Edward planned to find a small rowing boat when he could or just walk all the way to the Swiss border. They were supposed to work alone but neither man could bear to split up. 'Not yet,' Walker said, firmly. 'Tomorrow will be time enough.' The moon in all its glorious brilliance hung huge on the horizon and helped them march through the night. They were free. For the first time in a year they were unfettered, and Edward could taste his freedom as they stumbled along riverbanks that night. It had been easy, far too easy, and waiting for it to go wrong was torture.

Ten days they had survived, walking at night, sleeping during the day, heading as best they could towards Switzerland and freedom. They still had one compass, but it was the homemade one. Edward cursed the dark overcast nights, but eternally damned to hell the ones that blew straight down the mountains and screeched through the valleys, making it nigh on impossible to navigate straight. The moon and stars were obliterated and risking striking a match in order to have enough light to see the miniscule 'x' that he'd liberated from his watch, ground their enthusiasm into the stony paths of the foothills of the German Alps. But when the wind blew, and the match wouldn't light, they might as well have been walking straight up the Wilhelmstrasse in Berlin for the good it did them. They were *bloody bollocking* lost, as Walker kindly put it.

'Have we any food left?'

'Don't. You know the answer.'

Edward swore again. Their British-issue overcoats that they'd had to leave behind in order to look more local would have gone a long way to keeping out the chill wind right now. They had knitted caps and gloves, and wool trousers dyed an odd shade of blueberry, but when their stomachs were hanging out of them from starvation it seemed irrelevant. They didn't even have a decent knife that they could have used to kill some kind of small prey.

'We're going to have to find a village or farmhouse.'

Walker refused to answer. They'd been round this conundrum too many times these last few days. Staying away from people was safer, but having no food meant they were running out of energy and more at risk of failure through illness or falling because they were exhausted. The paths they'd stuck to so far had worked – staying in the tree line when they could, avoiding the flat bottoms of the open valleys during daylight. And they'd evaded capture so far. But how long before their luck ran out?

Walker groaned and sank to the ground. Daylight was beginning to filter through the forest, and they had stopped at the opening to a cave. Both of them were unsteady on their feet, but neither wished to admit it and both plagued with the indecision that filled their every moment. Even the glorious colours of late autumn – the russets and earthy ochres of the mixed forests – was not much solace when they were so hungry. They would have eaten raw fish if only they could have caught the pesky things. 'Tonight.' He breathed heavily. 'One farmhouse. One. And we'll take enough to keep us going for a couple of days. But I don't like it.'

'You keep saying.'

'Shut up. I'm going to try to sleep.'

The pair of them were hunkered down in a damp cave, backs up against the driest wall, bracken and dead branches piled up to keep them more hidden should anyone come past. They dozed off, trying to save what energy they had left.

A deep, guttural voice woke them. Both men were alert within a split second, ears pricked trying to assess the situation. Then the whine of a dog, picking up their scent. They could visualise it even if they couldn't yet see the owner or the dog.

They were trapped low down in a hollow and, worse, in a cave. Inside his head, Edward named every single swear word he'd ever come across. Ever.

The man spoke in German. 'What is it, boy?' The dog whined some more. 'Easy, easy. Hey! Schneider … hey! Hey! There's something down here.'

Edward's German was better than it had been a year ago; still useless for regional variations, but even he didn't need it translated. They'd been found. Walker's breath tickled his ear. 'Don't move. Brazen it out.'

More shouting seemed to come from above and around them and the sound of boots on the mountain path increased.

One man became two, and then were joined by two more. The Germans shouted amongst themselves about something in the cave. Hot sweat burnt through Edward. Damn the bastards. He couldn't be caught now, he just would not. There was still a chance they could escape. Every muscle in his body was alive, tingling, ready to flee. Panic raced through him. No! No! He wasn't going to just give up. He needed to get home to Isobel. He must! He couldn't bear to be stuck, impotent, back in the camp again, knowing what evil Werner would inflict on him.

The sound of boots scrambling down into the hollow and the scratchy noises of a dog, straining and whining at the end of a leash, was the last straw. Suddenly it barked and Edward could never recall why that was the moment he chose to flee, but it was the catalyst. One second he was crouched, hiding, the next he darted towards the light and the green glow of the overhanging evergreen trees that surrounded their cave.

'Halt! Halt!' echoed in his ears, but he never registered their meaning. He scrambled as fast as he could up the side of the small hollow, desperate to get away. Then the bang. Then more shots. He fell backwards, slamming his head against rocks and debris at the base of the hollow, rolling over, frantic to try once more. And then he was face down, eating larch needles, pinned down by a large hound, teeth sunk into his thigh and his sight blinded by the blood flowing over his face. His blood. And then it went black.

Chapter Thirty-Six

Bad Helberg POW Camp, Germany, January 1916

'This man.' A smart, well-dressed Swiss doctor stood his ground, facing the camp kommandant and tapping on the official document he was holding. 'Lieutenant Edward Dunwoody. I've been told he has a brain injury. A bullet wound to the side of his head. We want him. He is absolutely no use to you. He will never fight again.'

The kommandant snorted, then coughed, hacking up great globs of mucus that stubbornly filled his chest. 'You don't need him.'

'We do. He needs proper medical attention. We have heard he has been barely conscious for the last few months. We are not leaving without him. An officer for an officer. It is a good trade.'

The kommandant snorted again and huffed a bit longer, but the large bottle of scotch pushed his way helped him to make up his mind.

He signed.

The doctor gave a curt nod and then exited the building, barking out orders to his team of orderlies as he went. He wanted that injured man in his ambulance and away before the kommandant changed his mind. A train was waiting at the village station for them.

Walker heard the news and hobbled straight to his bedside.

'You're going home, Woody. Home. Just what you always dreamt of. Hang in there. I know you can hear me, deep down. You'll see Isobel again one day, and your wee nipper. Ignore what Werner told you.'

Edward lay motionless on the small, stinking bed frame. There was no fat left on his body in the slightest. Walker winced even trying to squeeze his hand to reassure him. 'She's still alive, mate. You must believe that. Hang in there and prove everyone wrong. And one day, you and I will meet up again in Ireland and we will chat about our escapades. Just wait and see.'

After Edward and Walker had been returned to their camp – Walker to isolation for three weeks and Edward to a hospital bed – Edward had been visited by Werner. The man seemed to take great pleasure in all of Edward's misfortunes, but the fact that Edward still hadn't woken from the gunshot wound above his right ear, didn't stop the bastard.

'A letter from your mother, Edward. She says this lady is dead. Izobel. Iz-obel. This is your lady-friend? Your lover? Your whore? Hey? Well, she's dead. Dead, I say.' He kicked the bed frame. There was no reaction. The stench within the makeshift hospital ward was appalling. Recently arrived Russian prisoners had caused an outbreak of typhus. The effects were debilitating and odious. Edward, even on top of his injury, now suffered from the same illness. And he stank, lying in his own bodily fluids. Werner clutched a large white handkerchief to his face. 'We killed her in a Zeppelin raid. So why don't you just do us all a favour now and die.'

Werner didn't stay much longer, the stench was too much even for his sadistic gratifications, but the damage had been done. If there had been a flicker of life inside Edward, now he gave up. The darkness was pleasanter than trying to fight his way up to the light and open his eyes. The purpose of his life, his heart, his soul had gone. He wanted to die.

Now Walker was by his side again, encouraging him. 'Come on, mate. Keep fighting. You're getting out of this hell-hole. Back to good old blighty. You must keep fighting.' A tiny squeeze on his fingers told him there was still life. 'I've put your photos in your top pocket. They are safe there. Isobel and the wee fellow. Keep fighting, mate, whatever you do.'

The orderlies that had arrived with the Red Cross doctor walked up the ward and stopped by Edward's bed, Walker explaining as much as he could about Edward's injuries. Gently, and as carefully as possible, they stripped Edward's body and washed him, before dressing him in clean clothes. Walker retrieved the two photos and placed them between Edward's thumb and finger. 'Hold onto them tight, mate, won't you? One day you'll see them again.'

There was a rousing cheer as his stretcher was set down inside the motor and the orderlies climbed in. Everyone had been terribly cut up when Walker and Edward had been returned to camp. Out of thirty-eight British escapees, only eleven were still unaccounted for. The boche had severely punished the whole camp and all letters and parcels had been stopped until after Christmas. How the Red Cross had heard about Edward's injury, no one knew, but it was immaterial. One of theirs was getting out at least.

'Keep fighting on, old chap!'

'Don't let the buggers get you down!'

'Believe she's still alive, Woody old chap.'

The doors closed shut but the sounds from the good-natured cheering could still be heard. Within the dark place inside his body Edward heard it, faint but clear. He was going home. Home to Isobel. 'Isobel,' he mumbled. 'Isobel.'

Chapter Thirty-Seven

No 5 British Red Cross Hospital, Abbeville, France, February 1916

One morning he could smell lavender and feel the comforting presence of pale blue and white, and hazelnut brown hair who sat close by.

'You can't go on like this.' The Irish lilt was soft in his ear. 'You need to get well by eating, but they keep sedating you. Don't struggle so. Let me help.'

He swallowed some soup. She seemed pleased.

Lavender, pink and hazelnut brown kept returning and spooning soup into him. He liked her reassuring calm presence. 'Your father visited again, but you were sleeping. Why don't you stay awake today?'

'My f-father?'

'Yes. Colonel Dunwoody.'

'Where's Isobel? I need to see her.'

'Shush.' She bent forward, wiping his mouth with a linen napkin and at the same time placing a finger on his lips. 'Shush,' she said, all serious and fixing her concerned expression on his face. Her eyes darted left and right. 'Shush. Don't say her name. Every time you ask for her, they sedate you.'

'But I want her. Where is she?'

'Your father doesn't want you talking about her. He gave us strict instructions. It makes you very upset, he said.'

He stared then, concentrating on the kind eyes which matched her hair. 'It upsets me, because I want her to know I'm alive and well. She's waiting for me. We have a son.'

The nurse, Miss Birch, considered his comment, her cheeks already pink, blousing up like a peony in full bloom. 'We're not allowed to talk about it. But... if you try and be good and not say it out loud, I will help you. I can write letters for you, anything you need. But you must be quiet.'

A surge of anger roiled in his stomach. They were keeping things from him. People. Controlling him. He'd spent long enough in prison camp to know what it felt like. 'Be calm?'

She nodded. 'It's the only way.'

She lifted the full soup spoon towards him. 'I'll call back whenever I can and tell you what I know.'

He opened his mouth obediently and swallowed. 'I'm skin and b-b-bone.'

'Yes, you are. And skeletons can't go gallivanting across the countryside searching for people, now, can they?'

He nodded, turning that thought over in his mind. His wrists and hands didn't feel like his own, lying on top of the hospital blanket. Protruding veins and bones created a map he didn't recognise. His own map, he supposed. The evidence of where he'd been. How hard he'd fought. But what of Isobel?

'I had photos! Where are they?' Panic rolled through him like waves on the beach at Crawfordsburn. This was important, he knew it was. He needed those photos.

She pursed her lips, shushing him again. 'Your father has them. Remember to stay calm when he visits. You held them constantly in your hands and called out for ... your,' she hesitated, picking her words carefully, 'your wife, all the time. Your father thought it best for you if he took them away.'

'She wasn't my wife.' He turned his head away, refusing the rest of the soup.

Miss Birch waited a little longer then stood up, leaning over his bed. 'I know,' she said quietly. 'But you loved her, and I want to help.'

Edward had to fight against slipping into the black waves that left him nowhere. If he had to act like he was calm in order to get home to Isobel, he would.

But he wasn't calm.

'Ah, there you are, old son. Welcome back!' His father arrived for a visit a few weeks later.

'Pops.' He watched him sit down on the small wooden chair sitting neatly beside his bed.

'Good to see you've pulled through all that bother. Matron says you stay awake most of the day now. Very bright, she says. Good show.' His large hands patted Edward's thigh through the blanket but hurriedly withdrew it. Edward was as skinny as a rolling pin. 'And you've been eating. That is good news.'

From his propped-up state, Edward scrutinised his father. More wrinkles, more bags under his eyes. An unhealthy hue to his skin.

'Are you well, Pops? Mother?'

'Yes yes. We are both well.'

'Wilfred and cousin Roger?'

His father tilted his head and cleared his throat. He became more interested in the badge on his hat than in looking at Edward. 'Wilfred's fit and healthy, thankfully.' His voice croaked. 'Roger...'

'Roger's dead?'

'Yes, I'm afraid so. He was at Bexley Hall in Norfolk. You remember the Finches?'

'Of course I do.' Of course he did. Did they think he was fragile in the head or something? 'When c-c-can I leave? I could visit Mother for you.'

'As soon as you are fit enough you will be sent back to England, but not yet. We just weren't sure how clear your mind was, Edward. You've been a bit ... Well, unsteady. Being in camp and such.'

'I believe I was injured t-t-trying to escape, Father. I feel so much better today.' He smiled, trying hard to prove it.

'Good. Excellent. Your mother and Wilfred will be delighted. Everyone's been under such strain, particularly your mother. All this worrying.' He kept fiddling with his hat on his knee. He went to say something but stopped.

Edward went to say something too, but held himself back.

'You see, Edward. It's been very hard on your mother, by herself. Worrying. And now with Roger's death coming so soon after his brother, I don't want her to be caused any more undue grief.' He didn't look directly at Edward, more to the left of him, or the ceiling. Anywhere in fact except at Edward. 'So, we won't mention the other thing again.'

Neither spoke again for a very long minute. The long wooden hut was noisy with the continual hum of deep male voices and firm, polite female voices. Edward focused on the sounds he found comforting. Someone humming a dance tune he remembered. The clink of a water glass being sat down on a metal tray. Birds outside filtering through the windows that were propped open for healing fresh air.

Isobel and his son were the other thing though, weren't they? The unmentionables.

'I n-need my photos returned though. *Please.* I'll n-n-never mention them again. Just the photos.'

His father cleared his throat, patted his rolling pin thigh bone, and half nodded in acknowledgment. He carefully pulled a small brown paper envelope from his jacket pocket, then held it over the bed. 'For your mother's sake, we're not mentioning this again. You are clear on that? This episode is finished.'

The last phrase was said using a tone Edward remembered from his childhood, reserved for serious misdemeanours and punishments. Edward got the message. 'Yes.' His eyes didn't meet his father's; they were fixed on the envelope as though it might vanish in front of his eyes, the same way Werner the prison guard used to taunt him.

'Good chap. I'll call by tomorrow. Your mother will be pleased we've cleared all this awkwardness up. New slate and all that.' He nodded and then was gone, leaving the envelope on the bed. His highly polished shoes squeaked on the wooden floor as he left.

Miss Birch was by his side, pretending to fix his sheets, as soon as his father departed. She placed one finger gently on the brown envelope. 'Calm, remember. Keep calm whatever you do.' Her eyes were on that envelope. Someone shouted *nurse* up at the far end of the hut and she slipped away, hurrying up the ward. She hadn't even made it to the far end when Edward's anguished voice ripped through the entire length of the hut.

'No!'

His bedside table was shoved clattering to the ground; glass shards splintering and scattering across the floor.

Footsteps came hammering on the wooden floor, another syringe, and then all was calm again. Miss Birch carefully placed her foot over Edward's two photos, hiding them from view. A short note from his father was soaked into the puddle of water next to his bed.

284

Edward,
 Isobel is dead, you do remember, please accept it.
 It's time to move on,
 be a good chap about this.
 It's for the best.
 Pops

Miss Birch pocketed the photos when no one was looking, ready to return them to Edward when she could, and also the short clipping from a newspaper reporting the death of a Mrs Dunwoody after a Zeppelin raid close to the Lyceum Theatre.

On days when the sun shone, they wheeled him in a chair to a window where the warm rays could soak into his shrunken bones. He was always cold. Parts of his hair had fallen out and a woollen cap was found to keep him warm. Memories swum about in his head – some good, some horrendous. He struggled to stay in the present some days, preferring to daydream about Isobel and Egypt.

Voices around him on the ward discussed the war. He listened. It was abhorrent to believe that for all the men that had been killed in September and October 1914, the front-line had hardly moved. They spoke of living and sleeping in soul-destroying mud-filled trenches and Edward could only sympathise. New prisoners that had arrived in Bad Helberg had kept them up to date with news from the front, but it was hard to fully understand the horror of it all, locked away as they'd been.

Letters came from his mother, telling him very little about Roger's death. Just one sentence. He'd have to ask for more details when she was ready. Wilfred wrote one letter, and said he was glad Edward was safe. Again, no news that he needed or wanted. Wilfred had been in touch with Isobel whilst he'd been imprisoned, lovely letters about how well she was and how much his son was the image of him, and yet not a word of her now. Not even a word of sympathy or explanation of her death. Nothing about his son; it was as though the two of them had never existed before. Gone. Wiped clear.

He asked Miss Birch about it when she appeared later. 'People are nervous of upsetting the other person, I believe.'

'But I'm already upset. I want to talk about her.'

Miss Birch shot him a nervous glance. 'Your father said we weren't to talk about her.'

'Because he's embarrassed. That's all. I want to remember all the wonderful things about her. Did I tell you what a talented artist she was?'

'No.' She busied herself around his bed, slowly tucking covers back in, taking his temperature and making sure he had fresh water to drink.

'She was, but she never saw it herself. She loved colours and big, bold landscapes and some would say it was ugly, but I just saw it as amazing – the way she saw things differently.'

'You don't stutter when you talk about her, did you notice?' She paused, smiling kindly at him.

'That's true.'

Miss Birch sighed. 'One day,' she said quietly, so only he could hear, 'I hope a man talks about me with such devotion the way you talk about her.' She moved on then, to the next bed and officer, to give them her attention.

Edward rolled onto his side. He was slowly gaining weight. He didn't look like the bundle of sticks as when he'd arrived. He'd write to his mother and talk about Roger, and he'd write to Wilfred and mention Alice, and ask him where Isobel had lived last year and how she'd spent her days and where his son was. He needed that information in the same way he'd needed decent food in camp; crumbs for a starving man. He craved any fragments of information about Isobel to keep her vivid in his mind.

Two weeks later, Edward was sitting in the sunshine on a beautiful spring day, where soft, fluffy clouds danced across the turquoise blue sky and blossom hung from every branch available. It was hard to imagine not fifty miles away the ground was so churned up not a living thing grew any longer and men drowned in the thick, cloying mud and rats feasted on human remains.

His father turned up to visit. He was more lined than Edward had ever remembered. 'You're looking much better, my boy.'

'I'm feeling better, Father. It won't be much longer before I can be back in uniform and back fighting the Boche.'

'Good. Take your mind off that … other thing.' His father reached for the pipe that he always carried around with him, lifting it out and a box of matches. 'Here.' He handed Edward a packet of cigarettes, before lighting his pipe.

'But I want to. Talk about Isobel, I mean. There's so much more I need to know.' The expression on his father's face stopped him in his tracks. Edward looked down at his hands instead of his father. If he pressed his fingertips together, it stopped the shake in his hands. 'Sorry.'

'It's unlikely you'll ever be fit enough to get back to the fighting. You're not quite steady in your mind. Forgetful and all that. Perhaps I'll pull a few strings and see if we can get you a desk job, just for a while. You need to stop all this carry on though, be a bit more manly.' He gestured towards Edward's limbs that trembled like a willow in a summer breeze.

'I c-c-can't it help it, Father. Things were a trifle sticky in there. I'm doing my best.'

'Glad to hear it. Anyway, how do you think your mother will cope if we lose one of you boys? She won't.'

'But I need to do my duty. Even when I went to Cairo, I always said I'd step up if there was a war.' His hands shook more and despite his best efforts to hold them still he couldn't stop the shaking.

'You made me look bad, did you ever consider that fact? Stop doing that.' His father leant over and slapped his hand, which trembled continuously. 'Can't you stop that? Have a cigarette, that will stop your nerves.'

Edward ignored the cigarette. For some reason he couldn't understand, even the sight of his favourite brand caused a band to tighten around his chest so badly he thought his heart would stop beating. 'Of c-c-course I did, but I couldn't live my life according to what you and mother wanted. I still c-can't. I must be my own man. Surely you understand that.'

'I need you at home looking after your mother for a while. That's an order.'

'I th-think you'll find it's not up to you.'

'Don't answer me back, boy. Why aren't you having a smoke? They're your favourites, aren't they? They'll stop that dreadful shaking damn quick. Stop it, I say.'

Ashamed, Edward sat on his hands, but he couldn't stop the building sense of panic rising within him. He nodded instead.

'Good. We can get you home soon hopefully. You and Mother can take some time back in Belfast together, get some rest and good food into you. Mother would appreciate you being home with her for a while, and it will stop all this silly nonsense.'

'I u-u-understand. Roger's death must have been very difficult. Where was he in hospital? Perhaps I could visit the staff.'

'Why on earth would you dream of doing that?' his father snapped. 'It's done with now. Over.'

'But not for me, can't you see.' Edward pleaded. 'I missed out on life being shut away. I need these things. Like Isobel. Won't you tell me more about her death? Only, in Wilfred's last letter he sent me a photo of George, my boy. He's alive somewhere and I want to see him.'

'He's not your boy now, he's Wilfred's, and I said we weren't talking about those people. Wilfred's another ruddy fool, after the wrong kind of skirt!' he roared, his moustache quivering on his top lip. He lowered his voice and hissed at Edward. 'You and I agreed, for your mother's sake. Not a word.'

'B-b-but I need to understand and Mother's not here. You c-c-can't command me to forget her.' Edward stood, shaking, but not backing down. 'You can't just erase her from my life. I won't stop asking about her until I know everything. I won't.'

Beads of sweat rolled off the forehead of the colonel, as he grabbed his hat from his head. He faced Edward, locking eyes with him. 'You defied me once, my boy, refusing to go to Sandhurst, and look how that worked out. I knew it was a mistake from the start. I blame that girl for it, turning your head. Men like us don't marry girls like that, do you understand?'

'No, I don't. I thought you and Mother liked them? We spent time with them in Belfast.'

'They had money, that's all. Money, but not enough to make them someone you marry. When this is all over, I expect you to stay in Belfast and look for a proper respectable job. None of this fanciful shop business. You need to knuckle down and remember your commitments to our family.'

'B-but what if she's not dead? Maybe it was a mistake. There's something I think I remember. Someone said it was a mistake – in the paper. Are you sure she's dead? Have you spoken to Wilfred? It said Mrs Dunwoody in that newspaper clipping. Did Wilfred marry her?'

'Stop it! Stop it, I say! Stop being a damn fool. That woman will never be a part of your life so just listen when I tell you she's dead. I showed you the paper and you still doubt me. How dare you question me?' His voice had risen so much that it brought a doctor and a few nurses running from the huts.

'Come away, sir. That's enough. It's not good for our patients,' Matron told the colonel firmly.

'You're hiding something from me. Isobel's not dead and you know it!' Edward shouted at the back of his departing father. All he could see of him was the erect shoulders and the skin at the back of his neck, which was beetroot.

'Shush now, shush.' Miss Birch tried to soothe him. 'This doesn't help, I told you. You're only upsetting yourself.'

'She's not dead. I can feel it.' He was rushed back to his bed, tucked in and given something to make him sleep. Sleep was a merciful retreat instead of the hole he always fell into when he imagined that she was still alive. He didn't see his father talking to the doctor, he was curled up and dreaming of the woman he loved. Isobel. His sweetheart.

Chapter Thirty-Eight

Special Hospital for Officers, 10 Palace Green, Kensington, London, May 1916

The upper windows looked out over Kensington Gardens. Edward could hear the familiar sounds of London floating up into his room, but he refused to engage.

He sent the soup bowl away untouched.

In the middle of the afternoon a silver tea tray and delicately cut cucumber sandwiches were sent up. He obstinately kept his face to the wall.

The dinner bell was rung at seven and he made out the shuffle of feet on the stairs as the other residents went down for dinner. He watched the clouds change from enormous banks of white fluff, to iridescent whirls of orange candy floss until it faded to a dark mass of indigo.

His door was rapped smartly before the owl-rimmed glasses of Dr Pettigrew peered round the door.

'Not hungry today, Lieutenant Dunwoody? You're missing a real treat. The chef was commandeered from the kitchens of the Ritz.'

'I'll eat when you stop pretending I'm mad.'

Dr Pettigrew nodded and came to perch on the end of Edward's bed, crossing one leg. He reminded Edward of his Classics professor when he'd been at Cambridge. All he needed now was the bow tie and the fair isle cardigan. But the warm London spring had decreed cardigans and sweaters unnecessary.

'No one says you're mad.'

'My father does, and he's the reason I'm here, isn't he?'

'You've been very poorly, you know that. And sometimes, under those circumstances, one might wish for things to be the case when they're not. Or one might imagine things are the case when in fact they aren't.'

'Mad. Like I said.' Edward turned away from him and concentrated on the bookcase that was in his room. Far too many heavy tomes and nothing for light entertainment. Not that he felt like reading, but he might have to resort to it.

'Not at all. Why don't you just join us for dinner. Eat something?'

'Why should I, when you all insist I am something which I'm not.' Beyond the open door a crash broke the silence followed by the roaring of one of his fellow hospital inmates. 'I am not like th-th-them.' He struggled so hard to get the word out. The frustration of it was like a huge wedge of wood stuck tight within his chest.

'Calm now, calm yourself.'

'Stop saying that! I never used to st-st-stutter, you know. Does that not interest y-y-you?' He shouted out the words. 'Not even in camp. Never.'

'So, when did it start then?'

'When my f-f-father insisted she was dead. Th-th-that's when.'

'Edward, may I call you that?'

Edward didn't deign to answer. He was curled up in the foetal position now, so tired of this continual back and forth, the lack of freedom to think as he wished. The conspiracy against him.

'You had a significant brain injury and you've been

bereaved, Edward. A dreadful bereavement. Accepting it will bring you relief and healing. It's like you are a train on the wrong track. When you change the signal, it will release the train.'

Poor Dr Pettigrew beat a hasty retreat when the first of the heavy tomes missed his head and slammed into the door. The second missed his foot, and the third thudded onto the Tiffany glass lamp, splintering it into a thousand pieces.

'I'm not mad!' Edward shouted through the door as he shoved the large wing-back chair against the door and tiptoed around the broken glass. 'Not mad. Angry. Furious. She's not dead!' The force of his own voice echoed around the room, but it felt better to let it out.

Out. There was an idea. He could just walk out. Well, not right now actually because they'd be watching out for him. He looked at the window. Daylight had retreated to an inky dusk, shadows falling long up and down the leafy street. He shoved the window up and looked out. A metal Juliet balcony, adorned with ironwork scrolls for useful footholds. Peering further, he could see the rib-like structure of the gutter and downpipe. He checked himself first. Pyjamas were a bit of a giveaway.

Once dressed he'd be able for it. Rushed voices outside his door intruded. Matron hammering on the door. 'Lieutenant Dunwoody, are you well? Are you injured? We heard something smash.' He sighed. Lord but this was going to be hard work. He wasn't mad, but he couldn't prove it until they stopped treating him like he was mad. Which they would continue to do if he kept losing his temper. Which he couldn't seem able to stop. And, if he was able to reason that all out himself, then surely that proved he wasn't mad? Or delusional. Just completely rational.

'Stop f-f-fussing. I'm getting dressed.'

Edward got dressed and went down for dinner a little late for the second course just to prove Dr Pettigrew wrong. He ate beef and drank wine and enjoyed the pudding. He chatted and made tentative friends with the other officers. He slipped outside when they weren't looking and walked into the garden behind the large house, just across the road from Kensington Palace. He didn't smoke any more, and he couldn't even pinpoint why, but tonight was one of those nights when he wished he did.

A nurse was resting on one of the benches. She patted the seat next to her. Reluctantly he sank into it but didn't want conversation, yet his legs were weary. His strength was still far from normal.

'You're our new patient, aren't you? Lieutenant Dunwoody? I'm Miss Seaforth.'

'Hello, Miss Seaforth. You've heard all about me, I'm sure. The one who insists he's not mad when everyone around can see he is,' he answered her, his voice dripping with sarcasm.

'I don't get to read the patient notes, Lieutenant. I just do as I'm told and look after you all. And, for the record, I don't think you're mad.'

Edward turned this time, assessing his bench companion. She was older than most of the VADs he'd come across on his long journey through France. Her face and features softened through age and experience and a touch of silver where her hair peeked out from beneath her nurse's veil.

'I came to nursing late in case you're wondering. Professional nursing, that is. My father succumbed to an illness of the mind and it took me and my mother to look after him at home until he died. You're not at all like him. Or the others who are here.'

'What am I then, in your opinion?'

She laughed; a deep, throaty laugh which conveyed a sense of authority which he liked. 'Matron and Dr Pettigrew would say quite rightly that I have no business nor qualification to give an opinion.'

'But if I asked for your personal opinion, and I didn't share that with them...?'

'Well, then I would say you are still suffering from some nervous distress from your time in captivity, from what I hear they are particularly harsh places – and you had a significant brain injury.' She nodded towards the thin white line above his ear. The place where his hand always sprang, doing his best to soothe the nerves beneath it. 'You were unaware of your surroundings for many weeks, the doctor said. That is significant damage.'

'I was shot. Escaping. Got within pissing distance of the Swiss border. Sorry.' He blushed. He needed to stop using bad language, but his self-control in many matters needed improving.

'You are also very angry and searching for the truth and people in authority are thwarting your ability to find it. And whilst that continues, this aggravates your mental stress.'

'I'm impressed, Miss Seaforth, that you managed to assess me so accurately whilst not having read my notes.'

'I have ears, Lieutenant Dunwoody. And a brain. And even I, a lowly nurse, can see why that might be distressing for you. But there. I have spoken too much.'

They sat in silence for a while, with just the late evening twittering of the birds in the trees above them for company, Edward's mind trying to make sense of what she'd said.

'The question is then, how do I prove I'm not unstable?'

'Well since I'm not allowed an opinion, nor to hand out medical advice,' she said with a twinkle in her eyes, 'I would gain their trust by complying and not getting angry. I would get lots of rest, and then I would ask Dr Pettigrew to let you find your own proof about the thing I'm not supposed to know about, and in so doing that would help you heal. But do stop fighting everyone. They're not a bad old bunch. Dr Pettigrew is a reasonable man and I do think you'll like him if you get to know him.'

Edward sighed heavily. How could he stop fighting them? They had him down on record as being mentally unstable.

'Your mind and your body are still suffering from your injury. You don't have the same neurasthenia as our other patients. Concentrate on getting that part of you healed at least. The rest will come.'

'My memory?'

'They must have treated you appallingly badly. Your memory is protecting you by shutting off those memories until you can cope with it, or it's from the injury.'

'I used to smoke, you know. Not a lot, but some. Now I cannot bear to think about holding one. Do you think that is important?'

'It could be, but don't fight it Anything that comes back to you, write it down or talk about it. I think if you all could talk about your fears, you'd discover you have a lot in common.'

'Talk? Men don't talk, we have a stiff upper lip and all that.'

'Well, I'd better go in now. I'm sure it's nearly time for cocoa.' She rubbed her arms. It was getting chilly. 'I'll go back first so I'm not seen with you. Matron is a real stickler for that sort of thing.'

Edward laughed. Miss Seaforth was probably twenty years older than him, and there was not much chance for 'that sort of thing'. 'Thank you though, for your honesty. I haven't had much of that recently.'

She nodded before departing, her pale blue skirts swishing in the still night air. Edward remained on the bench a while longer, listening to the distant sounds of London – still amazed that he'd survived to experience it once again. He just wished it was under a better set of circumstances. If he felt better, stronger, then he could make a run for it. But he was exhausted, and his brain felt like the glutinous pudding they had served this evening. Information, thoughts, facts – everything he needed kept slipping through holes in his brain like a colander. Perhaps he was delusional. Perhaps his father was right. He could remember people, things from his earlier life right up to Cairo, but day-to-day things were a struggle and last year was a complete blur, a shifting mass of tiny fragments.

Tomorrow he'd be strong enough.

Edward knocked on the door to Dr Pettigrew's office. 'Come in,' the voice inside called out. Edward grasped the handle and pushed it open. The doctor was perched on his desk, sucking at his empty pipe, which he used to direct Edward to the empty seat.

The office could hardly be called that. The study was better, or a library. The walls were lined with books upon books. The floor was a highly polished marquetry and a detailed Persian rug was placed in front of the marble fireplace.

'That's nice. I had one similar.'

'At home?'

'No. In Cairo. I worked there. I ran my own business, alongside an uncle who lived there. I miss it.'

'Is that where you were when the war broke out?'

'It was. It was also where I fell completely and utterly in love with Isobel.'

'Ah. Tea?'

'Please.' Edward sat down in the cosy chintz armchair opposite Dr Pettigrew and watched him pour two cups from the silver teapot. Strange how he could remember the rug instantly, but not what he'd done yesterday.

'Milk?'

'I'll take it black if you don't mind. I got used to drinking it without milk over the last while.' A memory shot into his head right then of his batman turning up with goat's milk. He wondered how he'd fared since then. He should write to him.

'So,' Dr Pettigrew said when they were both nursing cups of tea. 'How's the memory coming along? Any better?'

Edward shook his head. There were gaping gaps that he waded through each night in his dreams. Some memories he didn't want back, and yet the one he was sure would help him lay just out of his reach. 'I can't smoke any more. Do you think that's significant?'

Dr Pettigrew's eyes widened and he put down his cup. 'Have you not looked at your body? At the scars that you have?'

'No.' Edward was perplexed, but by the way his heart rate doubled he knew instinctively that it was important. 'I need to remember, don't I?'

'Steady on. Do it in your own time. But the fact your brain isn't letting you remember it, is for a reason.'

It was the way he said it that struck Edward. 'What do you know that I don't?'

Sighing heavily, the doctor appeared to consider his response before answering. 'The notes that arrived with you told me a good deal about what you'd experienced physically during your time in camp. Not everything, of course. But there were easy clues.'

'Like what?'

'You had a bullet wound, above your ear, but it was only a flesh wound and unlikely to have caused your memory loss. Do you remember anything else about the day you escaped?'

Edward shook his head. 'I ...' He tried hard to remember. Him and Walker. It was dark. They were hiding. Scrambling to escape. No, he couldn't remember any more.

'You fell apparently after being shot. The same injury as if you'd been thrown many feet by a blast. A lot of men here suffer the same memory loss after an event like that. You also had hundreds of sores, some healed over, but others were just open wounds. They initially thought all of these were from the lice; you'd scratched at them. You were brought in with typhus which causes memory loss and confusion. But some clever chap figured out that most of your scars were cigarette burns. Hundreds of them. I'm not surprised you don't want to smoke any more. Are you all right?'

Edward dropped his cup into the saucer where it spilled. Sweat poured from him and he struggled to loosen the collar of his shirt. The doctor was talking but his voice was like he had his head stuck in a fishbowl – it swirled and spilled all around him.

One word, one burn; you choose.

His letters. Werner. A slice of a memory flooded his brain and he clutched his hands to his head. He hated Werner with every fibre of his being, but he had to remember. It wasn't just the burns. It wasn't just the torture. It was the words themselves.

'Who is this vuman, Iz-obell. Who is she, Dun-Voodie? Eh? Is she a slut? A girlfriend? You want her words?'

'Yes,' he yelled. 'Yes.' He craved information from home. He needed to hear from Isobel. How she was. How his boy was. He needed that information to survive.

'You ready, Dun-Voodie? One burn. One word?'

'Don't do it, Woody. Don't let him get to you. It's not worth it.' Walker pleaded with him. 'Just let it go. Walk away, please. I'll write to her for you.'

He shook his head. He had to know. Werner confiscated all his letters when they arrived from home as another punishment and refused to allow him to write home. Or to Isobel.

Werner puffed away, making it as hot as he could. 'Ready!'

'Don't.'

Burn. The cigarette was held against his arm and he could even hear his skin sizzle. He forced himself to not cry out. Werner pulled the stub away, sucking on it again.

'Believe.'

Burn.

'Anything.' *Burn.*

'In.' *Burn.*

'The.' *Burn.* 'Do you give up? Do you want more?'

Edward tried to make sense of the words even as his arms and back burnt with pain. Don't believe anything in the … In the what? This was important, he knew it was. 'Yes.' He forced the word from his lips. He had to know.

'Newspapers.' *Burn.* Werner held the cigarette butt to the skin on the inside of his elbow – he must know how sensitive that place would be, how it would never heal.

Don't believe anything in the newspapers.

'Enough. Enough.' He gasped. It was something but he couldn't quite make sense of it. Isobel was sending him a message, that was enough.

When Edward came to, he was lying on the floor of Dr Pettigrew's study floor, the Persian rug beneath him, a blanket over him and the anxious faces of the doctor and Miss Seaforth, who was sponging his brow with tepid water.

'I remembered.'

'Remembered what?' Dr Pettigrew asked gently.

'I remembered why I don't like cigarettes and also why I'm convinced I'm not mad.'

Later, lying in bed with the curtains drawn and a cold cloth on his head, the doctor came to visit him again. Edward had taken the powders he'd been given to try and dull the headache that he knew by now would afflict him for hours or even days.

'How are you, old chap? That was a bit of a going-over you had.'

'But it was important, I know that now.' He pointed to the desk in his room. 'There's an envelope in the drawer. I want you to get it out please.' The doctor found it and returned. 'Open it.' Edward spoke softly, protecting his blinding headache.

The doctor pulled out a pile of newspaper clippings that his father had given Edward back in France. 'I've seen these already, old chap. I know what they say.'

'Did I shout out or speak earlier in your office?'

'You did. You said, and I quote, *Don't believe anything in the newspapers.* And you mentioned the name Isobel. And the name Werner rather a lot, only not terribly politely.'

Edward tapped the envelope of newspaper cuttings. 'Isobel

wrote to me in camp, before I tried to escape. She said specifically "don't believe anything in the newspapers." I didn't understand exactly what it meant, but it stuck with me. Then I escaped, and got shot, and have had a faulty memory ever since.' He tapped the cuttings again. 'See. She was telling me not to believe it. Why? Because it's not true. I have to write to her family and find out the truth, can't you see that?'

Dr Pettigrew didn't speak for a while. He stood up and paced the floor before replying. 'How about we make a deal, you and I? A deal I couldn't possibly offer to anyone else, so don't mention a whisper of it.'

'A deal?'

'You continue to work with me, and rest, and get your strength back. You need to meet up with the War Office and file a report about your mistreatment at the hands of the enemy, and, so long as we can keep your headaches under control because you're not getting upset, then I'll let you take a trip back to Ireland before I discharge you. The trip is part of your recovery. How about it?'

'You'll let me write a few letters to people who could help me?'

'So long as I can see them first.'

Edward briefly closed his eyes and breathed heavily. 'Done. But I must be able to write.'

'Done.'

'And you will give me a clean bill of health if I prove to you that I am not delusional, like my father says.'

'I will be prepared to write down, in black and white, that you are recovered sufficiently to be discharged, but not ready for the front yet if at all, if, and only if, you bring me back sufficient evidence to support what you've just asserted. Something. Anything. I don't even care.'

'I don't have to prove Isobel's alive?'

'No. Because even though you don't want to hear it, I don't think she is; but just enough evidence to show that you had *reason* to hope that she might be. I know you got that letter, but it could have been weeks old. It could have meant something completely different.'

'Excellent. Can I sleep now?'

'Yes.'

Dr Pettigrew found Miss Seaforth in the corridor later. Her eyes were shining. 'Don't get excited, nurse. There isn't enough of anything to suggest the wife, the lady, is alive.'

'But there's enough to show he's not of unsound mind. That all his suppositions and his belief that she was alive were based on reason, slim as it was whilst he was in hospital, and that's the key part, isn't it?'

'Yes. It is.' He stuffed his hands deep into his pockets. 'He's suffered enough with the injury, and the trauma of being imprisoned but then there is a separate part to this that his parents are involved with. If I can wipe his record clear, I'll be a happy man.'

Chapter Thirty-Nine

10 Palace Green, London, July 1916

A gentle knock on his bedroom door roused him from his stupor. Dr Pettigrew called hello and put his head around the door. 'Your mother's here to visit. How do you feel about that?'

Edward sighed heavily, rolling himself up to sitting. He'd been lying on his bed part dozing, part doing nothing but concentrating on the ceiling. 'Down in the dumps. Is that allowed?'

Dr Pettigrew looked serious and came right into the bedroom, closing the door behind him. 'Well, it is certainly allowed, but do you understand why you feel this way?'

'Because ...' Edward started, then stopped. He couldn't explain why exactly. It would be the first time he'd seen her. He shrugged. 'My cousin Roger's dead now. And his brother Maxim. My brother is fighting in France. She'll expect more of me. Both of them will. That's why I liked being out in Cairo. I got to choose how I lived.'

Dr Pettigrew looked thoughtful. 'Families have their own peculiar dynamics, I suppose, but you are a grown man. You still get to make your own decisions.'

Edward snorted; that was a luxury that he had got away with in the past but he didn't expect it to carry on un-impeded. 'Where is she?'

'We've put her in my study. Tea is being made.'

'Hang around then or come and chat – I bet you one of your good cigars that she starts to exert demands that I'm not ready to accede to.' He got up then, smoothing his hair down in the mirror and breathing deeply, preparing himself. The sooner he got it over with, the better.

Miss Seaforth was carrying in the tea tray when Edward walked in. 'Hello, Mother.'

'Oh, Edward, let me see you. How thin you are.' She burst into tears and hugged him tightly. 'Dear boy, dear, dear boy.' Dabbing her red-rimmed eyes with her handkerchief, she released him and sat back into the cosy armchair as Miss Seaforth returned with a plate of sandwiches for them both.

'I'm sorry about Roger and Maxim, Mother. I wished I'd seen them both once more, before … well. Before.'

Mrs Dunwoody couldn't speak, her face was buried in the white lace which she held tightly in one hand, her other hand gripping Edward's.

Neither spoke for a time. Edward had no energy to make conversation. He poured the tea instead, concerned for his mother. Roger's death was hard on them, her in particular. He'd been the youngest of the Dunwoody cousins and Mrs Dunwoody had been very fond of him. Grief buried itself deep inside you. He knew that much. 'Where did he die? I remember very little when Father told me. He was back in England, wasn't he?'

She nodded, muffled words getting lost in the fabric.

'Once I'm well enough to travel we'll go back to Belfast and visit his grave together, would you like that?'

Again, she nodded. He stirred his tea for something to do and lifted a sandwich.

'Have you seen the Finches at all? I keep meaning to write to them or visit. I'm sure they have a house in London.'

'No, you mustn't.' She spoke forcefully, spilling her tea. 'They are terribly busy; they've turned their home into a hospital. Run off her feet, Mrs Finch said.'

'You've seen them, then? I just wondered how they were. They must miss Alice dreadfully.'

'I suppose they do, she never said. Lucy Hartington was asking for you. She's in London. Why don't you come out for tea with us one afternoon? I'm sure your doctor would allow it. Get things back to normal.' She waved her spare hand in the air.

'I'm not ready to meet her, nor do I want to, Mother. I miss Isobel. That's who I want to see. Not Lucy Hartington.'

'Stop it, Edward! If you knew what that girl has done to us, you wouldn't even mention her name in my presence!'

Edward slammed his cup and saucer down and got up, hands shaking already. 'W-w-what do you mean? What has she done to you?'

His mother's face screwed up into undisguised hatred for Isobel. 'She used our name, parading herself about London pretending she was married to you of all things. And pregnant! The shame of it, Edward.'

'W-well if I'd had more sense, I would have insisted we were married before she left Cairo. The only reason I didn't was because I knew how badly you'd react if I got married without you. I'm glad she used it. She had a boy, you know, called George.'

'Don't even mention his name. He is not your son. Why do you insist on bringing it up? Wilfred is his father now, not you.'

A vein in Edward's neck throbbed so hard, blood whooshed through his head making it hard to think straight. 'Just tell me, Mother. Did Wilfred marry Isobel? No one tells me the truth anymore – not you, not Father, not even Wilfred!'

'Yes!' she shouted. 'Wilfred had to marry her because you … got her with child. So now we have a … a child of hers who is ahead of you to inherit things. God knows why Wilfred did it!'

His head pounded. It was true then. It had happened. 'I asked him to look after her. He was only helping me out. I still want to see him, he's my son, I will be his father. Who is looking after him? Are you? I must see him, I *need* to.'

'You will have nothing to do with that child. If Wilfred is killed, God forbid, we will cut them both off and never see them ever again!'

'Father insisted Isobel was dead, but the way you said that makes me think she's still alive. Is she alive? Are you hiding things from me, Mother?' His head pounded; the pressure building until he clutched his head, trying to stop the pain.

'She's dead.' Her voice reached a higher octave. 'Your father told me he'd shown you the paper. Her death was in the paper. It's all there.'

'If you are lying to me, I will never forgive you.' His voice had reached such a crescendo that the door opened and Dr Pettigrew and Miss Seaforth burst in. Miss Seaforth was straight by his side, keeping her voice low and gentle.

'I will not have that woman accommodated in my family, do you hear me, Edward? I forbid it. Not her and not her bastard child.'

'Out.' Dr Pettigrew's face was hard. He held the door wide open and looked directly at Mrs Dunwoody. 'You need to leave now; your son needs calm visits. Not this. We will arrange your next visit by letter. Off you go now.'

Edward paced the room, his head bursting trying to think it through. What had she said? Had he imagined it? It was so hard to remember things. Miss Seaforth moved the tea tray and returned with water and some powder for his headache, which she always anticipated for him. 'Did I imagine that?' he asked her, when he'd drunk some of the cool liquid. 'Did I? It sounded to me like she knew all about Isobel and that she is alive.'

She made him sit down again, mindful of the times he'd blacked out. He didn't need any more head injuries, on top of what he'd already suffered in prison camp. 'Well, Miss Seaforth? Did you hear anything from outside the door?'

She blushed. 'Dr Pettigrew was concerned, you understand. He didn't go too far, then, when we heard you shouting, we were waiting outside the door. I'm so sorry.'

'But did you hear? I'm so mixed up.'

The door opened again, and the doctor came in. Edward looked hopefully up at him. 'Did she say anything else?'

'I got the distinct impression she was ...' he hesitated. 'She was not being fully truthful with you.'

'I think Isobel is alive, definitely. The way she said it, well, shouted at me. She said it as though they were both alive. I need to find them.' Edward missed the look the doctor and nurse shared.

'I think you're right, Edward. I do. But this is all going to take a heavy toll on you. If she was in London, where might she be? Did she have friends that might help?'

'Just the Finches, that I know of. They have a house here. She could have been painting and earning money.'

'Was there anything else your mother said, when you think back now, that might give us another clue?'

Edward lay back, eyes closed against the glare of the afternoon sun shining through the window. 'She was angry with her. She said Wilfred had married her, so she was using our family name in London.'

'So, she's a painter, going by the name Mrs Dunwoody, possibly in London,' Miss Seaforth recapped. 'Perhaps I could search out some shops that sell paint. What did she use? Sorry, I've no idea.'

'Oils. She painted enormous landscapes when we were in Egypt. She went through so much paint. And canvases.'

'Well then, she'd need to buy those, wouldn't she? That's a start. Have you a photo of her? If we could narrow down where she might be living, I could call into any art shops and ask after her.'

'Wilfred should tell me, but I haven't had a letter from him in months.'

'Why don't you just ask the Finches?' Dr Pettigrew asked.

'Of course. That's it. Right now. If I'm quick, I'll get it into the evening post.' Edward stopped then, half-turned on his way out the door, staring at the large painting that stretched across Dr Pettigrew's study wall. The colours, the shapes, the style of it. He leant in, looking for a signature. Just three letters: I H D.

'This painting! Doctor, where did you get it from? It's hers. I'm almost sure of it.'

'Are you sure?' The doctor was thoughtful.

'Well not completely, but it looks like her style. Did you buy it?'

'I did. And before you ask, I do remember where. I promise I will call in tomorrow and make enquiries.' He returned the smile plastered all over Edward's face. 'Don't get your hopes up too much though, but yes, I think you might be on to something.'

Chapter Forty

Isobel was upstairs painting when the sound of footsteps scampering up the stairs reached her. 'Just walk, Agnes. Remember!' The maid had a habit of flying all through the house when sedate walking was fine, but she seemed to live her life at full throttle.

The two of them had both suffered dreadfully in the Zeppelin blast last autumn. Mrs Finch had packed the pair of them off to her sister in Scotland for months, far away from any potential raids. It had even been reported in the papers that Isobel had died. She might as well have. The minute her broken and bruised arm had healed enough, she'd dashed off a quick letter – *don't believe anything in the newspapers, I'm not dead, it was a mistake*. She'd included her new address, but she'd never received a single letter back from him. Not one.

The shiny, pink-faced maid burst into the room where Isobel was poised, paintbrush in hand in front of her easel. 'Beg pardon, Mrs Dunwoody. Letter for you. Says War Office on it, see.' She tipped her head and pointed at the words.

'Thank you. I can read it myself.' Isobel snatched it out of her hands. The news in the papers had been full of this new battle at the Somme, wherever that was. Dreadful numbers of men killed. She ripped the envelope open, not daring to breathe, scanning the words as fast as she could. She let out her breath. She couldn't get her head around the words on the page. Her knees wobbled as she backed into a chair for support. She had prayed this would never happen to him, but here it was in black and white. 'It's Wilfred. He's been badly injured. I must go to him.'

'Yes, miss.'

Isobel gazed out at the bright green leaves fluttering in the gentle breeze of a London summer. Her second summer away from her own family. Her heart ached for the way things used to be. Cecily had written to say she'd be in town soon, she'd had notice she'd be sailing for a new nursing position in Alexandria. How much things had changed in such a short space of time. And now this awful news of Wilfred. Despite her previous opinion of him, she had come to be very fond of the serious, kind man. He wrote beautiful missives about how they would set up home together when the war was over. His latest idea had been moving back to Summer Hill in Ireland. Peace and quiet and the waters of Strangford Lough to soothe his nerves. He never forgot to enquire about her and George, no matter what he must have been going through. The poor, poor man. She would do whatever she could to bring comfort to him, even if her stomach constantly churned with the emotional double life she led.

'Make me up some food to bring with me please, Agnes. Ask Cook for bread and scones and some of those nice biscuits she makes. I'll be away overnight I expect, so not to keep dinner either.'

'Yes, miss. Anything else?'

'Send Minnie up, please.' Agnes did one of her quick bobs and not one of her dramatic-pretending-to-curtsey-for-the-audience curtseys, for which Isobel was grateful. Her heart couldn't have taken it. Poor Wilfred, he hadn't written himself which suggested it was worse than normal. How he'd managed to escape the war so far with just minor injuries was a mystery. Whenever she wrote to him, which was frequently, she reminded him that he was just lucky, not charmed. There could still be something just around the corner for him and not to take any chances. He always answered her by saying that he'd never take chances, not whilst he had to take care of her and George. A grateful pang echoed in her heart for the steady man, a faithful and solid presence in her life this past year and now he was probably gravely injured – yet her immediate thought had still been of Edward. The guilt she carried was unbearable. Poor darling Wilfred, yet it was still Edward she shed her tears for at night.

Minnie tapped the door lightly. 'Bad news, miss?'

'It's Wilfred. I've to go to Netley. Would you make up an overnight bag for me please?'

'Would you like me to come with you? I know you don't need me as such, but just for the company.'

'That's very kind, but not today. Once I see how he is, I might send for you tomorrow. I may stay on longer.' She exhaled loudly. She had to put aside her own feelings now and be there for her husband.

'Not looking forward to meeting his mother again, I presume?'

She smiled wistfully. 'You read my mind. But Wilfred told me last year he'd put me down as his next of kin. So, if this has arrived it must be serious. I owe it to him to visit as soon as possible.'

'I understand. Well then, you better get those hands washed and your clothes changed. Mrs Dunwoody would hate to meet you smelling of paint. You might get to see Cecily if you're down that way?'

'Yes, I might. Although we're expecting her next week.

I'm sure she's as busy as ever. Why don't you post her a letter, explaining what's happened? Tell her I'll do my best to book into The Swan, just in case.'

'Right then.'

Isobel took a cab direct to Waterloo station and caught the afternoon train. She wasn't sure whether she'd get to Netley hospital today, but if she booked into The Swan for tonight, then she'd be able to see Wilfred the day after. Poor man. She prayed it wasn't too serious, no matter how ghastly the Dunwoodys had been to her over George, no one deserved to lose their son. No one.

The sun burnt through the clouds early the next morning and Isobel slipped into a light pleated skirt with matching short-sleeved blouse. She had surprised herself how quickly she'd taken to the new styles. She patted her cropped bob.

Clutching her handbag, she steadied herself outside the main entrance of the hospital. It stretched out either side of her as far as she could see. She had no idea of where Wilfred might be. It took a long wait in the main corridor before she was sent to the correct ward, but was told to come back after lunchtime when the ward would be open to visitors. Isobel promptly ignored that; Wilfred could be hanging by a thread and she had to be sure he'd still be alive if she came back even three hours later.

He was in hut twenty-four and she knocked sharply on the correct door and opened it, stepping into a small hallway. 'I'm looking for Captain Dunwoody, please. I'm his wife,' she said, smiling brightly and waving the official letter she'd received.

The nurse to whom she'd addressed barely stopped but said she'd speak to Sister. Isobel sat down on a lonely wooden chair and waited. Forty-five minutes later, she was called.

'We weren't expecting family today, Mrs ...'

'Dunwoody. Mrs Dunwoody.'

'You're his wife?'

'Yes.'

'I see.' By her expression, Isobel guessed she thought numerous incorrect things about her, but no matter. She was here.

'Might you tell me what state he's in? His injuries? I just got the letter from the War Office. There's no indication of how severe it was.'

The Sister appeared to size her up once more and then explained. 'He's lost both legs and has multiple other injuries, but he is awake and has been asking for you. The artist, I understand.'

If the news hadn't been so upsetting, Isobel might have snorted at the lady's pronunciation of the term 'artist'. She made Isobel sound as bad as a lady of the night.

'Follow me.'

Isobel steeled herself for the extent of his injuries as she followed the erect back of the dark blue uniformed sister. As they walked past the two long lines of beds, she kept her eyes firmly on the trailing ribbons of her pristine apron until they stopped at Wilfred's bedside. He had one small bandage around the top of his head, his left arm was heavily bandaged, and most of his torso but other than that it was still him. Just the missing space under the covers where his legs would have been.

'Hello, Wilfred. It's me.' She sat down in the wooden seat next to him and gently touched the only space of unbandaged skin that she could see on his right hand.

'I knew you'd come.' His voice was groggy and drawn-out.

'I came as soon as I could. I'll stay nearby for now.'

'Mother will turn up, I imagine. Best not.'

Every time he spoke, she could tell he struggled to get the words out without suffering.

'Did you let her know?'

'I sent her a telegram as soon as I found out. I just wanted you to know I cared. You've been very kind to me over the last year. Now it's my turn to reciprocate.'

'Thank you. Long road … back to full health. Come back though.'

'I will. Of course I will. I had no idea how things were with you. Might I come back tomorrow, then? I could come daily, avoiding your mother of course.'

He shook his head briefly. 'Write.'

'I will. One of the nurses can send me a letter back. You'll get better, Wilfred. I know this is a big set-back for you, but we'll get through it.' She wiped away the tears that seeped from her eyes.

'Your hair.' Only his eyes moved, she noticed; he kept the rest of his body as still as possible.

'I know. I rather like it. What do you think?'

'Hmmm.' He couldn't speak any longer; the pain must have been unbearable. She squeezed his hand once more then stood up, kissing him lightly on the cheek.

'Take care, Wilfred. I'll send lots of letters, I promise.' Tiptoeing away from his bed, she noticed a nurse beckoning her over. Isobel went to her. The nurse led her outside to the hallway before speaking.

'Sister wants to see you. Wait, please.' Isobel sat on another wooden chair and waited. And waited some more. She determined she'd go and ask, perhaps she'd been forgotten, but then she heard the efficient tip-tapping of someone approaching.

'Mrs Dunwoody?'

'Yes.'

'I have Captain Dunwoody's personal belongings here.'
She held them out to Isobel. A small bundle of letters tied
up in string, his watch, gold ring, and a pristine cream envelope on the top, in a hand she didn't recognise. Sister was
still speaking, but she couldn't concentrate. The envelope
had a name and address for Lt E Dunwoody, somewhere in
London. She moved the bundle in her hands, so she could
read it all.

'Did you hear me?'

'Pardon. Sorry … this letter … where has that come from?'

'One of the VADs took it down for him this morning. He
was most insistent it should get posted today. But since you
are now here, you can see it gets delivered for him. Now, did
you hear what I said about Captain Dunwoody?'

'Yes … no. Injuries?'

'Substantial. He is very sick. Very sick,' she reiterated. 'You
need to be prepared for the worst. He has internal damage
as well as his legs. Have you notified his parents?'

The words were swimming around in her head, mixed
up with Edward's address. London. Edward was in London,
yet Wilfred was here and critically ill. She was wracked with
guilt even thinking of one brother when the very one she
was married to needed her more than ever. 'I sent his mother
a telegram.'

'Good. Tell her to come immediately. You may return
tomorrow afternoon. Where are you staying?'

Isobel fumbled about, pulling out one of her cards from
her purse and the pencil she always carried. She scribbled
down the name of the hotel and handed it back, dislodging
the parcels of letters onto the floor. She apologised and bent
down to scoop them up. Stained with mud and blood and
lord knows what, she recognised the handwriting on them

316

as they lay scattered on the floor. Some were from her, and some were from … Edward.

From *Edward*. From him, when he was … where exactly?

'Mrs Dunwoody?' The authoritative voice echoed above her. The sharp tones reminding her of Lavinia Dunwoody.

'Yes?' she said, looking up.

'Are you quite well?'

'Yes, yes, of course. I'm fine. I might sit here a little longer to gather myself, if you don't mind.' She wasn't fine, far from it. To the rest of the world, she looked like a dutiful wife, yet inside she was exhilarated to find an address for Edward. She must be a dreadful person.

'Hmm. I'll send someone out with a glass of water,' she said in the sort of tone that suggested it was an imposition and not a kindness. Turning smartly on her heel, she was gone almost immediately, leaving Isobel on her knees in the corridor, weeping.

Isobel climbed back into the empty chair, her legs wooden and numb. She smoothed the address with her finger, over and over, 10 Palace Green, Kensington.

10, Palace Green, Kensington.

She could walk to it. Any day at all during the summer when she'd been in London, painting, she could have walked over in the morning. Half an hour. He had been so close. Why hadn't she known?

Why hadn't Lavinia Dunwoody told her?

The envelope wasn't securely fastened. Her finger found its way to the hole. The rest of the noises in the hospital vanished, washed away by the effect of this envelope before her.

One tug, it flapped open.

A letter to a brother, from a brother. She was prying. It

317

was none of her business, but she still did it. She slid the cream paper out, neatly folded. Immaculate.

One page, four quarters. She unfolded it slowly and stared at the words.

Royal Victoria Military Hospital, Netley
July 16th, 1916

Dearest brother,
If I should die, I want you to know I did my very best for her as agreed.
If I live, you need to know I'm not giving her up without a fight.
I love her with all of my heart.
W.

Her chest burnt so badly she wanted to smash her fists down on his stumps and hurt him, the same way her heart felt right now. Raw. Bloodied. Damaged.

But she didn't.

He was already in pain.

And she had Edward's address.

As agreed? What did that mean? She wasn't a parcel the brothers could shift between the two of them. She read the letter thrice over, concentrating hard on the meaning of the words. She had no answers unless she was also being unfavourable about Edward – but she just couldn't.

When was she *agreed?*

She slipped back into the ward and sat, watching him sleep. Watching the terror race across his features as he faced down some unknown demon that she could only ever imagine.

Her throat gagged on the smell of dried blood, and she tried to banish visions of Edward lying somewhere just as helpless. Was he disfigured in the same way? Broken? Incomplete?

Unable to gaze any longer on his mutilated body, she found peace instead in a small vase of flowers on the side table next to his neighbour. Bright blue cornflowers entwined with sweet peas in every shade of girls' dresses that you could ever paint, and then lavender, freshly cut from someone's garden. His mother's perhaps? A wife? The soldier next to Wilfred was bandaged so thoroughly that it was obvious he'd never make it home to see any of that precious garden again. Would Wilfred?

And Edward?

Isobel remained in the hard wooden chair until he stirred, his eyes opening, registering panic whilst he struggled to remember where he was. Had Edward ever done that?

Her heart, beaten as it was, softened as she registered the physical, then mental anguish that lay thinly beneath Wilfred's skin. She made soothing noises and stroked his uninjured hand.

'You're still here.'

'I am.'

'Thank you,' he whispered. Her presence alone seemed to give him relief from his demons.

'Tell me truthfully, Wilfred.' She struggled to keep her voice modulated. 'Did Edward ever ask about me?' She couldn't stop the tear that accompanied the words sliding down her cheek.

Guilt surfaced then. Guilt as hard and as fast as a bullet from a German Mauser was etched over his face. Instantly, she regretted it, but it was done.

He swallowed, eyes swivelling to the corrugated-iron roof before he spoke. 'You know?'

'They gave me your letter to post. I read it. I'm sorry.'

A fat bumble bee flew in through the open window and circled the perfumed posy next to them.

'All the time. Isobel...' He stretched out a finger as though to beg her not to abandon him. She moved a fraction away.

'Does he ... does he know about George?'

'Yes. Yes, and it kept him alive, Isobel, I promise. The hope of you and George. He stayed alive because of the two of you. As it keeps me alive.' His eyes were wet now and he turned his head toward the bee that consistently nudged and searched for its just rewards. 'Don't leave me, Isobel. Please. Forgive me. I just wanted to keep you for myself. Was that so very wrong? I love you. Stay.'

Slowly she stood up, the precious letter between finger and thumb. 'I'll return when I've found him and not before. You hurt me.'

'I know.'

Satisfied, the bumble bee stopped buzzing and nestled inside an open flower. The perfume it released pretending that, just for a moment, this was a normal day.

'If I can find a way to make this work with the three of us, I will. I care for you so much; you must understand that. Your presence in my life over the last year has been such a help, and, as soon as I can, I will bring George to visit you. Rest now and conserve your strength. I'll be back as soon as possible. Goodbye, Wilfred.' She bent, kissing him gently on the forehead; the only uninjured part of him. As she walked out of the ward the fragrant flowers faded and, once again, she gagged on the smell of dried blood and bodily fluids. She just made it outside the hut before she retched and her breakfast splattered on a patch of dried grass.

Chapter Forty-One

She packed up her belongings in Southampton and got the evening train back to Waterloo. She checked and double-checked the address on the letter. She re-read the letter, plenty of times. She even thought of reading the older letters, but couldn't. Whatever was between Wilfred and Edward should stay that way. She had the address she always wanted and, for now, that would suffice. She departed the train station and went to a taxi cab that was waiting.

'Ten Palace Green, Kensington, please.' Even saying the address out loud hardly made it real. She whispered it again and again. *Ten Palace Green.* How long had he been there? Days? Weeks more likely, if Wilfred had the address. Virtually around the corner.

The cab pulled up outside the tall red and cream brick building, set back off the street with its own drive and manicured gardens. She could have walked past it many times and not known it was a hospital.

The driver held her door open and placed her suitcase by her feet. She handed him the money and then stood on the pavement, riveted to the spot. It was late. They'd be having dinner, she presumed. It wasn't even a suitable time to visit but yet she couldn't have gone home. Not yet. Not when he was so close.

She opened the gate and took two steps closer to the entrance. Breathe, Isobel. He might not be here at all.

Two more steps and she was in front of the immaculate front door. The highly polished knocker was in the shape of a lion. Palms perspiring, she reached out and tapped it. Then instantly worried in case it was too loud and would scare the men, or too quiet and nobody would hear.

But they did.

A VAD answered the door, her uniform all crisp whites and blues. 'Yes?' she asked, smiling at Isobel.

'I'm ... I'm looking for someone. I believe he is here.'

'A name?' the nurse asked when Isobel didn't continue.

'Sorry. Sorry, yes. Lieutenant Edward Dunwoody. I have a letter from his brother, you see. This is the address I was given.'

The nurse seemed to wrinkle her nose before hesitating. 'The officers are at dinner right now, and we don't accept visitors except by arrangement...'

'But is he here? Is Edward here?'

'What name shall I say?'

'Mrs Dunwoody, Isobel Dunwoody.'

'Isobel?' She repeated Isobel's name in such a way that suggested it meant something to her. 'Wait here, please.' The door clicked shut with a definitive bang.

It had been a long day and Isobel knew her emotions were bubbling very close to the surface. If they said he was inside, would she be able to go home without seeing him, or would she cry right here on the doorstep and demand to be let in? She hoped she didn't disgrace herself.

She was aware of a noise a split second before the door was flung open. A man with a cheery bow tie and tweed jacket opened the door. 'Hello. Miss Seaforth said you were looking for someone. I'm Dr Pettigrew.'

'Yes. Edward Dunwoody.' She pulled the letter out of her bag once again. 'His brother has been badly injured, and he wanted this delivered. I thought ... as I was so close ...' She stopped and stifled a sob. 'Please, tell me, is he here?'

'Your name, miss?'

'Mrs Isobel Dunwoody.' She pulled a handkerchief from her pocket. 'He would know me as Isobel Harris.' Even trying to explain that was like a knife to her heart. 'Please, is he here?' Her tears fell now; so much had happened today.

'You'd better come in, Mrs Dunwoody. But please, this is unorthodox at the very least – you must not make a fuss. Agreed?'

'Yes.' She nodded.

'Allow me.' He kindly lifted her suitcase and carried it inside the double-fronted townhouse. He led her directly to his office and closed the door behind. 'Please sit. Tea? Something stronger, perhaps?' He perched on the large desk that dominated the room.

'Gin, if you've got it. It's been an emotional day.' She wiped away the tears that kept creeping into her eyes and watched as he opened bottles and poured them both a drink.

'Did you come straight here?'

'From Netley. Yes. His brother Wilfred has very ... substantial injuries.'

'I'm so sorry.' His voice was soft and reassuring and made her cry more. 'Will he ... is his life in danger?'

'Probably. I'm not sure. It was such a shock and then a muddle when I found Edward's letters and you see I've been waiting so long to find Edward and Wilfred knew all along where he was and never told me!' Her voice increased until she was wailing and beseeching the doctor. 'Just put me out of my misery. Is he here or not?'

He looked down at his feet as though considering his reply before answering her. 'He is, yes.'

At long last, her body softened. The burden that she'd

carried for the last two years shifted. She breathed in deeply and out again. 'Thank you.' She was satisfied to sip her gin now, letting the alcohol do its magic and seep into her bones, reaching all the aches and pains she'd been carrying.

'Have you eaten?'

'No.' She watched him push the bell and shortly after the same nurse tapped lightly on the door and peered around it.

'Miss Seaforth, could you arrange for a tray for us both to be brought in here please? I shall be eating in here tonight with Mrs Dunwoody.'

'Of course.' The nurse departed and the door closed shut again.

'I married his brother. It's all such a mess. I used to be his fiancé until he disappeared. I thought he was dead, you see! The family said he was dead!' She burst out crying again.

'It seems we have a bit of a problem then, Mrs Dunwoody. There seems to be more than one misunderstanding.'

'Call me Isobel, won't you? It's all very difficult. I just want to see Edward for myself and explain things.'

Pulling his pipe out of his pocket he chewed on it before replying. 'So, you are his sister-in-law then? Family?'

'Yes. I wish I was his wife, truly I do, but things worked against us. Tell me truthfully, is he well?'

'He asks after you daily, Isobel, and that is the truth. He has a very small photo of you and another of a baby.'

'George. His son. He's such a dear thing. He's so blond, just like him.'

'The thing is, Edward thinks he's well, but he's not. This is a Special Hospital for officers, do you understand what that means?' She shook her head, the words sending a shooting pain through her head. 'It's for men, officers, whose mind is not what it should be. They are generally physically well, but they are still suffering in some way. Nerves, neurasthenia, shell shock, memory loss, all of these things.'

'What about Edward?' she whispered.

'He was shot in the head when he was trying to escape. The bullet skimmed the side of it, making him fall; this injury triggered some of the damage, but he endured a lot of... unpleasantness... during his captivity.'

She dabbed at yet more tears that still persisted to wet her face. 'He has a rug like that, back in Cairo.'

'He said.'

'Will he recognise me?'

'Oh, of course. That doesn't seem to be a problem.'

'So, what is his problem, exactly.'

'Flashbacks – unpleasant ones. An uncontrollable rage at times, although that does seem to have abated for now once we promised to look for you. Memory loss is his worst problem. Sleeplessness... I could go on.'

'He doesn't remember things?'

'Yes. That is the main problem.'

The door opened again and a tray appeared around the door before the eager face of Miss Seaforth. She set the tray down on the large desk before handing a plate over to Isobel. 'Salad tonight. Quite warm weather we've been having. You're the artist, aren't you?'

Isobel looked up, surprised. 'I am. How did you know?'

'Edward never stops telling us how good you are.'

Isobel dissolved into tears again. 'Oh, my poor boy. I just want to see him; can't you arrange that?'

'We will, of course. But I need to do it slowly, you must understand. Prepare him. I'm positive a surprise won't be good for him. Let's eat first, and then I'll talk to him,' Dr Pettigrew said.

'I'll be back with your pudding. I couldn't carry everything.' Miss Seaforth left.

Isobel tried to eat, but it was awkward sitting with a man she didn't know. Dr Pettigrew kept up a general chit-chat, asking her about Cairo, telling her things Edward always talked about.

'One thing I must ask you about if you don't mind, is that his parents kept insisting you were dead. They even had a newspaper with your demise in it.'

'It was a mix-up. I lost my purse when a German Zeppelin dropped bombs near the Lyceum in Covent Garden. I was injured, but my purse ended up next to another woman who was killed. But his parents know I'm not dead. I've seen his mother since then. I'm married to his brother. They would know if I was dead or not.'

'It has caused him undue amounts of stress. Have you any idea why they would persist with this lie?'

'They don't like me. They want him to marry Lucy Hartington. I don't know.' She wailed again. 'Mrs Dunwoody is unusually vocal against me, she always has been. How long has he been in England for? I know nothing. Even Wilfred kept it from me.'

'He's been with us a few weeks. Not long, but he's not ready to leave here, not for a long time. I must be clear on that.'

'Please!' She looked up at the doctor and her eyes filled again with tears. 'I love him so much. I need to see him. I'm sure I can help him. Please can't it happen tonight?'

He chewed on the end of his pipe, his other hand stuffed deep into his jacket pocket, eyes cast to the floor. 'I'll go and speak to him, Miss ... Mrs ...'

'Isobel.'

'Isobel. But I have to be the one to decide if he's ready for this. What about your marriage?'

'Don't mention it yet. I'll find a way to tell him.'

'Wait here.' He nodded again and then left.

Isobel slumped back into the chintz armchair, trying to stifle her sobs, but it was useless. It had been a very long, emotional day. Edward was so close, within touching distance, but none of the circumstances were ideal. It was all a mess. Her mind kept jumping back to the letter. *As agreed.* What did that even mean?

'Hello, old chap.' Dr Pettigrew approached Edward as he slumped in an armchair in the large sitting room. The evening air was warm, daylight still lingering, and London sparrows were still swooping around outside in the street. Edward had taken to chewing an empty pipe for want of giving his hands something to do. 'Fancy a walk?'

This was something different. All his senses alerted, he sat up straighter. 'Yes.' Dr Pettigrew said little but indicated with a tilt of his head and a jab of his pipe which way they were to go. They went outside.

They walked in silence at first, listening to pigeons arguing over the few scraps they'd come across and the motors spluttering and coughing up the road. 'How's things, Edward?'

'Fine. Today I am fine.'

'Good, good. No headaches?'

'Not today, no. Have you found her?'

'Why do you ask?'

'You're acting strangely.'

'Ah.' The doctor sucked on his pipe a bit more. 'The thing is, we never talked about what would happen when we found her.'

Edward's skin prickled. 'You have found her, haven't you?'

The doctor made one of those strange noises that was neither a yes nor a no. 'Well, let's just say she has found you.'

'She has? When, when can I see her? Is she here? In London?' He twisted his head round, looking back at the townhouse as they kept walking the other way.

'Calm. Calm. Let's talk about what might happen if she came to visit and straighten out any misconceptions you might have.'

'What are you talking about?' Edward stopped on the pavement and stared at him. 'I need to see her, I must see that she is well, and not struggling and that she knows I love her. I must!'

'Yes, yes, all that. But you also need to understand that just because you've found her, that when she visits you here, that... it's not an instant fix and you get to go home with her. We need realistic expectations of what might happen.'

'I understand.' His heart raced even though his mouth spoke words that sounded calm. 'But she found me? She was looking for me?'

'Yes. She found your address very recently. Today, if you must know. She contacted me straight away.'

'She still loves me?'

'I believe so. But, as I am your doctor, I need to manage your expectations. Things... well, after such a long time separated, don't expect things to be exactly the same. Do you understand?'

Edward nodded, but his eyes darted up and down the street. She really was here, close by. His heart could barely cope. It would explode within him. After all this time apart, they would be together again.

'Edward, your relationship with her will have changed. People change. You have changed. All those things make the situation... delicate.'

'When can I see her? Tomorrow?'

'Edward, listen to me.' Dr Pettigrew made his patient look at him. 'Yes, you can see her, very soon, but do you understand you will still be a patient here, under my care for several more months? Are you listening to me?'

'I am. You're not letting me out just because she's turned up. That's it, isn't it? I'm still a bit forgetful and not fit, I know all that. But I can see her?' he persisted, an enormous smile plastered on his face.

The doctor sighed heavily. 'Yes. You can.'

'Tomorrow? I'll never sleep.'

'How about tonight?'

'No! She's here? Actually here? Right now?' He looked back up the street. The sky had magically changed colour; where before it had been a murky white, it had imperceptibly flushed rose pink. *A fitting tribute to the way I feel now*, he thought. The sky matched Isobel's hair.

'I'll speak to her, shall I? No running away together though, heh! You're not the young man you think you are.'

'I'd miss breakfast,' he joked. Which was a running joke between the two of them because every day Miss Seaforth checked if he'd eaten his morning porridge. And some days he'd eaten twice. He still had days when his memory completely vanished, and he couldn't claw it back from whatever dark crevice of his brain it had slunk into. They were almost back at the front steps.

'So where do you want to see her? Have you any thoughts? Outside? Inside?'

The clouds above London were intensifying into the most abundant display of Isobel's paint palette. Pink, salmon, rose, gold. 'Here. Just here on a London street,' he answered, his voice quiet and resigned.

The doctor nodded and slipped quietly up the couple of small steps to the front door. It opened almost immediately, and Edward knew someone was watching for them. He could wait though. This moment; he had to imprint it on his defective brain, knowing that somehow it would slip through the cracks of grey matter that was inside, but it would still be there. He'd learn how to find it again. He had to remember it all.

The door opened again – a person was waiting just inside, hidden at first, as the lights were off due to the black-out. Then came a female, with a light-coloured dress flowing around her body, making a delicate whooshing sound as she moved. A small cream hat was hiding her face, but the strange light that surrounded them now lit up the hair that had escaped from under it. Rose gold. Isobel.

'Edward?'

They stood, a few feet apart, each smiling at the other, drinking in the other's appearance, checking for changes, for things that were the same. He removed his peaked cap so she might see him better.

'Isobel, my love.' Two steps and they were within touching distance. Edward lifted his hand and she met his – fingertip to fingertip – then pressing further until their palms connected. 'I've dreamt of this moment so many times.'

'It's really you.'

'It is.' He moved his fingers now, clasping her whole hand, stepping forward another step, hardly daring to breathe in case she wasn't real. He pulled her fingers towards his face and kissed them, gently, savouring the feel of them. 'Linseed and turps.' He laughed. 'Still the same, Isobel.'

She laughed, then cried, an anguished sob escaping from her throat and her other hand stretching forward, reaching for him, grabbing his lapel. 'Hold me. Are you real?'

'I'm real. I love you.' He reached around her, holding her tight, drinking in her scent, her warmth, her softness. 'Get rid of the hat, I can't see you!'

Isobel laughed again through her sobs and wriggled in his arms just enough so that she could toss away her hat. 'There. Is that better?' She leant back a little, scanning his face, searching for the features she remembered, and those that were new. 'My darling boy. You are safe now. Safe.' Tears rolled down her cheeks in profusion and she couldn't have stopped them if she'd tried. He held her tighter now, his cheek pressed against hers, his lips kissing her ear and her hair.

'You cut it?' he laughed.

'I did. Such a nuisance.'

'I like it. I can't believe you're here in my arms.'

'I am, my love. Right here. Kiss me.' She leant back now, tilting her head, watching his eyes and then their lips connected once more.

He kissed her gently.

He kissed her softly.

He kissed her as though his life depended on it.

They rested then, safe within each other's arms, inhaling the scent of the other. Not wanting this, their first moments reunited, to end.

'You're shaking, Edward.'

'It's not so bad as it used to be. Are you ready to go back in? I need something to steady my nerves, and I want you to meet someone.'

'Of course. Whatever you think is best.' Not letting go, he led her back to the front door and up the steps. Miss Seaforth and Dr Pettigrew were watching from the front window.

331

'Ah. There you are. Come in, come in.' They were directed back into the doctor's study where Edward sank onto the sofa.

'My legs. I do beg your pardon, Isobel. I'm not quite myself yet.'

'How's the head?' Dr Pettigrew interrupted, looking directly at Edward.

It brought it straight back to her, though, that Edward was still a patient. She had both of the brothers to look after now.

'It feels relatively fine, for now. I won't be able to sleep though. When will you be back, Izzy? Where are you living by the way?'

'Tea, anyone?' Miss Seaforth interrupted, smiling at them both.

'Something stronger, if I'm allowed. We need to celebrate, do we not? Have you two met, by the way?' Edward asked.

'Not really,' Isobel said.

'Miss Seaforth has been very helpful. She found one of your paintings.'

Isobel was surprised. 'Which one?'

'I bought it actually,' Dr Pettigrew replied. 'It's behind you.' Speechless for a moment, Isobel twisted in her seat. Her painting, *The Returning Soldier*, was behind her on the study wall. 'Very fine it is too.'

'Good heavens. Do you like it?'

'It is very accurate. It touches something deep within me. Everyone comments on it.'

She was touched. The very painting that she'd laboured over and cried over and thought of Edward constantly whilst she painted, was actually *here*. Her first instinct was to be embarrassed, but she stopped – reminding herself that here, in this building, were the men she painted it for. 'How did you know it was mine?'

'Well, a bit of sleuthing, if you must know. Edward thought it was your style, and just the initials there, we were still trying to find you though...'

'But then I found you,' she replied. Edward smiled back; his old, boyish smile that she remembered so well. His eyes hid something else though; a pain, or a terror, locked deep within. She'd seen it so often when she'd been at Bexley or at Waterloo Station. The unknown of what had happened to him buried itself deep within her. She prayed she'd be able to help him recover.

'Where do you live, Izzy? Wilfred never gave me your address. I fear it's getting late and although I don't want you to leave, I don't want you travelling too late.'

She flinched. He'd been looking for her just as much as she'd been searching for him. The whole family, Wilfred included, had kept them apart. 'Russell Square. Not far. I'll get a taxi cab soon. The thing is, Edward...' She looked towards the doctor for help. He nodded as he poured them a little nightcap. 'Wilfred's very poorly. He's at Netley. I was there today and that's when I found your address. I need to go back down tomorrow and probably stay over for a few days, just until I see how he fares.'

'I see. Do my parents know?'

'I'm not sure. I sent a telegram to your mother at the Belfast address.'

'She's not there, though. She's in London.'

'I need to let her know then. I'm so sorry. I had no idea. I'll go straight round on my way home.'

'How bad is he?' he asked quietly, his hand and leg quivering on his right-hand side.

'I think you need to prepare yourself for the worst. I should go now. Might I come back tomorrow, Dr Pettigrew? Before my train? Perhaps you have strict visiting hours.'

'Not for you. But don't tell anyone,' he said, winking at her. 'I'd have thought Netley had strict hours though.'

'They do. I ignored them. I'm so sorry, Edward. I want to stay, but I owe it to your mother to let her know.'

'Isobel, we've found each other again. That's all that matters. I will be right here when you come back. Have you a new photo of George? Mine is so old and tattered.'

'I don't have one with me, but I'll get you one. He's at Bexley Hall with Mrs Finch. She's a dear to him. Treats him like a grandson. He's so like you, Edward, I can't wait for you to meet him. Is that allowed?' she asked the doctor again, who had edged his way to the door. 'Can I bring our little boy to visit? He's a baby, but he's awfully good.'

'Perhaps not inside. Sudden noises are uncomfortable for a lot of my patients. But Edward could meet you outside again. You could walk into Kensington Gardens. Would that suit?'

'Absolutely. Do you have a telephone? Or else I will send a letter advising you of the time. Afternoons would be best though; he still naps in the morning.'

'I shall look forward to it. Now, perhaps I could walk you to the road? Much as I hate to see you go, I can't face Mother myself.'

'I'm well used to your mother.'

He laughed. 'You always were the brave one. I'll carry your case and get you a cab.'

All of a sudden, it was over. Their first reunion. Dr Pettigrew trailed behind; Isobel wasn't sure if he was afraid of Edward disappearing, or if Edward's health was worse than he let on. Edward carried her case in one hand and held her other hand as they walked side by side together. 'Did you shrink, Edward, or have I got higher heels on?'

'It's me. No muscles left. I'll be fighting fit before you know it.'

She knew that's what he hoped deep down, but even the walk down to Kensington to hail a cab seemed to tire him. She was grateful the doctor was with him when they said goodbye.

She cradled his face with her hand, kissing him lightly on the other cheek. 'I found you, my love, and I'll be back tomorrow morning. We won't be separated for long and soon you'll be well enough to come home.'

'Where is home, Isobel?' His eyes clouded just then, a shadow racing across them.

Her heart constricted right then. She couldn't bear to check if he'd truly forgotten or was just asking for clarification. She smiled harder, fighting back the tears. 'Home is wherever George and I are. And Wilfred when he's well enough to come home too. It could be in Ireland, or in London, or back in Cairo. Even in Norfolk with the Finches. Wherever you think we'll be happy, my love, just tell me. Good night.'

Their hands lingered, separating slowly before, reluctantly, Isobel let go and climbed into the cab. She gave the address for the Dunwoodys' house and slowly the cab set off. She waved madly through the back window, not looking away until he was out of sight. She broke down then. Huge gasping sobs as though she would split in two. The cab driver made comforting comments and was kind, but there was nothing to be done until she was all cried out.

'We're 'ere,' the driver said, a long time after her sobs had stopped. 'Want me to wait on you, or are you stopping?'

'Wait, please.' Climbing the steps and ringing the bell was worse than waiting to see Edward. The door opened, the housekeeper let her in and called her mistress. Mrs Dunwoody appeared at the door, frowning.

Isobel ignored her expression. 'It's Wilfred. He's badly

injured and he's at Netley. I've seen him today but it's imperative we return tomorrow – we can travel together if you want, only I'm going to visit whether you like it or not. Oh, and I've found Edward, so we can also discuss why you told him I was dead all this while. Now, shall I leave, or not?'

Mrs Dunwoody opened and closed her mouth a few times. 'Stay,' she finally said, her eyes filled with tears. 'Please.'

This must be the strangest day ever, Isobel thought as she ran lightly down the steps to retrieve her suitcase and pay the driver. The best and the worst of her life, colliding.

Chapter Forty-Two

Lavinia Dunwoody gestured for Isobel to go into the drawing room. It was dark, as though Mrs Dunwoody had already retired for the night, except she was still fully dressed. She busied herself by turning on a couple of lamps and seated herself on the edge of an armchair before looking again at Isobel. 'Tell me about Wilfred,' she demanded.

Isobel perched on the sofa, uncomfortably. 'I saw him today. He is very poorly.'

'Yes, but what exactly? Very poorly is what nurses and doctors say. Just tell me *exactly* what is wrong.'

'Fine.' It wasn't hard to hear the steely flint in her voice – the bit that protested Isobel's very presence in this house. 'He's lost both his lower legs, presumably in a bomb blast. The rest of his body seems burnt or badly injured too. He was awake and able to converse with me freely, but in a lot of pain.'

Lavinia rocked silently in her seat, clutching her arms to her body; her sobs silent to start with, before a high-pitched keening noise filled the room. Isobel sat awkwardly on her side of the room, not ready to cross the boundary to offer the woman comfort. If she was being honest, she hated her. She was prepared to be of service to her, to get her down to Netley tomorrow, but warm, sympathetic feelings towards her? No.

Isobel got up a rang the bell. 'Perhaps a restorative drink

might help?' Lavinia didn't seem to hear her and continued, engulfed in her own grief, isolated on the armchair.

The maid arrived. Isobel asked for something for Lavinia and herself, and, even though it was completely rude of her, she asked for something else to eat. The night had been exceptionally long so far and she could see it stretching further. She hadn't been able to eat much before she saw Edward, but now her head swam – with hunger, with weariness or just grief, she couldn't say.

The clock on the mantelpiece had ticked round an entire half-hour before Lavinia made any further attempt to speak to her and Isobel had cleared a plate of sandwiches and a slice of sponge cake.

'How was he, in spirits, I mean?' Lavinia Dunwoody finally spoke.

What could she say? He was badly injured. He'd obviously had surgery recently. He was also suffering from guilt, or remorse, or … what exactly she wasn't sure but it was not easy to explain. 'He was holding up remarkably well.'

'Good. These things can have such a dent on a man's pride you know. I've seen it before. My friend's son. He shot himself rather than be a cr …' She slugged the amber liquid down her throat. 'But he has a lot to look forward to, doesn't he? I mean, he still has his … hands?'

'Oh yes. His mind seemed undamaged too. Just his legs …'

Lavinia nodded again; there seemed nothing to dispute. 'You and he will still find a way,' she gulped, 'to be a man and wife? You have George.'

Isobel inhaled, then exhaled. How to explain … things. 'I'm not walking away from Wilfred. I will be there for him in whatever capacity he needs me. We will find a place to make a home that suits his needs. George is starting to walk

338

now, that will amuse him. There will be lots to look forward to.'

'Good, good, I'm glad. I didn't know how things... were, between you.'

'You never asked. George is your grandson, you know. You can see him whenever you want so long as you don't make demands about how he's brought up. He's a dear little fellow and you are missing out. I'm going to bring him to see both Wilfred and Edward as soon as I can.' Lavinia flushed then, but Isobel didn't care if her words wounded her. 'So, why did you tell Edward I was dead? He didn't deserve that, not after all that he's been through.'

The older woman folded and unfolded her legs, keeping her gaze away from Isobel. 'You can't just demand to upend my family, you know. This was my family first. These are my boys. *Mine.*'

'Who are grown *adults*. Who deserve to make their own life choices and decisions, even if that goes against what you think is acceptable.'

'No they can't!' She leapt out of her seat, glaring down at Isobel. 'They can't. You think you can behave exactly as you like, and everything will be fine, but it won't. Our lives are built on firm foundations and everyone knows how things work. You can't just force your way in and toss it all away.'

'Society has changed, Lavinia. When will you see that? Only your generation hasn't kept up. And yet you will join the ranks of widows and mothers whose sons have perished or who have been eternally broken. That changes society, can't you see? It will tear a huge, gaping hole that we can never cover up again. Your sons will still make their own choices, even now. If Wilfred manages to survive this, you better make damn sure you stand back and give him space to make his own decisions – not demand he move back home with you. If ever anything would emasculate a man, it's having no say in his future. So, we come back to Edward. Why did you lie to him?'

'I was trying to protect *him* if you must know. Because I love him dearly.' Every word was enunciated so clearly and coldly, Isobel shivered in the wake of the woman's frosty tones.

'I love him dearly too, but you never asked me what was best.'

'Love him? You married his brother! How is that love, tell me? Their father and I discussed it, and both felt, with everything as it was, that saying you were dead was better than saying you'd betrayed that love.'

Lavinia's words hit her as painfully as though she'd been slapped. She couldn't defend herself because she felt the same. 'Wilfred asked me to marry him if you need to know the truth. It was his idea all along, in order to give George a proper name.' She stopped, thinking of that letter and what it actually meant, but she wasn't going to discuss it with his mother. 'Now, am I staying the night, or shall I go home?'

'Home?' Lavinia scoffed, her face screwed up in disgust at Isobel's words. 'Every home you have has been given to you by someone else, and yet you still act as though you are the one who's been wronged. When will you learn you are the one behaving badly, with such ugly morals you could bring society down single-handedly? I was going to offer you a room for the night, but I can't bear to have you under my roof a moment longer. You can see yourself out. I would ask that you stay away from my boys, but for reasons I cannot understand they both seem to need you.' She stormed out of the room.

A burning pain hit Isobel square in the chest. She clenched

her hands together for fear she might start throwing the vases or ornaments sitting around the room. How was it possible to hate another person so badly when all they'd used was words as their weapons? Slugging down the last of her own drink she barged out, grabbing her suitcase which still sat in the hall, and yanked open the front door. She vented her anger by slamming it shut and hoped the neighbours would complain. She marched on, not looking left or right or even noticing which direction she was going. Damn the Dunwoodys. Damn them all.

At some point she focused enough to hail a cab and returned to Russell Square. She lay on her bed fully clothed, thinking about everything. She'd found Edward. Edward! He and Wilfred were what she needed to focus on, not Lavinia Dunwoody and her barbs.

Isobel waited as long as she could bear the next morning before phoning Bexley Hall. She left a message, knowing Mrs Finch would still be in bed.

Wilfred badly injured in Netley and I've found Edward in London.

She sent a note to Mr Finch via his club in case he was there. He'd want to know the news too. Her suitcase lay in the hall exactly where she'd left it last night, but her purse, and Wilfred's letters were next to her. She'd forgotten to even give the letter to Edward after all that. Perhaps it would be a way to ask him its meaning.

The other letters were still in her purse; a small bundle tied up with string. She sat down on the second from last step on the staircase and turned them over and over. The top one was addressed to Wilfred, from her. She recognised it of course. Methodically, she pulled the string loose, holding her breath, refusing to consider the consequences. One, two, three more from her, which she lifted and piled up on the step next to her. Then two more with handwriting she didn't know. Two more from her. Another one she didn't know. And the very last. Edward.

Edward writing to his brother. The stamp was French. The edges were tattered and worn, as though it had been carried around for a long time. Slowly she pulled the letter out of the envelope and unfolded it.

2nd Bt, Royal Irish,
Northern France,
October 5th, 1914

Dearest brother,

It pains me to have to ask this of you, but I will.

Things are not as we expected here. The Huns are more plentiful, more aggressive and more determined to invade France. I have been here only a month and already I've written over twenty letters home to parents and wives, telling them their son or husband has died. One day it could be me.

I promised Isobel I'd be home for our wedding. Right now, I can't see how that could be possible. I beg of you this one thing – that if I should perish here, in this foreign land, that you will look after her. I know you love her. Maybe not in the exact way I do, but I know you do.

If, for reasons that are hard to put on paper, she needs to get married (he had underlined it several times)*, and I cannot be there, I beg that you will step into my shoes and do just that, on my behalf.*

If I die before I ever see you again, know that I am

proud to have you as a brother, and look up to you and hope that I can bring honour to our family on the battlefield. I pray to God that he will keep you safe and that we will all be reunited one day in the future.

Your loving brother,
Edward

The page fluttered to the floor. She didn't deserve either brother, they were both doing their best to look after her. Edward had asked Wilfred to marry her. When Wilfred received the letter was hard to tell, but since he'd been steaming home to Liverpool through the Mediterranean at that point, she imagined the post hadn't caught up to him and his battalion until he'd left for France again. And Edward was already missing by then. He could have said, couldn't he? All this time she'd carried this burning burden of guilt within her heart, believing she'd betrayed Edward, and yet Wilfred had done as his brother had requested him to do. A bitter taste rushed up her throat. She had been angry with Wilfred. He could have confided in her, eased how she was feeling even a little. But no.

Two other letters lay in the pile. She had no shame any longer. She would read them.

Dearest brother,

So, I am a father! I am so proud and grateful to you for looking after them. The photographs bring joy to me every time I look at them. He looks like me, doesn't he? I ask and ask, but you never tell me. Where is she? Please give me an address for her. I must write to her myself. Also, you never answer my questions about what will happen when I get out. I think of these things all the time in here, for we have little else to do.

Thank Mother for the food parcels. Tell her to keep sending them – I know that some of mine don't get through. I depend on them to keep me alive. Cigarettes, books, socks, shirts, a new scarf for winter. A razor too, please. Pass all the requests on, please, I can never be sure my letters get through either.

An address, please!

E.

Abbeville,
France,

My dear Wilfred,

Against the odds, I have survived. I escaped but was recaptured and heard from no one until I was rescued by the Red Cross. I have seen Pops a few times now. He says Isobel is dead. I don't believe it. I can't believe it. Tell me it's not true. Are they lying?

I beg you would put me out of my misery, for I cannot see the point in living if she is no longer here.

What of my boy? Pops refuses to discuss anything.

I am desperate for news,
Your brother,
E.

She imagined him in the hospital, injured, emaciated, desperate for answers; for her. And everyone lying to him. Poor man.

She cried silent tears, holding herself tightly, eyes screwed shut, wishing she could remove those images from her mind. He'd wanted her all this time and the family had lied. She didn't know how long she sat there.

The doorbell rang so she answered it, wiping her face as dry as she could muster. Mr Finch.

'I came as soon as I got the message. He's here?'

'He is.' She dissolved into tears again, but the dear man bundled her into his arms and held her tight.

'There now, there.' He led her into the lounge and rang the bell. 'Tea please,' he said as Agnes put her head around the door.

'So, tell me then. Edward is here?'

'He is. I saw him last night.'

'He's well?'

'Well enough. He's suffered badly, he was shot in the head and has trouble with his memory. He recognises me though. He doesn't seem too bad on the surface, but I've not had enough time to be with him, you see.'

'Good, good. I'm so pleased. Wilfred?'

'Wilfred is touch and go, I'm afraid. His injuries are extensive. Poor man.'

'Poor man indeed, but you know we'll do whatever we can ...'

'I do.' She breathed heavily in and out, trying to fill her lungs. 'You already do. It's just ...' Her voice quivered. It was so hard dealing with the anger she was holding on to.

'What else?'

'The Dunwoodys have been lying to me at every verse end, Mr Finch. All of them. I know they don't like me, but even Wilfred has!'

'People do strange things, Isobel, when they feel threatened. Lied about what, exactly?'

'Wilfred had Edward's address all along, well mostly. He could have told me he'd been rescued and was back in France; let me write to him myself. I have letters here which explain.' She blushed then, for she'd forgotten she shouldn't have read them. 'But once Edward was rescued, they told him I was dead. *Dead*. I can't understand why they'd be so cruel. After all he'd been through, why they would persist with that?'

'Oh, my dear! How awful.' He shook his head, brows furrowed and eyes etched with pain. 'That poor man has suffered enough.' Mr Finch came to sit next to her, patting both her hands. 'I can't understand nor explain their behaviour because it seems excessively cruel, but you've found him now. That's all that matters for now. When will you see him again?'

'Now. I'm going to call over before I get the train to Southampton again. As angry as I am at the family, Wilfred still needs me. Both of them do.'

'Good. Might I come with you, my dear? My motor is here. Whatever you need this morning, I'm here to help.'

'Thank you.' She meant that. Truly, she'd have been lost without the Finches. 'I just need to get packed again and then we will go.' She rubbed her forehead trying to erase the piercing headache that had lodged there and the awful feeling that she and Edward had been dealt an exceedingly poor hand, by the very people who claimed to love him the most.

Chapter Forty-Three

Edward was waiting for them, sitting in the room which overlooked the street. He was smartly dressed in his uniform and hat in his hands. He waved and then went to the front door and was down the few steps and straight to Isobel, squeezing her tight in his arms.

'Isobel, my love. I was scared I'd dreamt it.'

'No. Not at all. I am real and so are you. Oh, Edward, it's so good to see you again.' She inhaled the scent of his shaving cream and soap, relishing its familiarity.

'Hello, old chap.'

'Mr Finch.' Edward loosened his hold on Isobel and reached across, gripping the older man's hand tight and pumping it up and down. 'So good to see you again.'

'Us too, Edward. You have a dear, dear boy you know. We've loved having him at Bexley.'

'Thank you. I want to say how grateful I am to you and Mrs Finch for looking after Isobel. I should have done it properly myself, back in Cairo. Totally my fault.'

'Water under the bridge now, old chap. Forget about it. We're just glad you're home safe.'

'Come on, you two. I want to introduce Mr Finch to your doctor, Edward. How easy is it for you to receive visitors? Mrs Finch could bring George up this week. I expect it will be a few days before I can get back.'

Edward looked puzzled. 'I've no idea. I don't have visitors, except Mother.'

'No one else?'

'No.'

Isobel glanced at Mr Finch. He looked as surprised as she was. Surely his old friends and extended family would have been to visit at some point?

Dr Pettigrew met them on the front step. Edward did the introductions, and then the doctor suggested that Edward and Mr Finch took a walk outside whilst he and Isobel had a chat about things. Isobel couldn't quite hear what the doctor said to Mr Finch, but she caught the word 'alone'. She waved off the two men and followed the doctor into his study, lingering a little in front of her painting.

'You have a very particular style, Mrs Dunwoody.'

'Isobel, please.'

'Isobel. Your blocks of colour are quite unique. They suggest the platform, the train and everything else that we know is there, and then the figures in the centre, the injured man, the nurse. All very poignant.'

'I shed plenty of tears over that.'

'I'm sure. Now, back to Edward, take a seat, won't you?' He wafted towards the seat she'd sat in yesterday evening. Even that event seemed so far removed from today, now she'd seen him in the sunshine rather than the dusk.

'So, the obvious things we need to talk about is Edward's health, but also the fact that you're not his next of kin.' She went to interrupt him, but he shushed her gently. 'It's fine, Edward's given me full permission to explain everything to you, and his desire that he be released from my care as soon as is possible.'

'And is that possible?'

'I'd like to give it at least a month, if you don't mind.

But we'll have another chat in two weeks, see how things are. So, the main things you are thinking about are what his long-term health problems are going to be?'

She nodded. She had tossed and turned last night with those exact thoughts.

'Right now, there are a few things: his memory, and the damage from the head injury. Both of which are connected. It may be that now you are here, the memory fixes itself, but until we know for sure, he is not to be left alone outside at all. We don't want him out for a walk and then disappearing again, now do we?'

'No.'

'Then we have the head injury. I'm afraid that too is unknown. I'd like to think it has been causing the memory problems and as it continues to heal, then the memory also heals. There are many new treatments being used, Isobel, and Edward will be able to seek them out, even when I sign him off, but...'

'But what?'

'But for starters he won't ever be going back to fight, and two, I think for the next few years, and possibly permanently, he will be better placed if he has a companion.'

'Like myself.'

'Yes. Or a friend, or a servant. Just to make sure he is well.'

'What about working, Doctor? He will find it imperative to return to running his business, having a purpose to his day.'

'Again, I'm not sure how much he'll be able to do independently, but as long as someone can double-check things.'

Isobel frowned. Edward would despise having someone following him around. He couldn't be that bad, surely?

'Miss Seaforth has a system here for the officers with memory problems in order to help them. She only sets out the correct number of bowls and plates at breakfast time, and they have to leave a card in the bowl to say they've had breakfast. That way she knows who has eaten.'

'And that works?'

'Mostly yes. Edward is fond of eating. He'd suffered badly from malnutrition. What you see now is nothing to how he was when he was first rescued.'

'I see. Maybe he was just hungry?'

'He didn't remember whether he'd just eaten or not.' She hated the pitying look on his face. He didn't appear this bad at all. The doctor carried on. 'Routines are key. Getting him to do the same things in the same order and incorporating a checking system so you know if he has or hasn't done it. Leave things in the same place, for example, say, paperwork. An in-tray, an out-tray, keeping the desk clear of other things.'

Isobel sighed. Edward needed to be treated as an adult. All of this 'organising' would leave anyone angry and frustrated. 'What about pain? You mentioned headaches, I think.'

'Bromide. It works reasonably well. But, also, we pre-empt occasions that might cause distress and, where possible, reduce it.'

'Like his mother?' She couldn't help noticing the twitch in his moustache.

'Let's just say, knowing who his visitors are, and what strain they might give him, are key. You seem to be restorative to his health.'

'His mother wasn't, I imagine. Speaking of Mrs Dunwoody, I must go. I am returning to Netley today to visit his brother. I expect to be gone several days. If it's pleasing to Edward, might Mr and Mrs Finch be allowed to visit, with the baby? I can't understand why he hasn't had other visitors.'

'His parents didn't want any unnecessary visitors, they said.'

'They meant me. They were determined to keep us apart.'

Dr Pettigrew looked thoughtful. 'Let's see how Edward is today after your visit, and I shall make a decision. Does that seem fair?'

'Thank you. I shall pop out and see him. The gentlemen will have had time for a catch up by now.'

Dr Pettigrew nodded and held the door open for her. She spied them outside on the drive. Edward's face lit up when she descended the front steps; he held his arms open to her and enfolded her within them before she'd reached the last step. He swung her around before setting her down beside him.

'I missed you.'

'So did I. Did you sleep well, Edward?' She scanned his face again for any sign that he was suffering. She spotted the white streak in his skin, just above his right ear, where the hair didn't grow the same any longer. A sharp burst of pain, like a white heat shot through her chest, as she imagined what might have been.

'I did. Or at least I believe I did. I felt rested and was up early. I couldn't wait to see you again. We've so much to catch up on. Have you time for a walk?'

'I do. Not long, I'm afraid, I need to check on your mother and see if she's travelling to Netley with me.'

'Mother's already gone. She stopped by this morning.'

'Oh, Edward. Did she upset you?' She could feel a tremor running through him, like an invisible lightning bolt, just beneath his skin. She couldn't tell if this was permanent, or the consequence of his mother. She had so much more to learn about him.

He smiled ruefully. 'Let's just say we had words.' He

laughed then at her expression. 'Come on, let's take another walk.'

He lifted her arm, tucked it through his and they set off down the drive and back towards High Street Kensington. Isobel didn't think the joy she had at such a simple pleasure would ever fade. Shoulder to shoulder, arm in arm, they walked along the pavement, her heeled shoes tip-tapping along the path and birds above their heads singing in the lime green canopy of the London elm.

'But you are well?'

'Isobel, I have found you again. Nothing Mother says could upset me. I promise. I believe you and her already had a little ding dong last night, am I right?'

Isobel flushed. A little 'ding dong' made it seem genteel, a disagreement among friends. It was so much more than that. 'What did she say? I hope she apologised!'

'She's afraid of so many things, Izzy, and losing her place in society jostles for place amongst losing me or Wilfred, or both. You frighten her!'

'I can't change how I feel. I'm not going to change how I behave. I love you and if I have to love both you and Wilfred at the same time, then I will. But I'm not losing you, not ever.'

'I asked him to marry you, Izzy, did he say?'

'No.' She sighed. 'But I read your letter to him. He kept it all this time. I felt so guilty, Edward, you must understand. I thought I was being disloyal to you.'

'After I'd been in France a few weeks and it became obvious things weren't as we expected, I feared you might be pregnant, and that I wouldn't make it back to marry you. I wrote and asked him to look after you if I didn't survive. I'm so sorry. I should have said.'

'Don't apologise. Perhaps I should have said no. We've an

awful mess to sort out now, and I always felt I was betraying you, my love. I never stopped loving you, ever, and we never ...' She couldn't articulate the words. 'He hasn't made it back since. He left for France the same afternoon. He suffered badly too. If only you'd seen him. I thought *I* was helping *him*. He wasn't truthful about you or your whereabouts either, but I can forgive him. Your mother, not so. And what are we going to do about *us*?'

'Let's not th-th-think of the consequences right now. Time enough for all that once Wilfred is better.' He held her tighter. 'I'm so sorry.'

'Don't be. I should have married you in Cairo when I had the chance, but I was scared.'

He stopped. 'Scared of me?'

'No, of marriage.' He locked eyes with her then, holding her close, pulling her hand to his chest. She felt his heart beating so fast, like the reverberations when a motorcycle is just about to set off. 'When I was young, I was up in the attic and I found a drawing book of Mother's. She was artistic, Edward. Yes, my mother!' The expression on his face said he thought otherwise. 'Mother had this book filled with dresses and dresses, all the styles of the day. She could have been good at it. Fashion sketches, they were. She said she learnt how to do them when she watched her father. He was a tailor before he opened his shop. She had such talent and yet when I asked why she didn't draw any longer she said she never lifted a pencil after the day of her wedding. Marriage was when you gave yourself over to the needs of the other and put your own wants away. I was scared, Edward. Scared of losing myself. I panicked. I'm so sorry. It was my fault – we should have got married back then when you asked me.'

Edward held her closer, cheek to cheek, saying nothing

for the moment, just being next to her. When they finally drew apart, he spoke. 'We are meant to be together, Izzy. I don't care if we never get married officially. I don't care if we cause a scandal, but I'm not giving you up. I love you always. You are my soul mate. You are the reason I fought to stay alive in the camps, you and George are my reason for being. We were destined to fall in love.' He stroked the contours of her face, as though he was tracing her features back into his memory. He leant in closer, kissing her gently on her lips. 'I love you, my darling girl, with all of my heart.'

Tears fell on Isobel's lashes and he kissed them away. She still felt the vibrations running through his body, but they were softer now, like a rumble of thunder on a sultry summer's afternoon. When their lips parted, they rested close enough together that their foreheads just touched, her hat having long ago fallen off. The familiar rumble of a motorcar and a toot of an over-eager delivery van broke their reverie. 'I must go back, Edward. Wilfred needs me.'

'I'm jealous, but I understand.'

She remembered the letter still in her pocket, undelivered. Well, it could stay there. Edward didn't need that extra burden with her or his brother. They say *time heals all wounds*, well, maybe she'd have to put that theory to the test.

Chapter Forty-Four

'Isobel!' the familiar voice of her sister carried across the street.

'Cecily, my love. How wonderful to see you.' She held her arms wide open, needing the solid warmth of her sister's unquestioning love for her so badly.

'I heard about Wilfred. I snuck in to see him, darling,' Cecily said, hugging her sister in return. 'And Edward! You must be over the moon after all this time. How is he?'

Isobel buried her face against the comforting shoulder of her sister. She couldn't speak, it was all too painful. 'Fragile,' was all she could whisper.

Her sister continued, 'Come, dearest. I have the afternoon off. Let's walk, we'll find a quiet bench someplace.'

They walked arm in arm. Cecily, still in her blue and white uniform, made eyes at the shorter length of Isobel's outfit and her cropped hair, teasing that she'd turned into Rosalie, who was always dressed in the height of fashion. 'I wonder when we'll see her again?'

Isobel couldn't even speak, her throat was too choked.

'Now, Izzy, this won't do at all.' Cecily led her to a corner of the park with an ancient oak tree providing a shady canopy under which they might hide themselves. 'Remember the old willow next to the pond at Summer Hill? I wonder when we'll make it back home?'

The afternoon sun filtered through the leaves, birds

hopped through the undergrowth and not far away little children squealed with laughter as they played in the pond, splashing water over each other. 'Do you remember when we were young like that and all we had on our horizon was to get married?'

'I didn't, though,' Isobel corrected her. 'I fought against Mother like mad.'

'True. And yet here you are married anyway.'

'If I could go back in time and change my decision, I would in an instant.'

Cecily pulled her close, just holding her and letting her tears fall until she had exhausted herself. After a while, when Isobel's sobs had ceased, she spoke. 'I can't say for certain what will happen, but I do know that you are just as strong as Mother but in a different, more loving way, and you will do the right thing. I've nursed lots of returning soldiers, and truthfully ...' she paused, deliberating over her words, 'I can't see that Wilfred has much of a chance. If he does make it through, after the war, I will come back to join you and help nurse him. We can't see into the future, Izzy, it just unfolds one day at a time. But right now, you are married to him, and you need to be strong and kind. Love him in the best way you can.'

Isobel's shoulders physically ached when she thought too much about the future, but she knew she deserved it. She would dig deep and do what she had to. She dried her tears and filled her lungs with the fresh summer air. 'Let's get some tea, shall we? I shall miss you when you've sailed.'

'Me too. And my nephew of course. Come on. Tell me what he's up to now.'

The two sisters stood up, and arm in arm retraced their steps through the park. It was extraordinary how much life had changed for them in such a short space of time. 'Did you ever hear how Tom was getting on?' Isobel asked her sister.

Cecily flinched a little, holding her shoulders straighter. 'He married another nurse some months ago after calling our engagement off last year. I've been determined not to be melancholy about it. I'd rather be nursing after all.'

'You're brave too.'

'We're both strong, brave women. We have new opportunities all the time and we shouldn't throw anything away.' They held tighter to each other and walked that little bit slower, cherishing their time together.

Chapter Forty-Five

Isobel bought herself a motor. She'd sold another painting and been commissioned for another large one, and what with all the travelling back and forth to the hospital and the train station, she thought it would be jolly useful.

Minnie was aghast when she saw her behind the wheel. 'You can't be driving that yourself, miss. It isn't ladylike,' the maid said, her mouth wide open.

'Of course I can. Times have changed, Minnie, and we have to change with it. I shall name it Bessie. She shall be awfully useful, don't you think?' There was a bit of huffing and puffing, but Minnie had to admit a few weeks later that they'd have been lost without it.

Wilfred hung onto life and Mr Finch had friends that they were able to rent a cottage from, and Isobel, George, Sarah and Minnie moved close to Southampton. Mrs Dunwoody was offered a room with them, but she declined. Everyone heaved a collective sigh of relief. Isobel had tried to build bridges, but it was not to be.

In the first week of September, Edward packed up a small bag and caught the train back to Southampton with Isobel. Dr Pettigrew had given his permission for the trip, understanding how badly Edward needed to see his brother.

'Let me go in first, will you?' Edward asked Isobel when

they arrived. 'I just need time to sit with him, get my thoughts together. How poorly is he?'

She winced. Wilfred had been steadily deteriorating these past few weeks and the patient, steady man she'd known was disintegrating in front of her eyes. Every time she visited, he'd lost more weight and his breathing was more laboured. It was hard to see how he could claw himself out of this, but she'd found it so hard to explain it all to Edward.

She kept an eye to make sure Edward wasn't tiring as they walked from Netley station to the hospital. She could never not be awed by its huge building, never mind the many extra wards built out the back. Her brain spun sometimes trying not to think about the number of men killed and injured in this ghastly war. And it still wasn't over.

The closer they got, the more formal they became with each other. They had to be on their guard; she was a married woman still. She directed him to the right ward and waited outside again – those wooden seats were becoming faithful friends. She didn't want to see their reunion. It was a private matter between brothers.

After a long time, Edward came back. 'I need a moment,' he said, his voice thick and croaky. She opened the door so he could get some fresh air and she knew even by the set of his shoulders it had been hard. *Oh, my love*, she thought, *if I could ease your burden even for one night I would.* He looked back at her, his eyes overly bright with that haunted look in them. 'He's asking for you.'

She stopped at Wilfred's bed. She could find it with her eyes closed now. His skin had taken on an unhealthy pallor. She glanced wildly up and down the ward. How long could he carry on like this?

'Hello, Wilfred, my dear. It's Isobel.'

'I ... knew. Your ... perfume.' His words were hard to

listen to because she knew how much it cost him in energy and pain. His lungs struggled to give him enough air, his stomach rising and falling with each breath, and that pulled on his broken damaged skin. 'Edward ... look ... after ... you.' He looked so sad and defeated. If there was one thing she could sacrifice for them that would fix all their problems, she would do it in a heartbeat.

She squeezed his hand as gently as she could so she couldn't possibly hurt him. 'I'll bring George tomorrow. Just for a minute so you can kiss his head, and if Matron doesn't allow it, I'll stand next to the window again and make him giggle. You liked that.'

He squeezed her hand once more before closing his eyes. She stayed by his side for a while longer until Edward returned, then they said their goodbyes and left. Matron was busy with another patient, but Isobel left a message to say she'd be back the next day and would like to speak to her or a doctor about Captain Dunwoody's prognosis.

'Home?' she asked Edward.

'Please. Our first night under the same roof. I still wish I wasn't due back to Palace Green tomorrow.'

'Me neither.' She paused. 'About Wilfred?'

'Shush. It's done. He looked after you when I needed him to, and he told me to look after you once he's ... gone.' He struggled on the last word.

Twice a week to start with, Isobel and Sarah (who held tightly onto a wriggly and excitable George), took the train from Southampton up to London and spent the day with Edward, each time spending longer together and going further afield. Sometimes they lounged in Kensington Gardens with a blanket and a picnic and she gave Sarah the afternoon off. Edward played with George, letting the baby get to know and trust him. Edward had missed over a year of his life and was determined he would miss no more.

Some days they walked up and down Oxford Street and Regent Street, looking in the shop windows, buying small gifts for each other, and picking out household items that they would use to furnish their own house one day.

One afternoon, when the weather turned inclement and angry lilac clouds hung low over London, they retreated back to Russell Square. George was ready for a nap anyway and he let Edward carry him the whole way up to his nursery where Agnes took over, changing his linen and putting him down to sleep. Isobel pulled Edward by the hand and showed him into the room where she painted.

Edward inhaled. 'It's like coming home; that smell is so you. It's everything I always treasured about you. Linseed and turps.'

Isobel laughed, gently pulling him closer, and slipping an arm around his waist. She pointed out the portrait of George that she'd just started resting on her easel. His large round head and baby blond curls had been pencilled in, but all around him lay blank.

'Where is he sitting?' Edward asked.

'Back in the nursery at Bexley. He has a tiny little baby chair that he sits in when he eats his dinners and he looks at me with such solemn baby eyes. He takes his dinnertime very seriously.'

'Good chap. I never realised how important food was until I was without it.'

'My love,' Isobel hesitated, drawing closer until they were nose to nose. 'I wish I could carry some of your burden for you. Would it help if you shared it with me?'

Edward took a deep breath. How could he ever hurt Isobel's soul with all that he'd been through? He couldn't, because whenever they would lay together, that's what she would remember of him – the bad parts. Not the love they shared. He shook his head a fraction. No, he couldn't share except for a few snippets now and then.

'Couldn't you show me then? Have you any injuries?'

'On my body?' She nodded, gazing at him so carefully he thought he could swim deep into her hazel eyes and it would wash him all clean. 'Well,' he said, stroking her cheek and then letting his hand graze down her shoulder until his thumb stopped over her breast. 'I do have scars. Plenty of them. I just don't want to scare you.'

'I won't be scared. Can I kiss them?'

'Maybe.' He waited, holding his breath, treasuring this moment. He cupped her breast with his hand and dipped his mouth to meet hers, kissing her deeply. He heard her utter a soft gasp as his thumbnail teased her nipple, and both of them pressed closer, both knowing that now was the time. Isobel reached up pulling at his tie, loosening it, frustrated it was taking so long. Skipping out of his arms, she dashed across the room, closing the door firmly behind her, and returned to his arms when he scooped her up and carried her to the chaise longue that was in the room. He kissed her now with an urgency and desire he'd only been able to dream of for two years. 'Damn these buttons!' He laughed as they both struggled to discard their clothes.

They both had memories of it before, back in Cairo, their first few times together. 'We are different people now, Izzy. Are you ready for this?'

'Our love is the same though, better for being apart and for having created our boy together. I've missed you so dreadfully much.' She discarded her blouse and skirt and managed most of the buttons of her chemise before he was naked in front of her. He bent his head to kiss the rosy tips of her breasts before letting his mouth trail further down her body.

'Hurry,' she cried. 'Hurry, Edward. I just need you right now. Two years is far too long.' Tears sparkled in her eyes as she took in the myriad of scars across his arms and torso. Edward could feel her hands circling his chest and tracing the lines on his back created by Werner – but he'd won. He was here, back in London, back with his love and nothing would ever separate them again. Their need for each other was strong and swift but, as Isobel kept whispering in his ear, it was just the first of many, many more times together. He'd survived, and he was home with Izzy safe in his arms, and his own sweet boy sleeping soundly just along the corridor. He'd lost two years of their lives, but now they had a lifetime together.

Chapter Forty-Six

In the last week of September, Edward packed up his kit bag for good. His headaches had reduced dramatically, and he was no longer burdened with the intense rage and mood swings. Being reunited with Isobel and meeting his son had been the best medicine of all. His health was not perfect, but Dr Pettigrew had suggested weekly appointments with him at first, gradually reducing them as the year went on.

'So, how does it feel to be released?' Isobel asked.

'Like heaven mixed with a good dose of normality. I know we said we wouldn't talk about the future, but right now, you and George are my future.'

She leant into him then, letting him surround her with his arms. For so long she thought this day would never be on her horizon – but now it was here. This man, the love of her life, the father of her child, was right beside her, and she'd have to keep pinching herself to make sure she wasn't dreaming. The only downside was that Wilfred his brother, her *husband*, was still incredibly sick.

'Come on, Izzy, let's catch that train.' They strolled down the wide leafy street, where the sycamores were already starting to turn shades of ochre and rust, and the first of the crispy leaves were lying beneath their feet. London carried on as it always did, regardless of bombs from Zeppelins, or bad news. Life carried on.

★

Sunday afternoon, Isobel drove them both to Netley hospital in Bessie. Wilfred had been moved to a corner bed and screens were pulled around him. George was up in Edward's arms, babbling a string of baby words and chuckling and pointing to everyone he saw. Matron spotted them coming and stopped Isobel, her outstretched arm directing her to the row of wooden seats that Isobel had come to hate. The matron looked flustered.

'Wait here, please. Captain Dunwoody already has visitors and they have indicated that they don't wish to be disturbed.' Her clipped tones were as business-like as ever.

Isobel noted Edward skirting behind Matron, and he went in anyway, still carrying George in his arms; his blond curls bobbing just above Edward's shoulder. 'I am his wife, Matron. I should be allowed in.'

'And you will. Soon. But this time you need to say good-bye.'

'I see.' Her lip wobbled and she was glad now of the sturdy seat to rest on. This was it then. Poor Wilfred. A life cut short when he had so much to offer the world. 'What about...' She couldn't bear to ask about arrangements, even putting them into words seemed disrespectful.

'His parents are here now, so I should leave everything up to his father, if I were you. They'll not thank you for interfering.'

Isobel felt the admonishment. She wasn't welcome, not by the Dunwoodys, that was for certain. She stayed on the wooden seat trying not to think about everything that had passed this last year, and the year before. The 'what might have been', and 'the what should have been'. Alice and Wilfred, two precious lives unfulfilled.

Edward came out, leading his mother by the arm and balancing George on the other. 'Go in now,' he said quietly.

Isobel swallowed down the panic that erupted in her stomach. His father would be there. She tiptoed into the ward, conscious of every noise her shoes made on the linoleum.

'Shush, can't you?' Colonel Dunwoody hissed at her.

'Sorry,' she whispered, sitting on another wooden chair. She tried not to move, nor talk but sat a few moments in silence, listening to the rasp of Wilfred's slow breathing. In ... out ... in ... out. Every time he breathed out, she sat, fingers gripping the chair to see if he took another breath. His skin, what she could see of it was mottled blue. His hands, placed by his side over the covers, were blue.

'C ... can he hear me?' she whispered as quietly as she could.

'Yes. Be quiet,' the colonel answered her, gruffly. He turned his face towards her, hissing. 'Look, just say goodbye and go, can't you? You shouldn't be here. Family only.'

She glared at him, but refused to be cowed. Instead, swallowing down her own impulse to cry, she leant forward and spoke softly to her husband, gently touching his hand. 'Wilfred, it's Isobel. I'm here, my love.' His breathing was so laboured she couldn't bear to watch. Each breath worse than the one before, and more time passed before he took his next one. She kissed him lightly on the cheek and stood up. A red admiral butterfly trapped in the corner against the closed window caught her eye. It too struggled and flapped, then stopped. Weary of its effort it rested against the wooden frame, its once-brilliant colours faded and tattered after its battle.

The colonel flapped his hand at her, gesturing her to leave. 'Send them back in.'

She was dismissed. She doubted if Wilfred even knew she was there. *Goodbye, sweet man, let it be quick*, she thought, for this was a horrible way to die. Fighting every fiber of her being to run away as far as she could, she held herself firm and tiptoed outside the ward again. Any kind of noise seemed an insult to what was occurring just yards away. Eyes blurred with tears, she sank gratefully onto the chairs again in the corridor. Edward placed a reassuring hand on her shoulder. She was strong, at least she thought she was, but it was the sight of Mrs Dunwoody with darling George on her lap rocking backwards and forwards, her head buried deep within his curls and keening in a high-pitched tone. 'My boy, my boy.' Backwards and forwards she went, eyes tight with grief, tears pouring down her face until George squawked because she was holding him too tight.

Curious, thought Isobel, *it's not my own grief that will break me, but watching another mother falling headlong into the crevasse of grief over her own son who only had moments left on this earth.*

'It's time, Edward.' Isobel couldn't say the exact words but waved ineffectively in the right direction. 'I'll take George.'

'Mother, come now.' Edward peeled his mother's arms off George and the baby lifted his chubby arms up to Isobel. 'Dadada,' he babbled then cried. Isobel kissed his cheeks and soothed him, tears streaming down her own face. A huge, ragged sob caught in her chest and she knew she must leave before she disgraced herself. She turned back just the once and saw Edward leading his mother back into the ward. Even before she'd turned the corner, the piercing cry of a mother seeing her son just departed this life sent a cold prickle right down her spine. Isobel could only hold George all the closer and walk steadily on. The Dunwoodys needed to be together right now, and they didn't want her present.

Chapter Forty-Seven

Summer Hill, Ireland, August 1920

Even the dragonflies found it too hot to stay out in the sun that afternoon, vanishing beneath the overlapping waterlily leaves at the edge of the water. The sun beat down on the little party that lazed on the banks of the pond, trying to find shade under the willow trees. Isobel sat hunched under her white lace parasol which she had ingeniously propped on the lower branches of the tree above her. The saucer-like brim of her summer hat still blocked her view, so she tossed it away and continued sketching. Edward reclined next to her, socks and shoes discarded, trouser legs rolled up, and his bare feet cooling in the muddy water below the bank.

'This is pleasant, isn't it?'

'It is. Are you comfortable, Ralph? Not too hot for you?' She checked on Cecily's husband.

'I'm fine. Stop asking,' he retorted, fanning himself with his straw boater.

'Honestly, Isobel,' Cecily said, looking at her sister. 'You're turning into Mother, all this fussing and continual checking.'

'I am not!' She beamed back at them, delighted that they had everyone under one roof finally. It had taken Ralph Walker, Edward's comrade and friend from the camps a little time to get orientated to the house and grounds in Ireland – the German guards had beaten him many a time before he had finally been released in 1918, and his sight had never fully recovered, nor had his right knee. He relied heavily on a stick these days, and Cecily of course. Isobel and Edward had looked on with joy as a romance had sprung up between the two of them almost as soon as Edward insisted on bringing Ralph back home for a visit. Now the two men, along with Cecily and Edward's maternal uncle, ran an import business bringing in the Egyptian cotton that Edward had sourced many years ago, and in return they exported Irish linen. There were plenty of things Isobel couldn't stop beaming about.

The others laughed, amused at her reaction. The sound of babies babbling echoed across the pond from the other side of the stables. 'Oh heavens, they must be awake already. Peace has vanished.'

'They'll be fine. The grandmothers will be fighting over who gets to push the perambulator.' Mrs Finch had become more of mother figure than her own mother ever would, but it had surprised both herself and Cecily how much their own parents wanted to see the grandchildren. Even Edward's parents had softened a little once they got to know George better.

'Not in this heat. Not Mother!' Isobel exclaimed.

'Well, all right, perhaps not pushing it, but you know she can't bear not to be with them when they wake in the afternoon.'

Cecily and Isobel had provided the grandmothers with three grandchildren now. George, the oldest at five, thought he was above playing with the babies as he still insisted on calling the little ones. Mr Finch and he had proved perfect partners for learning everything about riding horses and sailing boats.

'Our children are totally spoilt, I hope you know that, Cecily.'

'Well it's not for too much longer. The summer soon goes past, and we must return to Cairo again.' A ringing sound echoed across the meadow. 'Heavens, afternoon tea already,' Cecily said.

'Ice-cold lemonade would be nice.'

'But we must walk to the far side of the house to get it,' Isobel groaned. Tea would be laid out on the tables on the terrace, just like it had been every afternoon all summer. Isobel adored the place and couldn't bear to leave it at the end of each summer, but today it was stifling hot, and the terrace was a good five minutes' walk.

'What's for tea?' Edward asked.

'The same thing we have every afternoon in the summer. Don't tease me, Edward. Salmon and cucumber sandwiches, a Victoria sponge and jelly. Come on. Get up, we'll walk back through the shade. Meet you on the terrace, Cecily.'

Cecily heaved herself up and dusted down her calf-length dress. The shorter-length dress and hairstyle suited her, even though she'd waited years before following Isobel's lead.

'Come on, Izzy, we'll walk back through the woodland, it'll be cooler that way.

'Let's have a look then.' Edward lifted her sketch pad out of her hands. He'd already moved and was kneeling next to her.

'We'll leave the blankets for now. The others might like to come down after they've eaten, but you can help carry my easel, Edward.'

'Certainly.' He went to lift it and her sketchpad flapped open, sending pages everywhere. They dashed about after them, gathering them up and rescuing them from the ducks who had come to investigate.

'You know you're rather good at this, Izzy.' Edward stared at her drawings of him and the children. 'Have you ever thought of exhibiting any of them?'

Isobel smiled fondly at her husband. 'I did, dear, last year. And the year before that. You've forgotten.'

'Have I?' His face clouded with pain. Isobel tried to gloss over it, never wanting him to realise how much his memory still troubled him.

'Never mind. So long as you don't forget I love you very much, that's the important thing.'

'I'd never forget that, would I?'

'Well,' she teased him gently, 'if you did, I could always remind you of it.'

He pointed out the half torso of his that she'd just drawn. She had concentrated on getting his head perfect, and the bone structure correct. Every hair was visible, and even the veins on his arms stood out. 'Can I keep it for my office?'

'Of course you can, my love. I was thinking of painting you again, to match the one from Mena House. Would you like that?'

'Of course.' He looked quizzically at her for a moment. 'Are we happy?'

'You know we are. We've a lot to look forward to. Even if Ireland doesn't stay the same, we've always a home at Bexley Hall, and in Cairo.'

'Ralph and I were thinking of setting up a warehouse in Nice, or somewhere on the Riviera, would you like that?'

'Really?'

He stopped dead in the path, anticipating her delight. 'Absolutely. It would be a good place for the children to grow up, I don't think we'll be returning to Ireland any-time soon, and Cairo is getting a little hot. You and Cecily could pick out a large house overlooking the sea and the grandparents could come for visits every winter. We'd never be lonely.'

'How could I ever be lonely, darling? I have everyone I need right here. You, our children, Cecily. The Finches. Everyone.'

'I agree. I have everything I need right now in my arms. Kiss me, my love. Kiss me.'

The End

Historical Notes

My fictional character, Edward Dunwoody, was a part of the OTC whilst at Cambridge. After war broke out in August 1914, Earl Kitchener published an appeal on 10th August, appealing for 2,000 young men to take temporary commissions in the regular army. Edward Dunwoody was one of those that applied and subsequently joined the 2nd battalion, Royal Irish Regiment, arriving in France in early September to replace junior officers already incapacitated or killed. If this route is incorrect, the inaccuracy is entirely mine.

When I first decided to write a romance set in the First World War, I wanted my hero to disappear in some way. After some initial research into Irish Regiments who were in the right area at the right time, I came across the events of the night of the 19th/20th October 1914 and the mystery of the 2nd battalion, Royal Irish Regiment, and immediately knew I wanted Edward Dunwoody to be a part of that missing battalion.

I read the war diary of the battalion, and as it says on the page, 'Unfortunately little evidence is obtainable of what occurred on this day'. I recreated my fictional scene purely from the regimental diary, and as such, and not knowing any different, I made the battalion surrender by early morning on the 20th, around 6 a.m. I didn't know that there were other, albeit limited, accounts available, and so I must apologise, as in fact the battalion fought on until four in the afternoon, after reinforcements were unforthcoming, and they were surrounded.

In my novel, the point at which the 2nd battalion surrender and any events after that were created purely from my own imagination. I devised the POW scenes from referencing John Lewis-Stempel's book, *The War Behind the Wire*.

I imagined a scenario where the Germans shot and killed any of the Royal Irish soldiers who were injured and unable to stand, and later threw them into a mass grave not far from the village and the battle scene. After I contacted Ronan McGreevy, *Irish Times* journalist and author of *Wherever The Firing Line Extends*, he was able to point me to new evidence that suggests that my fictional account is far closer to the truth. There may well be a mass grave close to the village, where the remains of the soldiers still lie in an unmarked grave. For the sake of their families, and in acknowledgment of the sacrifice those men gave, it would be right and fitting if, one day, they could be found and given a proper, respectful burial.

As it says in Ronan McGreevy's book; 'On 19 October, the strength of the battalion had been twenty officers and 881 men. Two days later, it was one surviving officer, a transport officer and 135 men.'

My fictional character, Edward Dunwoody, was eventually rescued from a POW camp, after surviving the surrender and made it home; the majority of the 2nd Battalion soldiers were not as fortunate.

Recommended reading:

War Diary: 3 Division 8 infantry Brigade Royal Irish
    Regiment 2nd Battalion January 1915 WO95/1421/314
    August 1914–31

John Lewis-Stempel – *The War Behind the Wire – The Life, Death and Glory of British Prisoners of War 1914–18*

Ronan McGreevy – *Wherever The Firing Line Extends – Ireland and the Western Front*

Phillip Hoare – *Spike island: The memory of a Military Hospital*

Andrew Humphreys – *Grand Hotels of Egypt in the Golden Age of Travel*

Acknowledgements

Becoming a published author has been a very long road. I first realised I had an itch to write as my oldest child napped in her cot – she's now twenty-six. They say it takes a village to raise a child, well, it takes a community to support a new writer on their path to publication.

Firstly, huge thanks to Charlotte Mursell (Orion) who saw the potential in my novel, and then to the steady, guiding hand of Rhea Kurien and the team at Dash. I am eternally grateful to you all and I'm utterly delighted with my finished novel and the stunning cover.

My journey to publication has been a long and winding path and the Romantic Novelists' Association has been a part of that journey for the past eight years, and I wouldn't be here except for them and their New Writers' Scheme. Many thanks to their voluntary team who have contributed so much over the years and especially the readers who have critiqued many versions of this book.

Many thanks to Alison May who gave me the proverbial kick up the backside during lockdown one and two and told me things that I needed to hear. My book is better because of you. And here's to the rest of the Romantic Novelists who have cheered me on over the last eight years: The Irish RNA Chapter, The Road Trip fab four; Karina, Ruth and Seána and also to Karen, Debbie and Kirstie, of L&S, who got me through 5k per week in Lockdown 2021 and who continue to be an amazing support. To Jenni Keer and Clare Marchant who I met at my first kitchen party and who always have the answer to any crazy thing I need to know. To Emma-Claire and Janet Gover and the rest of the New Writers – thank you!

Before I joined the RNA, I was part of Carmel Harrington's *Imagine, Write, Inspire*. I'm eternally grateful to Carmel and the rest of the group who believed in me from my very early days. Thank you also to Sharon Thompson and her writing group, *Indulge In Writing*. Sharon, who never stopped believing in me, is currently holding up a banner which reads, *I told you so*! I'd be lost without Sharon and Bernie and our daily check-ins. And to Anstey Harris and the Tuesday night group, just keep making shit up!

Many thanks to Dr Paul Atkinson for answering my questions about head injuries and typhus. Any inaccuracies are purely mine.

Thank you to Ronan McGreevy, who gave me permission to quote from his book, *Wherever the Firing Line Extends*, and shone light on the events of 19th/20th October 1914 and the devastating consequences on the men of the 2nd battalion, Royal Irish Regiment.

Thank you to my sister Clare who helped with my research of Cairo in 1914 and to Emma, Lina and Minna who travelled the same journey as Isobel, Cecily and Alice, and left behind their words and memories. A little piece of them lives again in my characters.

My deepest gratitude to my husband and my children who supported me even amongst my disappointments and tears. Lots of tears! The highs and lows of getting published are not for the faint of heart. But remember this: you are never too old to chase your dreams.

And last but definitely not the least, to all who will read

this book. I hope you fall in love with Isobel and Edward just as I have. If the story has touched your heart, please leave a review so that Amazon can do its thing and other readers may find a little bit of escape as they dive in and read about my characters who were destined to be together.

Printed in Great Britain
by Amazon